EGYPTIAN BOOK OF THE DEAD HIEROGLYPH TRANSLATIONS Vol. 5

TEMPLE OF AMUN-RA
&
EGYPTIAN
BOOK OF THE DEAD

Hieroglyph Translations of the Panels Containing the Egyptian Mysteries of Cosmic & Mystic Identity

by
Dr. Muata Ashby
©2020

Egyptian Book of the Dead Hieroglyph Translation Series

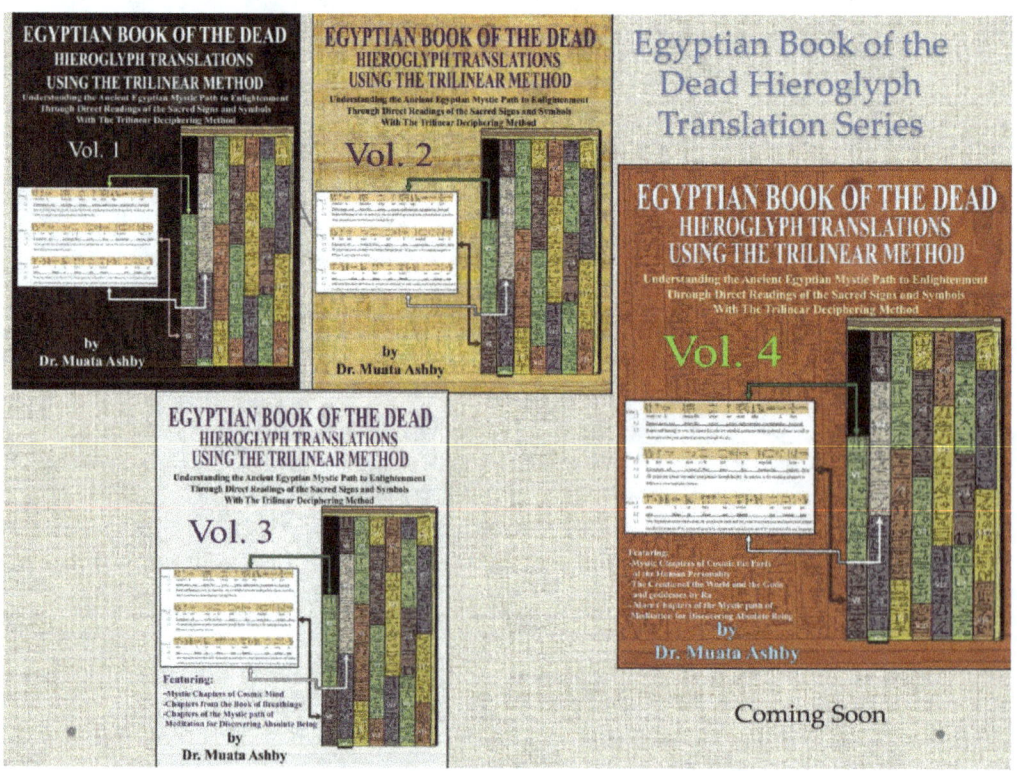

https://aerbook.com/store/Egyptian_Yoga_Books

EGYPTIAN BOOK OF THE DEAD HIEROGLYPH TRANSLATIONS Vol. 5

Copyright © 2020 Muata Ashby, Sema Institute of Yoga

All rights reserved.

ISBN: **1-884564-36-4**

https://aerbook.com/store/Egyptian_Yoga_Books

www.Egyptianyoga.com

www.Egyptianmysteryschool.org

To see the full presentation that this book is based on GO HERE:
https://www.asarucollege.org/2019conference

EGYPTIAN BOOK OF THE DEAD HIEROGLYPH TRANSLATIONS Vol. 5

DEDICATION

To Aset, daughter of Nut and Geb

ACKNOWLEDGMENTS

To my spiritual partner Dja Ashby, and my students, who have all supported and made this work possible and sustainable.

HTP(Peace)

EGYPTIAN BOOK OF THE DEAD HIEROGLYPH TRANSLATIONS Vol. 5

TABLE OF CONTENTS

Contents

THIS BOOK IS A COMPANION TO THE 2019 NETERIAN CONFERENCE ON THE HIEROGLYPHIC TEACHINGS RECORDED IN THE VIDEO SERIES AND PRESENTED FROM THE 360 Degree Video Presentaion & 360 Degree Virtual Temple Web Site 6

PREFACE 7

TRANSLATION FORMATS USED FOR PRESENTING THE TRANSLATIONS WITH THE TRILINEAR METHOD 7

    Conventional Interlinear Format 7

    Trilinear Contextual Format 8

    Reading the Philosophy Embedded in Ancient Egyptian Hieroglyphic Writings 10

PART 1: Introduction to the Temple of Amun Ra at Abu Simbel 13

    2015 Neterian Pilgrimage to Kemet Group at the Temple of Amun-Ra at Abu Simbel – visit led by Dr. Muata Ashby 14

    Temple of Amun-Ra at Abu Simbel Threefold Layout 24

    Temple of Amun-Ra at Abu Simbel Floor Level Elevation 25

What is Conditioning? 27

NETERIAN WISDOM ON THE CAUSE OF CONDITIONING-Stele of Abu (11 Dyn.) Teaching: Duality in life causes a life based on desire and hatred leads to the impetus for human incarnation. Cause of ego and reincarnation 28

    Chapter 30A of the Ancient Egyptian Book of Enlightenment (Book of the Dead) 30

What are Identity and Identification? 33

    Three Sources of Social Conditioning that induce identification-According to Ancient Egyptian Philosophy 35

Neterian Wisdom: How to break through Social and Egoist Conditioning? 36

    Teachings of Amenemopet Chapter 2 V-Turn Away from Negative Experiences, Thoughts, and Feelings that Negatively Condition the Personality 36

    Teachings of Amenemopet Chapter 9XI-EXPOSE ONESELF TO THE GOOD/TRUTH 37

EGYPTIAN BOOK OF THE DEAD HIEROGLYPH TRANSLATIONS Vol. 5

- FORMS OF AMUN-RA 44
- PART 2: Wisdom of Identifying with the Human Being 46
  - Panel -#1 Honoring the Human Royal Person 50
  - PRESENTATION OF PRISONERS TO THE DIVINE FAMILY 53
    - Deliverance of Prisoners to Amun and Family 54
    - PRESENTATION OF RAMSES AS UPHOLDER OF TRUTH AND ETHICAL CONSCIENCE 67
  - Meeting the God Ptah and Receiving the Emblems of Royal Personhood 70
  - Delivering Prisoners to the God Amun 79
    - How to meet the Criteria of Being Recognized as a Royal Person and Receiving the approval of Ptah, the God of the Earth Plane and Physical Creation and the Granting of the Royal Person Status in the form of the Heka, Nekaku and Chepesh/scimitar 83
    - Teachings of Amenemopet Chapter 4 85
    - LIVING MANIFESTATION OF THE DIVINE, a Royal Person (the human accepting and honoring the higher expression of one's own human being, the becoming of a Royal Person. Temple of Amun-Ra at Abu Simbel –[location Branch #4-east wall] 87
    - Panel 1.5-Adorations of the Royal Person to him/herself as a 88
    - Forms of Lord (God) Djehuty-God of the Moon, Intellect, Serpent Power and Writing 110
    - Below, the God Djehuty who cleanses the Eye of Heru and the Eye of Hetheru (Hathor) . 111
    - Insights Into the Concept of the "City of the Eight (FROM 2017 Neterian Conference)..... 121
    - 8 Cosmic Principles of Khemenu and their Implications 123
    - PMH Pert em Heru Chapter 8- Making a passage through Amentet and going into the light realizing Osiris Identity and Djehuty identity in enlightened consciousness 126
    - Wisdom of the Moon and the Source of Human Divine Energy Consciousness 130
- Part 4- From Identification as a Human to Identification as one of the Gods and Goddesses .. 132
- From Identification as a Human to Identification as one of the Gods and Goddesses 133
  - Panel 3- The Royal Person is Part of the Family of Gods and Goddesses 134
  - The Divine Family of Amun-Ra, Mut, Khonsu is also the Divine Family: Asar, Aset, and Heru . 153
  - Panel #4- The human Royal Person is the Great Divinity-– [location Vestibule #2] 157

EGYPTIAN BOOK OF THE DEAD HIEROGLYPH TRANSLATIONS Vol. 5

A final note on Panel #4 162

Panel #5 The Royal Person is the Unbound Higher Self of His/Her own existence AND their own parent. 360 Location-Temple Location Branch #5 163

Panel 5 The Royal Person is also an Unbound Entity who is their own Parent 167

-- 168

Adoration by the human Royal Person to THE GREAT DIVINITY who is also Horus/Ra, the Royal Person's own Higher Self" –[location Branch #1] 170

Panel #6: Adoration by the human Royal Person to THE GREAT DIVINITY who is also Horus/Ra who is the Royal Person's own Higher Self" 172

Panel #8-- The Human Royal Person is the Living Manifestation of the UNBOUND SELF and the GREAT DIVINITY–[3600 Location, Temple Location Branch #4] 180

PART 3: Wisdom of Identifying with the Unified Cosmic 189

    SPECIAL STUDY OF AMUN-RA-PTAH-From Papyrus Salt 194

    Configuration of Cosmic Divine Principles from Papyrus Salt 195

THE CONCEPT OF OM AS A DESCRIPTION OF MANIFEST WITNESSING CONSCIOUSNESS IN ANCIENT EGYPTIAN PHILOSOPHY 202

From Subtle to Gross-The Absolute Manifesting as Three: Principles of experience: Amun-Ra-Ptah 204

HYMN TO AMUN-RA, The Hidden Awake and Aware Among Us 208

Stele of Adoration to Ra-Herakty & Tem as One 212

    *Cross-reference- HYMN TO AMUN-RA, The Hidden Awake and Aware Among Us [VERSE C] 212

    Precepts of Ani- Pray in silence with a loving heart 215

        *Cross-referencePrecepts of Ani (below)to- HYMN TO AMUN-RA, The Hidden Awake and Aware Among Us [VERSE E-above] 215

Temple of Amun-Ra at Abu Simbel Sanctuary Text Translation 217

    Temple of Amun-Ra at Abu Simbel Sanctuary Translation 226

PERTEMHERU CHAPTER 176-Going Into the Hidden Chamber of the Un-manifest and Coming Out as an Enlightened Spirit Being 232

    Chap 176 Pertemheru chapter 176 becoming Neberdjer on the day of uniting 2 lands if known becoming Shining Spirit 234

EGYPTIAN BOOK OF THE DEAD HIEROGLYPH TRANSLATIONS Vol. 5

ADDENDUM 242

    Panel #7- My Unbound SELF is THE GREAT DIVINITY, WHO ALSO IS MY FATHER" –[3600 Location, Temple Branch #4] 242

    Col. 5 246

INDEX 248

Other Books From C M Books 242

https://aerbook.com/store/Egyptian_Yoga_Books 242

EGYPTIAN BOOK OF THE DEAD HIEROGLYPH TRANSLATIONS Vol. 5

THIS BOOK IS A COMPANION TO THE 2019 NETERIAN CONFERENCE ON THE HIEROGLYPHIC TEACHINGS RECORDED IN THE VIDEO SERIES AND PRESENTED FROM THE 360 Degree

Video Presentaion & 360 Degree Virtual Temple Web Site

This book has been coordinated along with a 360 Degree Temple Web Site where the selected images can be seen online to better view the panels in their temple locations and for a better understanding of the contexts presented in this book that provide even greater philosophical insights through the 360 spherical experiences.**

**For anyone interested in in a more detailed discourse on the extensive Wisdom teachings and philosophical implications introduced in this volume, follow the link to view the live presentations given by Dr. Ashby that cover the slides contained in this book as well as the extended commentary on the translated texts by Dr. Ashby presented by him at the December 2019 Neterian conference. This includes access to the 360 Degree Temple Web Site

[https://www.asarucollege.org/2019conference/]

PREFACE

TRANSLATION FORMATS USED FOR PRESENTING THE TRANSLATIONS WITH THE TRILINEAR METHOD

Conventional Interlinear Format

The conventional or regular interlinear format of translating Ancient Egyptian hieroglyphic texts presents a phonetic transliteration of the Ancient Egyptian hieroglyphs and transposes the hieroglyphs into the characters of the language they are being translated into. The second line presents a word for word translation. This level of translation can sometimes result in a limited, choppy, and less intelligible presentation of the original intent of the script. When the translation is between languages of dissimilar structure and cultural references such as the difference between the Ancient Egyptian language, which is rich in metaphor and iconographical implied wisdom versus the European languages which are based on a stricter alphabetic matrix, the structural differences along with differences of culture mean that a strict word for word translation can be insufficient to convey a full understanding of the intended meaning. So, while the conventional interlinear format is useful to a certain extent, a more comprehensive translation matrix is needed to gain the deeper richness of the meaning and import of the original hieroglyphic text.

Example of the Regular Interlinear Format:

Verse 1.   ORIGINAL TEXT

    1.1.   Transliteration into the phonetic letters of the language of the reader

    1.2.   Translation into the words of the language of the reader

Ex:

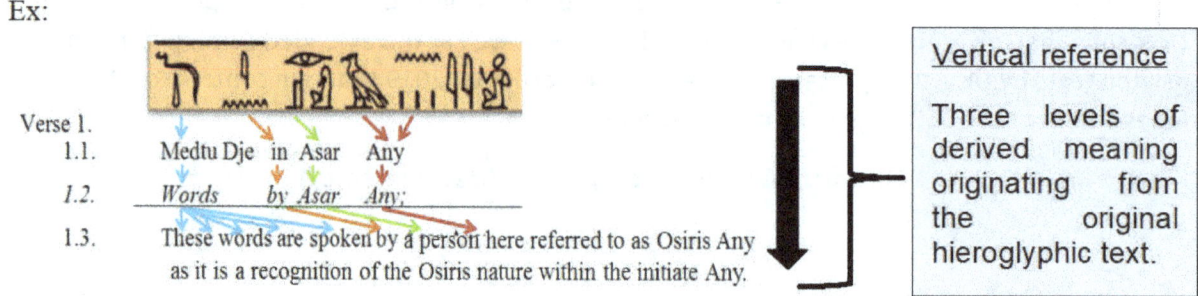

EGYPTIAN BOOK OF THE DEAD HIEROGLYPH TRANSLATIONS Vol. 5

Trilinear Contextual Format

The Trilinear Format for translating the Ancient Egyptian writing is a method as well as, to some degree, also a decipherment protocol that allows a layout for viewing the meaning from its source through layers of meaning extraction to the final rendition. The term "decipherment" is used because to the modern mind, whose concerns are often far removed from the world and philosophy of the Ancient Egyptians, the contexts and philosophy of the ancients are akin to more than a mystery, but also as a scarcely fathomable idea that is like a code or formula to be discovered to unlock the secrets of life, death, and the afterlife. Over the years, Dr. Muata Ashby has developed a format of translating Ancient Egyptian hieroglyphs into the native language of the reader that incorporates three levels of translation instead of the two levels of the ordinary conventional interlinear format. In a few cases, the conventional interlinear format is used in this volume. However, in most other cases a Ternary System will be used. The Ternary System devised by Dr. Muata Ashby adds a third layer of translation to the work that includes a contextual translation beyond the word for word translation. This added layer of the translation may be termed "Contextual Translation" and all together constitutes the ***Trilinear Contextual format***.

The Trilinear Form (which is a ternary system) of translations is a format developed by Dr. Muata Ashby for translating the Ancient Egyptian Hieroglyphic texts. It contains a *tripartite* arrangement composed of three translation sections or layers/levels. The <u>first level</u> is a phonetic transliteration. The <u>second level</u> is a direct word for word translation from hieroglyphic to the native language of the reader. These two levels generally constitute the "Conventional Interlinear Format" of translation. The Trilinear Format adds a new level of translation. The <u>third level</u> of translation is a contextual translation bringing out the meaning in an informal colloquial context in prose style incorporating:

A- the Ancient Egyptian Sebait (philosophical) tenets along with

B- the Ancient Egyptian Matnu (mythic) references and Ancient Egyptian "Maut" (morals or takeaways of the myth to which the text appertains) contained in the text in order to better reveal the intended meaning for the reader's language and culture.

C- In this volume, a new feature has been added to the trilinear system; the last translated verse will also include, where possible, a summary making contextual sense of the wisdom presented throughout the text, with particular focus on the beginning verse so as to clarify the takeaway by recalling the status of the spiritual aspirant at the beginning, then the transformation experiences throughout the text in its key hieroglyphic expressions and concluding with the outcome expressed in the final verse.

EGYPTIAN BOOK OF THE DEAD HIEROGLYPH TRANSLATIONS Vol. 5

Example of the Trilinear Format:

Verse 1.   ORIGINAL HIEROGLYPHIC TEXT

    1.1.   *Transliteration into the phonetic letters of the language of the reader*

    1.2.   <u>Translation into the words of the language of the reader</u>

    1.3.   Translation with contextual insights which may include philosophical and or mythological and/or historical background insights with colloquial references.

Ex:

Verse 1.
1.1.   Medtu Dje in Asar Any
1.2.   Words by Asar Any;
1.3.   These words are spoken by a person here referred to as Osiris Any as it is a recognition of the Osiris nature within the initiate Any.

NOTE: Each level of translation is designed to be both a reference to the other levels (vertically) but also to the previous and next statement in each level; so, for example, Verse translation Level 2.1 relates to 2.2 and 2.3 (vertical) but 2.2 also relates to 1.2 and 3.2 (horizontal). Therefore, if all the Level 2 translations are read by themselves or Level 3 translations are read by themselves one after the other, there will be a continuous and coherent rendering of the text

Example

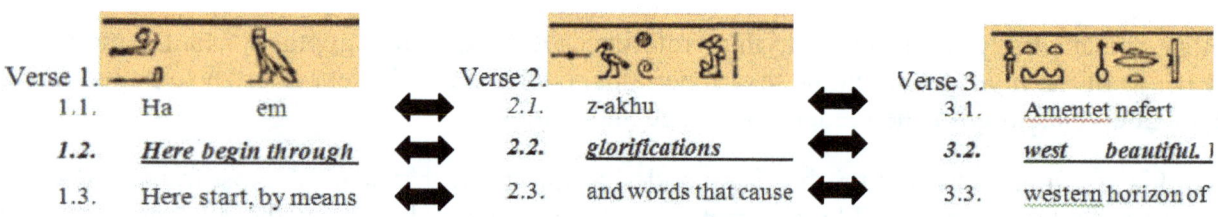

(Horizontal relationship)

In this way, the readings of Verse 1.2 followed by Verse 2.2, followed by Verse 3.2, translations, one after the other (ignoring .1 and .3 levels), horizontally, provide a continuous and coherent word for word narrative of the translation.

Also, the readings of Verse 1.3 followed by Verse 2.3, followed by Verse 3.3, translations, one after the other (ignoring .1 and .2 levels), horizontally, provide a continuous and coherent prose narrative of the translation.

EGYPTIAN BOOK OF THE DEAD HIEROGLYPH TRANSLATIONS Vol. 5

Note: When some text appears in red it is because the original hieroglyphic text was written in the same way. This was done to highlight certain parts of the text or to highlight the chapter titles of the text. See the example below.

Verse 1.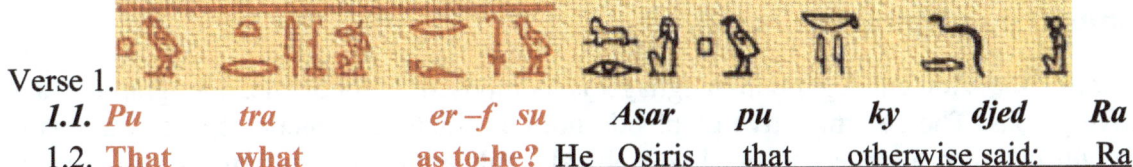
    1.1. *Pu*   *tra*   *er –f su*   Asar   pu   ky   djed   Ra
    1.2. That   what   as to-he?   He Osiris   that   otherwise said: Ra
    1.3. **What is that personality that is being talked about?** That personality is Osiris. Another way of thinking about it is that Osiris is also Ra…

Reading the Philosophy Embedded in Ancient Egyptian Hieroglyphic Writings

Here I will provide two examples, using two of the most important hieroglyphs to demonstrate why and how the philosophy of the Ancient Egyptian Mysteries is determined in the texts to be read. As stated earlier, reading the Ancient Egyptian texts in a literal way, ascribing meanings that relate to the culture of the reader is a disservice to the ancient culture and also it is a distortion of the meaning of the texts and the legacy of the original priests and priestesses who created them.

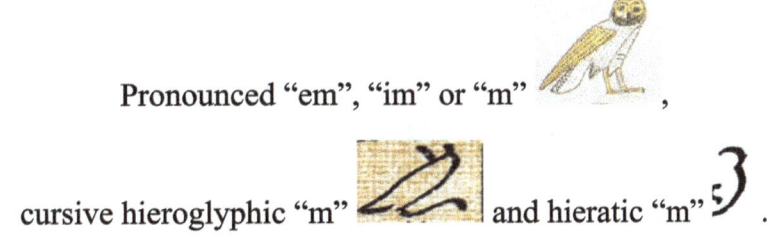

Pronounced "em", "im" or "m", cursive hieroglyphic "m" and hieratic "m".

The first glyph is the owl. Perhaps one of the most important glyphs, unlike determinatives, which do not convey phonetic aspects to the word, the owl has a phonetic and philosophical meaning. Whenever the owl appears the meaning can range from "in, within, inside, though, as, in the form of. This means that it is a pivotal term especially when it relates the person for whom the text has been created to any particular or general Divinity [god or goddess]. It, therefore, means that such a person is being identified with that divinity or with an aspect of divinity or they are being recognized as "becoming, or appearing or manifesting as". This, of course, signifies a movement of transformation either in progress or already attained. This glyph is seldom interpreted in such a manner and thus the overall outcomes of such neglectful translations will render a mundane and or erroneous insight into the Ancient Egyptian hieroglyphic writings.

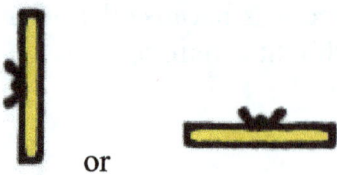 or

Another important glyph is the scroll.

Generally, the Ancient Egyptian language is composed of phonetic, ideographic, and determinative glyphs. The determinative glyphs do not contribute a phonetic aspect to the word but rather contribute a reference and or philosophical implication to be inferred by the reader. The scroll is a determinative glyph that, when appears, forces the application of a perspective abstractness that allows a vision of a meaning that transcends a strictly mundane or specific application. This is a reading that incorporates a philosophical and or conceptual basis to the meaning of the particular word. An example of how to apply the scroll in reading a word or sentence or passage is that its conceptual abstractness is to be applied to the regular meaning of the world, and the abstractness relates to the Ancient Egyptian philosophy of the spiritual mysteries that affirms a transcendental nature of life that goes beyond physical reality.

As a group, determinatives provide a similar function and constitute an integral and essential means of understanding the deeper wisdom and intent of the Ancient Egyptian written language. Below are some of the most important determinatives.

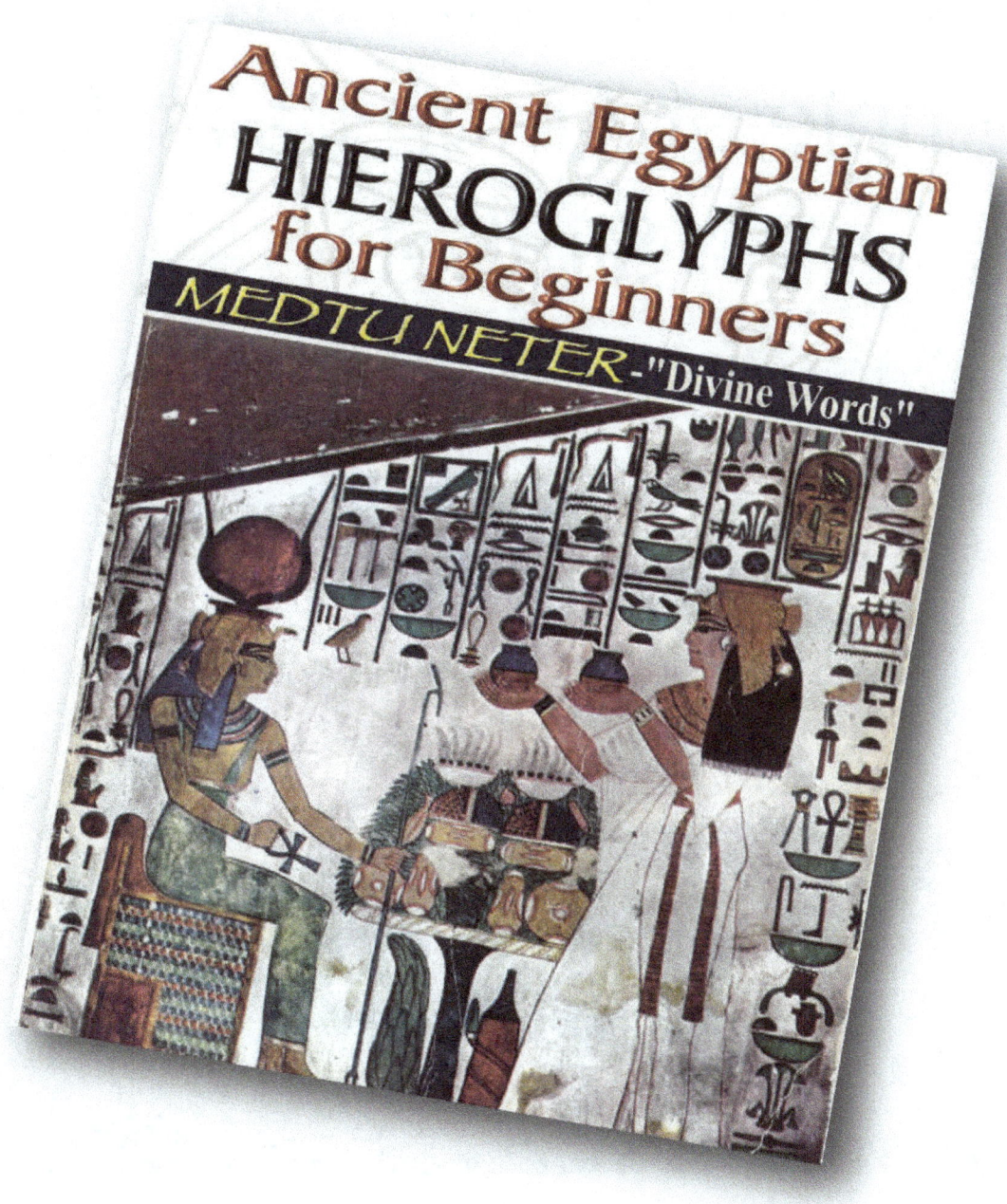

For more on the Ancient Egyptian Hieroglyphic Writing see the book *Ancient Egyptian Hieroglyphs for Beginners* by Muata Ashby

PART 1: Introduction to the Temple of Amun Ra at Abu Simbel

-Above: Temple of Amun-Ra at Abu Simbel, Egypt.

2015 Neterian Pilgrimage to Kemet Group at the Temple of Amun-Ra at Abu Simbel – visit led by Dr. Muata Ashby

The temple of Amun-Ra is a construction dedicated to the Divinity AMUN-RA. Amun-Ra is a unified Creator Divinity unifying two mythic divinities, Amun and Ra. They, together with another god, Ptah, constitute the Great Cosmic Trinity of Kemetic/Ancient Egyptian religion: Amun-Ra-Ptah. This Temple incorporates all three divinities but highlights the role of Amun and Ra and especially an aspect of Ra named Ra-Herakty (Horakty). The Temple is located in the southernmost area of present-day Egypt, close to the border with the country known in modern times as Sudan, which was, in ancient times, known as Kash/Kush (Nubia). Therefore, in ancient times, it served the spiritual needs of the people in the region, which were Kemetans/Kamitans/Ancient Egyptians and Nubians. Today, the immediate location area where the Temple is located is known as Abu Simbel, which is a town/village. The Temple was originally located several meters below its current location. It was moved in the 1960s in order to save it from the rising waters of the Nile River after the creation of the Aswan Dam.

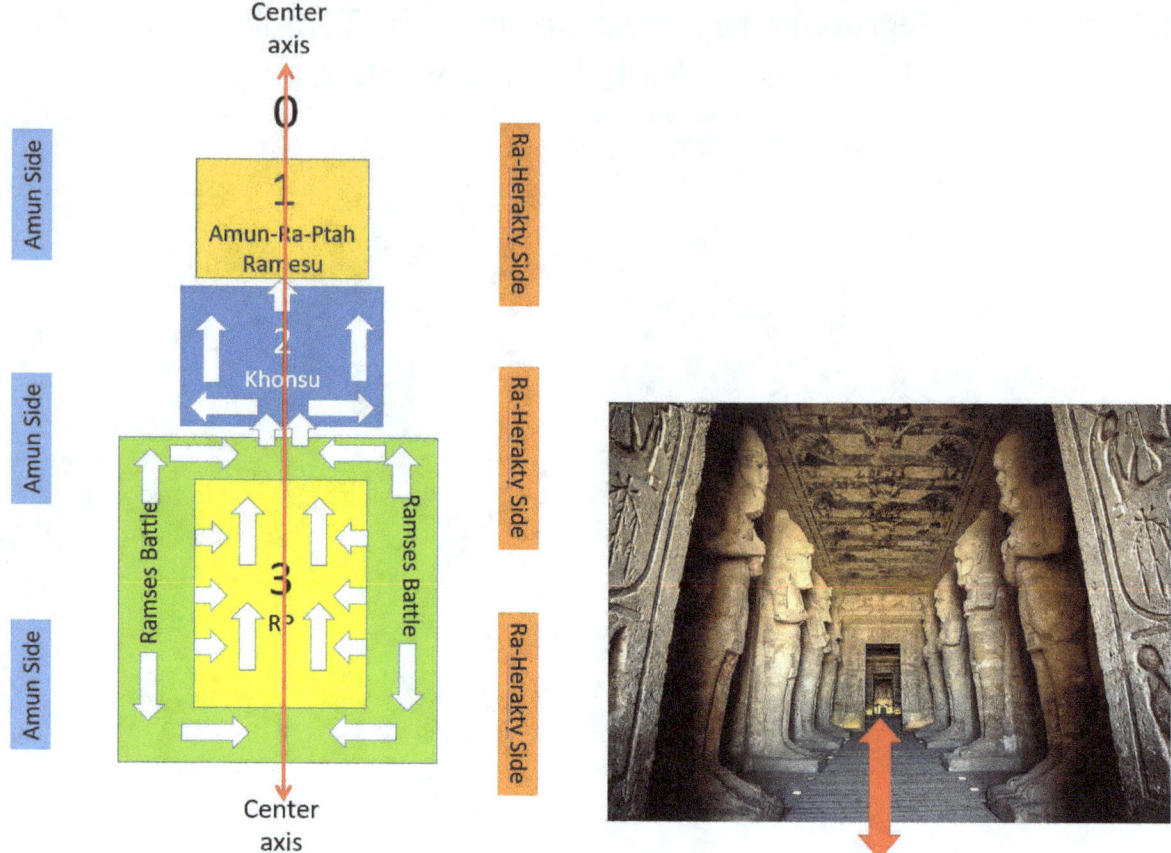

The Temple architecturally consists of four main chambers along an east-west central axis which divides the temple down its center, into two halves. Each half is dedicated to each aspect of the unified Divinity; so, facing the temple, looking from east to west, the south side (left) emphasizes the aspect of Amun, the Hidden Creator Spirit, and the north side (right) emphasizes the aspect of Ra as Ra-Herakty, the sustainer of Creation. The placement of the temple in the south of the country fits the notion expressed in the temple, of Amun being a god of the south. The temple was constructed in a period (New Kingdom era) when the god Amun was in prominence and recognized as the king of all the gods and goddesses. The temple was carved into solid rock, into a mountain on the banks of the Nile River.

EGYPTIAN BOOK OF THE DEAD HIEROGLYPH TRANSLATIONS Vol. 5

Description for Map of Egypt

This is a basic map of Egypt showing the main cities and municipal areas of the country. In order to get to the temple of Amun-Ra at Abu Simbel, Egypt, it is necessary to travel to the south of the country just north of the border of the country today known as Sudan which in ancient times was known as Kush (Nubia). It is part of Ancient Egyptian legend that the Ancient Egyptians were originally colonists who came from the land of Kush, that is, from the south to the North Eastern quadrant of the continent of Africa.

EGYPTIAN BOOK OF THE DEAD HIEROGLYPH TRANSLATIONS Vol. 5

Description & Summary

The next series of images or color paintings are from the early 19th century. The first two are from David Roberts in 1838. They show the state of preservation in which the temple was found at the time.

Abu Simbel David Roberts 1838 c.e.

EGYPTIAN BOOK OF THE DEAD HIEROGLYPH TRANSLATIONS Vol. 5

Description & Summary

This description is for the following temple floor plan image and the concept of likening it to a palm tree. In Ancient Egypt, there were three main types of columns that were used in the Ancient Egyptian temples. There was the type with Lotus capitals, having the lotus flower at the top where it rises to the ceiling. There was the type with the papyrus column capital and there was a type with the palm capital.

Now, In the Temple of Amun-Ra at Abu Simbel, the columns do not have either the Lotus, papyrus or palm capitals. However, this analogy of the palm tree is very pertinent when the 2D image of a palm tree is compared to the floor plan of the temple. When the floor plan is compared to a palm tree, we will see that, like the trunk palm tree, the temple has a main central section (the center of which is the temple axis). From that central section, several halls can be seen coming off of the main central axis of the temple, like branches coming off the trunk of a tree. As we will see, through the study of the panels of the temple that provide insight into the philosophy of mystic identity, the branches of this Ancient Egyptian temple hold several inscriptions and varied iconographies that contain standard presentations and also special ones, like having palm frond branches with leaves and also fruits in varied locations seemingly at random.

There is another concept that is useful for thinking about the wisdom and operations of the Ancient Egyptian Temple. As alluded to in our studies (see the book *Temple of the Soul* 2019), the Ancient Egyptian temple may be likened to a computer wherein the physical structure is the "hardware" and the iconography and hieroglyphic texts of the temple are, as if, it's "software".

So, in this computer analogy, the physical aspect of the temple may be likened to its hardware. The images, statues, and reliefs and accompanying hieroglyphs are the software. The human beings equipped with the understanding and spiritual purity, who enter into the hardware and experience the software, are called the "wetware" since they are the "Living", conscious and aware interactive aspect that connects to the software and hardware of the temple so as to activate its functions and achieve its purpose of facilitating spiritual enlightenment. As human beings traverse through the temple they will see many images just as one can see several aspects of palm leaves and fronds in a palm tree. In some parts of the palm tree, fruits can be seen; in the same way, in the branches of the temple, there can be seen several forms of iconography and hieroglyphic texts that are the fruits, that give special enlightening teachings to be consumed by the initiate. These iconographies and texts contain both Pro-forma (standard) as well as non-standard, special mystic wisdom teachings.

As we engage the study of several panels of iconography and hieroglyphic text we will see how those fruits are manifested, in the spiritual program of the temple, that reveal a mystery of mystic identity that is to be discovered by the human person who participates in the mystery of the temple. This is to be done to discover the nature of the true Self, beyond the strictly human understanding.

The temple of Amun-Ra and the concept of a palm tree for better understanding

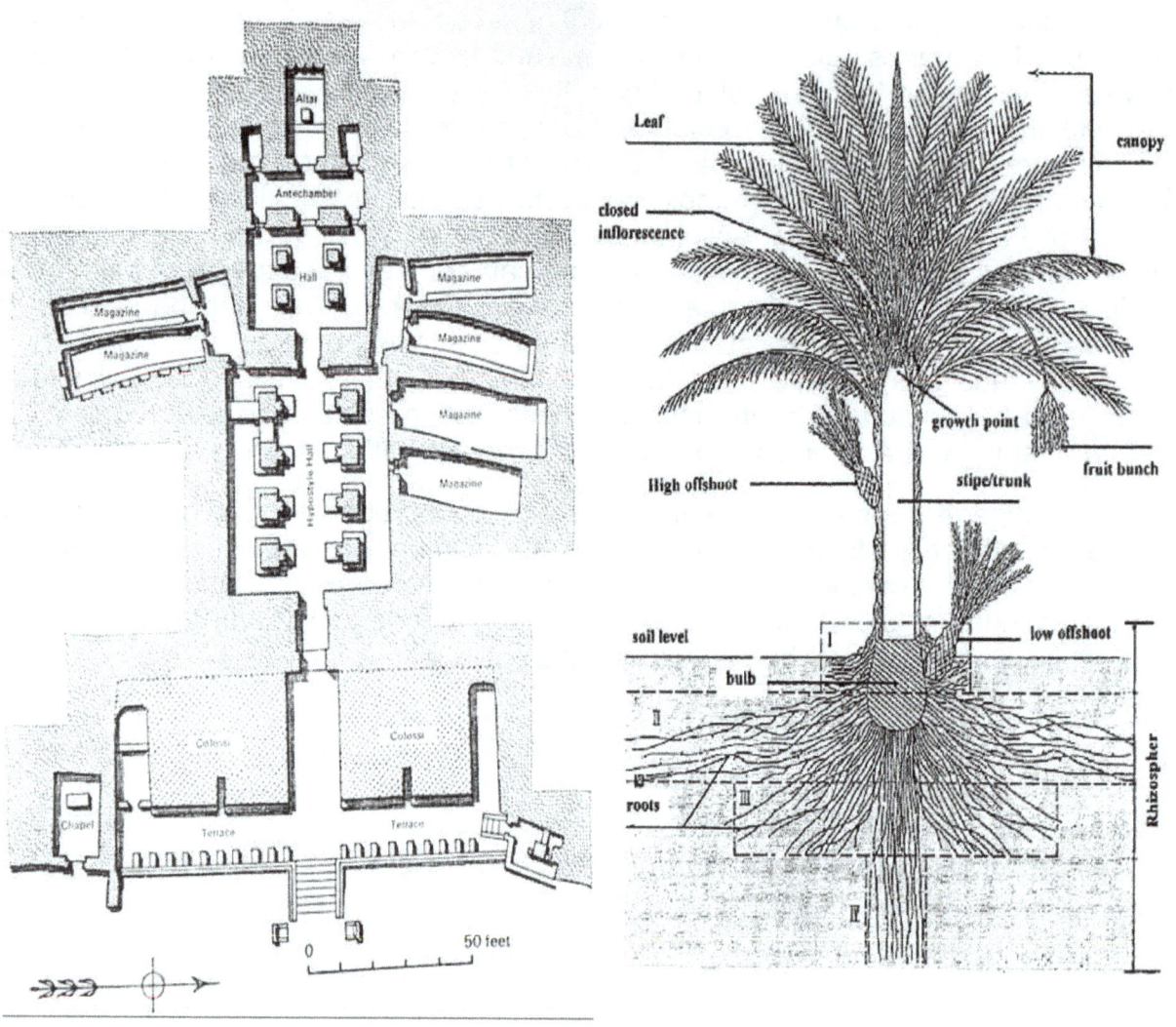

The next image depicts palm tree column capitals from another Ancient Egyptian temple.

EGYPTIAN BOOK OF THE DEAD HIEROGLYPH TRANSLATIONS Vol. 5

Description & Summary

The next images depict palm trees from the Ancient Egyptian text known as The Egyptian Book of the Dead.

Description & Summary

The next image shows the temple floor plan on the right showing the central section of a temple which has three main sections two vestibules and 6 branches. On the left, the three main sections are highlighted showing the aspect of the human being to which each section relates. The section colored in green relates to the physical body; the section colored in blue relates to the astral body or the mind. The section colored in gold relates to the causal body or the source of individual consciousness. The idea is that throughout the movement of the temple each of these bodies is to be purified and harmonized. The harmonization process includes the dissolution of the grosser aspects of the personality into the subtler aspects of the personality. Therefore, the conscious awareness of physical body identity is to be dissolved into the conscious awareness of the astral body. And likewise, then the conscious awareness of the astral body is to be dissolved into the causal or cosmic being. Beyond the causal nature, there is a transcendental absolute that is to be discovered once the three bodies are dissolved. This is the fundamental and philosophical basis of the temple that will be studied through our examination of several special panels and their hieroglyphic texts.

EGYPTIAN BOOK OF THE DEAD HIEROGLYPH TRANSLATIONS Vol. 5

Temple of Amun-Ra at Abu Simbel Threefold Layout

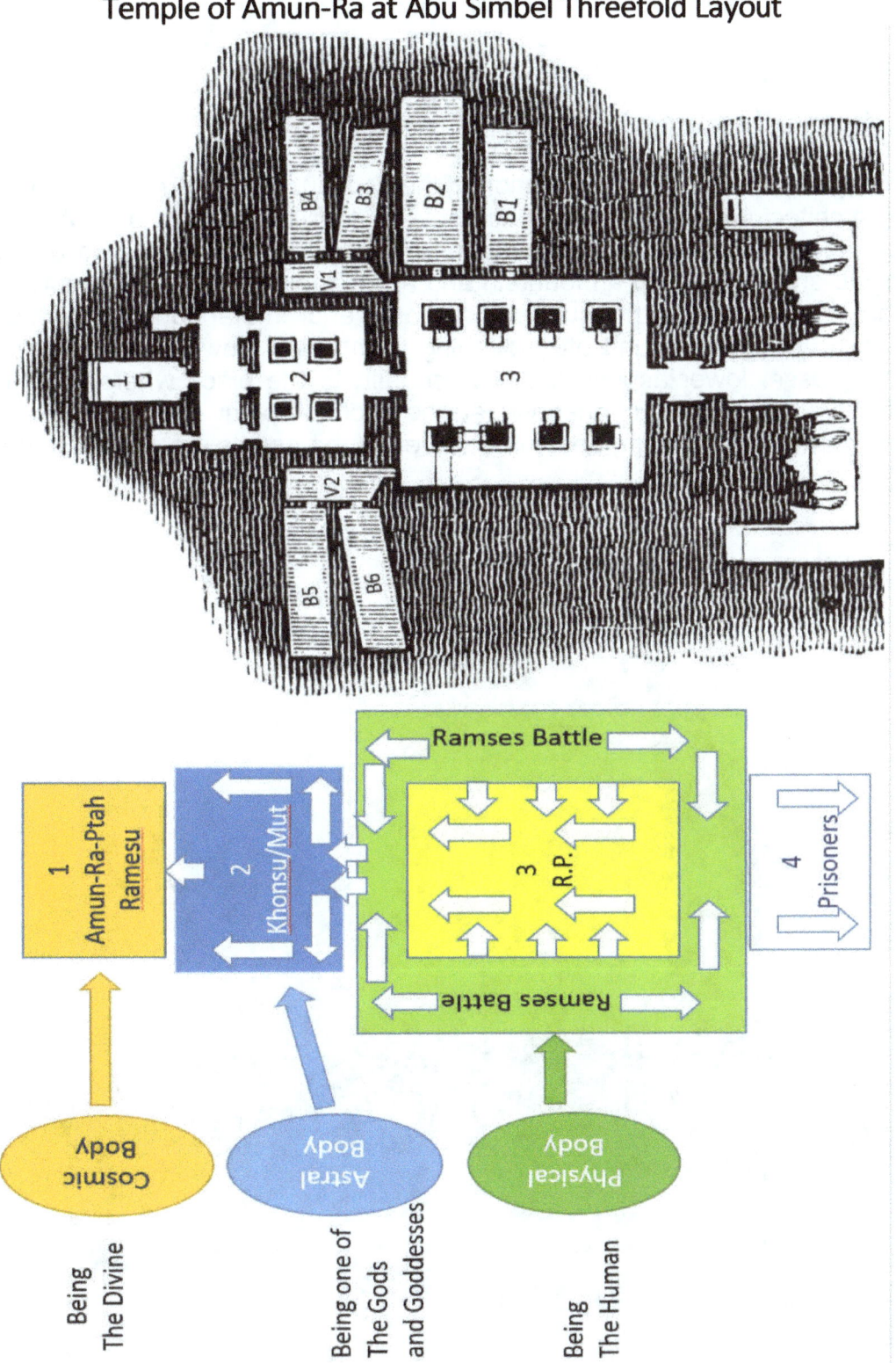

EGYPTIAN BOOK OF THE DEAD HIEROGLYPH TRANSLATIONS Vol. 5

Temple of Amun-Ra at Abu Simbel Floor Level Elevation

Description & Summary

The image below shows the elevation of the sections of the temple. In typical Ancient Egyptian architectural format the elevation of the floor level at the front of a temple, the entrance, is lower than the inner sanctuary or holy of holies. This is an allusion to the idea that we are climbing up a mountain and at the mountaintop, the divinity is found at the highest point above the surrounding land and, metaphorically, closest to the heavens. The divinity is found after climbing from below (lower elevation) from where exists the grosser lower aspect of the personality to the place where time and space have dissolved into cosmic oneness at the highest point which is located in the sanctuary room. This teaching becomes clearer as the panels are studied in detail.

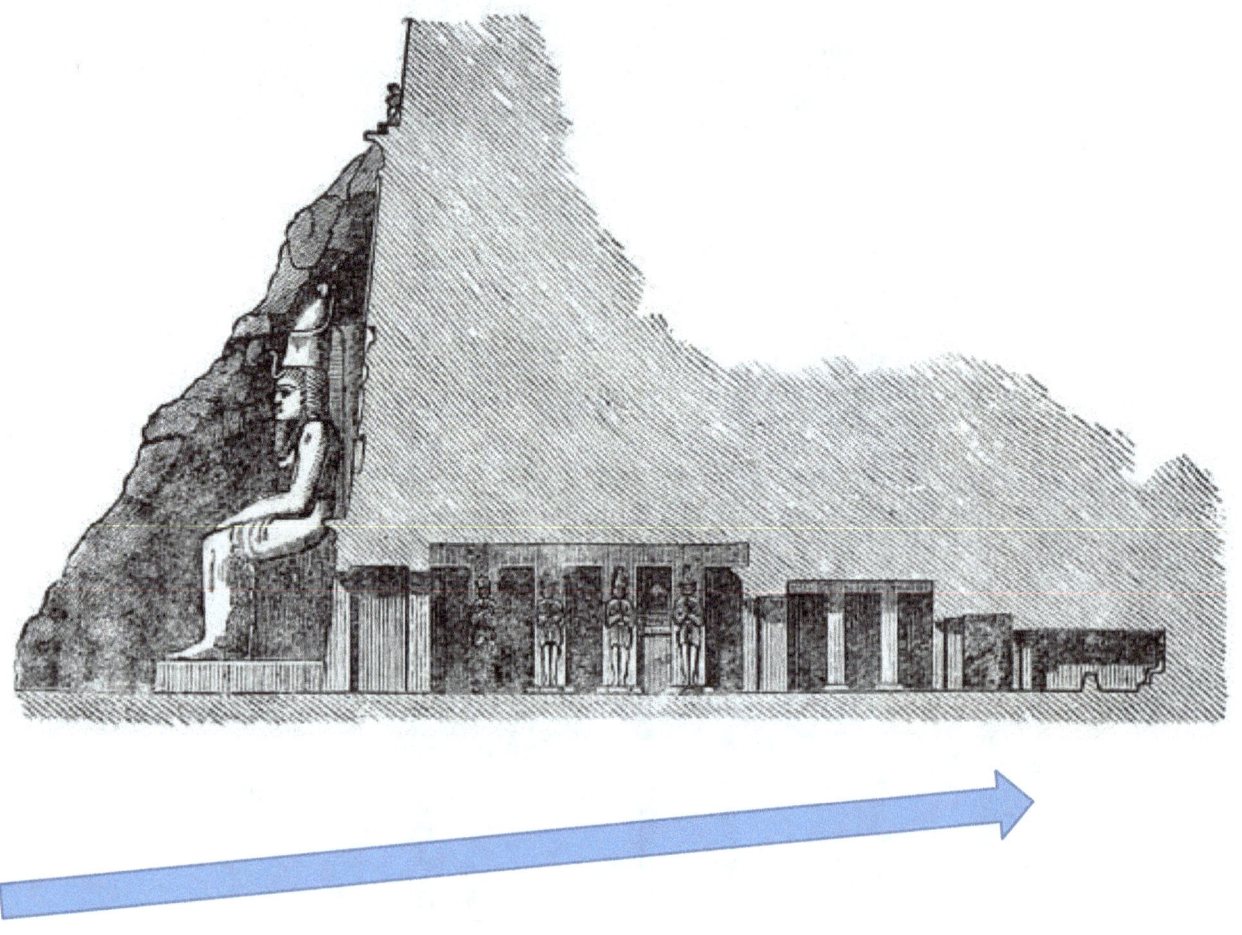

EGYPTIAN BOOK OF THE DEAD HIEROGLYPH TRANSLATIONS Vol. 5

Description & Summary

The following image contains the floor plan of the temple on the left side. On the right side, some of the most prominent iconographical panels are described and their locations are shown. Also, this image clearly shows how the temple is divided in half. The left side is related/dedicated to the God Amun. The right side is dedicated to the god Ra-Herakty. This setup of a temple introduces the idea that we are dealing with a divinity that has two aspects. Specifically, the God Amun represents witnessing consciousness. The god Ra-Herakty represents mind and Ptah, the manifestation.

Therefore, the three sections of the temple relate to the three divinities (Amun, Ra, and Ptah) and the meaning of their psycho-spiritual principles. Thus, as a human being traverses the three main sections of the temple they are to discover and experience those principles from the 3-human perspective, 2-the perspective of the gods and goddesses, and finally, 1-the perspective of unitary conscious awareness. Therefore, at the same time, they are to discover the nature of their own being as gradually and increasingly having higher levels of divine identity.

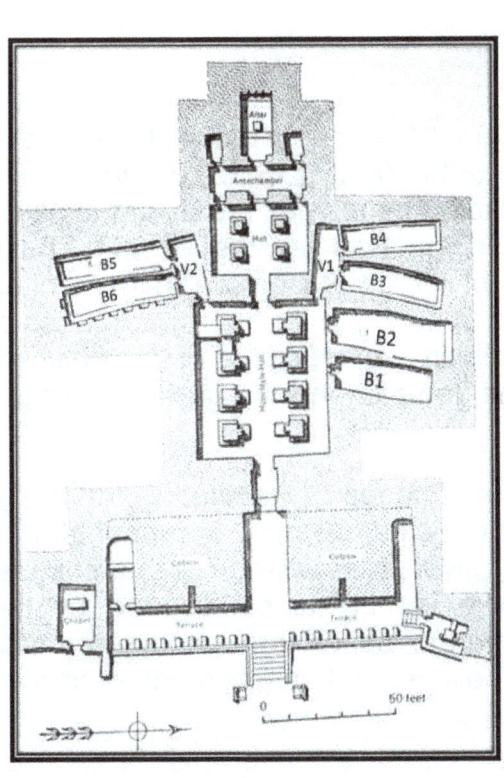
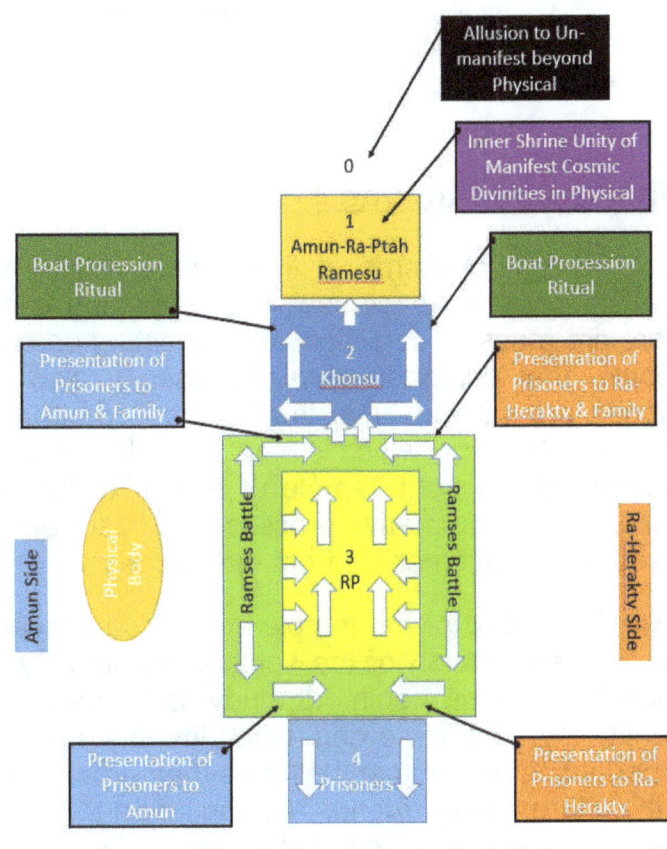

What is Conditioning?

What is conditioning?

The central theme of this temple relates to the concept and teaching of mystic spiritual identity. As we saw, in the opening images of the front (façade) of the temple, there are massive depictions of four sitting personalities. The images are all of the same people, that personality was Ramses II also known as "Ramses the Great." These images are said to have inspired the construction of Mount Rushmore in the United States of America, which is a nationalistic symbol, as opposed to the massive images of Ramses at the front Temple of Amun-Ra facade, which are reflective of a significant spiritually transformative process that occurred in the Temple, and the greatness of the personality that emerges from that process.

In the context of the temple architecture façade, the images of Ramses II, represent the final expression of the spiritual personality that projects out from the inner shrine. Therefore, we will begin our study of the panels that give us the wisdom about spiritual identity by first reviewing what identity is and how identity is conditioned by the experiences of a human being as they grow up in time and space through involvements with culture, family, friends and their own thoughts, feelings, and opinions gathered over the current and many other lifetimes.

In this section, of our study, we will first look at the definition of conditioning. Then we will look at an Ancient Egyptian text called "Stele of Abu". This original translated text provides insight into how a human being's conscious awareness becomes conditioned and normalized to the idea of experiencing duality and egoism. Then we will look at some modern interpretations or definitions of identity and identification. That will be followed by more spiritual concepts but through the Ancient Egyptian hieroglyphic translations from Ancient Egyptian texts that teach about the nature of the highest human identity and how to break the social and egoistic conditionings in order to achieve or restore the original highest human identity.

Ancient Egyptian wisdom about the cause of conditioning

NETERIAN WISDOM ON THE CAUSE OF CONDITIONING-Stele of Abu (11 Dyn.) Teaching: Duality in life causes a life based on *desire* and *hatred* leads to the impetus for human incarnation. Cause of ego and reincarnation

Verse 1.
1.1. **A   ankhu   tep   ta   merru   ankh   mesdjed**
1.2. Listen!   Life   on   earth   loving   life   hating
1.3. Hear this important teaching. Those people who are alive, living on earth, the physical plane, who live life clinging to being alive and hating the idea...

Verse 2.
2.1. **chept   im   merr   tjen   oah   tep   ta   djed**
2.2. death   by   desire   that   of planting   on   earth.   I Say
2.3. ...of death; that way of life, their perceived experience of living, emphasizing human existence as an abiding, desirable and not illusory reality, this way of thinking and feeling is the cause of the desire to plant oneself, to establish oneself on earth perpetually and this desire causes reincarnation since no one can live on earth continuously forever. To those people, I say the following:...

EGYPTIAN BOOK OF THE DEAD HIEROGLYPH TRANSLATIONS Vol. 5

Verse 3.
- **3.1.** ten   chat   ta   nu   en   amakhy   abu   er   ra - per
- **3.2.** to you: thousands   loaves, drink, to   revered   bull   of [all] the temples
- 3.3. …Turn away from the deluded notions about life, as if illusory desires could ever be fulfilled thereby, ignorantly and instinctually living by love or hate, desire or repudiation, like a thoughtless instinctual animal, a way of life that intensifies duality, dualistic thinking, mental agitation, ignorance and egoism, conflict, frustrations, combativeness, and suffering. The desires of love and hate cloud the mind and prevent a higher vision of existence and lead to control by ego (Set) and to reincarnation. Instead, do what I did, turn to the temple and its teaching; turn worldly love into temple devotion by making offerings of thousands of loaves of bread and drink to the sacred mascot of Asar (the Apis bull) and to the temples and thereby engage in devotions and temple rituals to cleanse the personality, and become worthy of the temple wisdom through association with priests and priestesses to become free from delusions of life so as to discover the true nature of existence beyond physical mortal existence.

Chapter 30A of the Ancient Egyptian Book of Enlightenment (Book of the Dead)

Description & Summary

In the following text, from the *Pert-em-Heru* or Ancient **Egyptian Book of the Dead**, also known as "The Book of Coming Forth Into The Light (Enlightenment), we find a teaching that complements the one presented in the *Stele of Abu*.

Chapter 30A (section) Pert-m-Heru: The Heart as Cause of Incarnation, Ma'at as the path of Enlightenment

EGYPTIAN BOOK OF THE DEAD HIEROGLYPH TRANSLATIONS Vol. 5

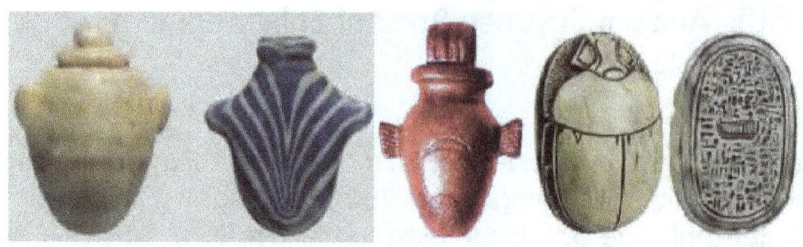

Verse 1.
1.1. Ab – a   n   mut - a   zep sen   haty ab – a   n   un – a   dep   ta
1.2. *Heart mine the   mother mine   repeat twice. Heart mine   cause of   existing-I   on   earth.*
1.3. My heart, my mother, my heart, my mother. My heart which is the mother which gives birth to my desires that cause my soul's coming into human incarnation.

Verse 2.
2.1. m   aha   er   a   m   meteru   rem   neb   chetu
2.2. *Manner rising   not   me   by   obstructing   as witness   in presence   lord judgment balance*
2.3. At the time of my judgment in the Hall of Maati, in the presence of the lord of the judgment, Lord Anubis (Anpu), when you step up to bear witness about me, oh my heart, the place in my unconscious mind, wherein are stored impressions of my past, the sum total of my thoughts, feelings and actions over many lifetimes, do not obstruct my spiritual journey by bearing witness about negative things I may have done while alive in the land of the living, since I strived to follow Maat and a life or righteousness, order and truth; so there should be no negative things to bear witness about.

Verse 3.
3.1. m djed   er –a   iu   ari n – f   zet   er   un   Ma'at
3.2. *Manner speaking about me   it is   worked he against the   about   absolute   right & truth, order, justice.*
3.3. When you speak about me, report about me as one who lived in a manner not against what is real, what really exists, the ever-presence, abiding reality, God, as what is real and not the illusory world of time and space as if it were an abiding reality. So do not speak about me as being an advocate of that which is egoistic, self-serving, against truth, such as the ideal of greed, callousness and the idea of physical vanity ignoring the ephemeral nature of life and dismissing the infinite and immortal spirit, Neter, beyond the ephemeral time and space relative reality of life. Bear witness about me as one who lived in a manner not against what is right & truth, order, and justice.

The Stele of Abu (above) presented the idea of how the human mind latches on to likes and dislikes which cause a predilection for building desires, in the mind, that cause forgetfulness about higher spiritual awareness of identity and in turn desiring for worldly pleasures, which necessarily means also repudiating that which is not pleasurable. Since it is only possible to experience pleasure in a physical human state of existence, thus, the desire to become and stay alive in physical form holds sway over the personality and thereby clouds the intellectual and feeling capacity to know of what is beyond the physical sensory experiences. That state of the personality is referred to, in the Ancient Egyptian Philosophical context, as mortal and ignorant. Associated with the sense of mortality is the fear of death, which was also highlighted in the Stele of Abu above ***mesdjed chept,*** about hating death.

This Pert M Heru text further explains that a heart (meaning unconscious mind) filled with the accumulated pressures from experiences of desire and repudiation builds up a cumulative momentum that pushes a human being to pursue incarnating into human form in order to pursue the fruits of the actions (fulfillment of desires)

impelled and compelled by the accumulated experiences of the past that seem to promise some form of fulfillment in the future, which of course can never happen since the realm of time and space is always changeable; therefore, any achievement of pleasure will inevitably end and lead to continuing pursuits for the fulfillment, in an endless cycle ending in frustrations followed by death. Thus, the heart is spoken of as the "mother", the aspect of the personality that gives "birth" to the personality in the form of a human being and consequently, it is the mother, that is to say, the mind(heart) that holds the error-based desires due to the residue leftover from memories through experiences of the past, termed ***aryu.*** It is those aryu, the residues of past experiences, feelings, and desires along with their pressure to long for or repudiate objects, situations or experiences, that maintain the ignorant and deluded state of mind, which need to be purified so as to break the cycle of spiritual ignorance that causes human beings to pursue endless lifetimes of failing to find peace and fulfillment instead of pursuing the fulfillment that the temple and the spiritual scriptures have to offer.

EGYPTIAN BOOK OF THE DEAD HIEROGLYPH TRANSLATIONS Vol. 5

What are Identity and Identification?

Social Identity Theory | Simply Psychology
https://www.simplypsychology.org/social-identity-theory.html
Social identity is a person's sense of who they are based on their group membership(s). Tajfel (1979) proposed that the groups (e.g. social class, family, football team etc.) which people belonged to were an important source of pride and self-esteem.

Identity Foreclosure definition | Psychology Glossary ...
https://www.alleydog.com/glossary/definition.php?term=Identity+Foreclosure+
Identity Foreclosure. Identity foreclosure is a stage of self-identity discovery in which an individual has an identity but hasn't explored other options or ideas. Most common in young adolescents, in this stage the individual has just adopted the traits and qualities of parents and friends.

What Is Ethnic Identity? - Developmental Psychology ...
https://psychology.iresearchnet.com/developmental-psychology/human-diversity/wh...
Ethnic identity refers to a person's social identity within a larger context based on membership in a cultural or social group. Research about ethnic identity has come from various disciplines, including psychology, sociology, and anthropology and thus has been conceptualized and measured in different ways depending on the discipline.

Modern definitions of "identification" in terms of human psychology

EGYPTIAN BOOK OF THE DEAD HIEROGLYPH TRANSLATIONS Vol. 5

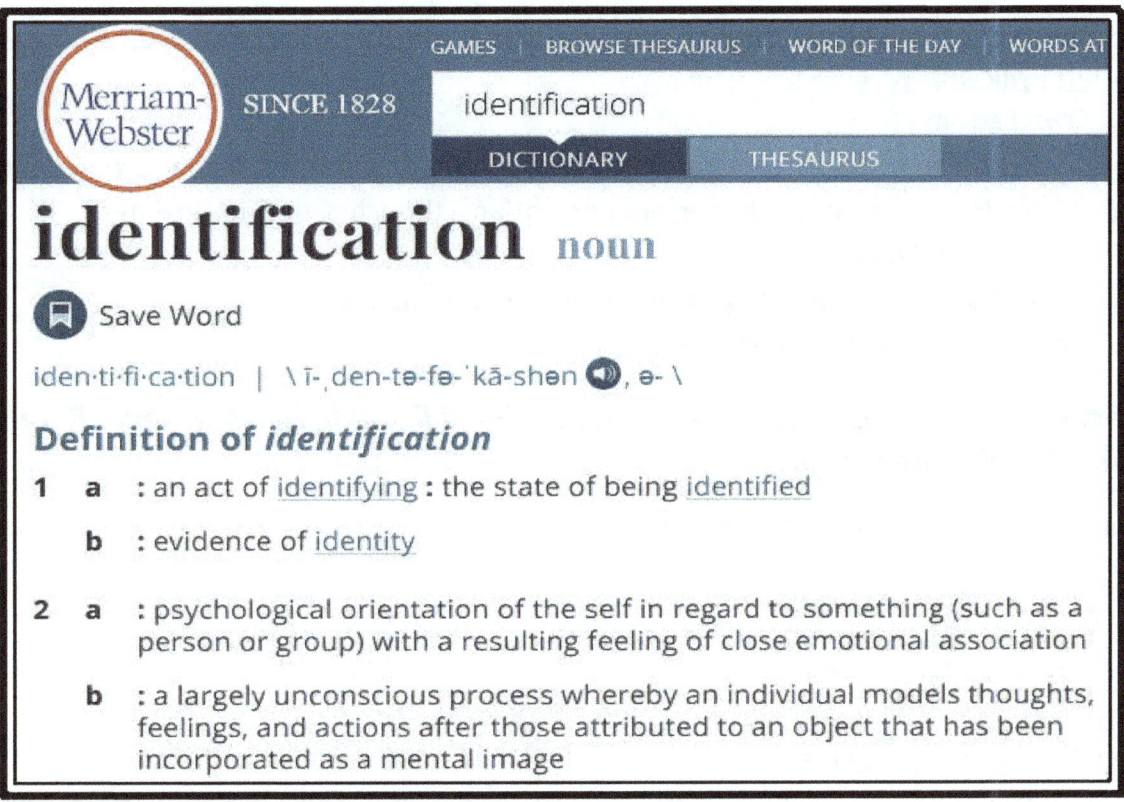

Three Sources of Social Conditioning that induce identification-According to Ancient Egyptian Philosophy

A. **Own Egoism**
   a. *Aryu* –residues from past perceptions, thoughts, desires, feelings, experiences
   b. New aryu formed by current perceptions, thoughts, desires, feelings, experiences
B. *Remtetju-* Other people's egos and their opinions and desires
C. *Neteru*-Nature and its movements

Neterian Identity concept – Source: *PERTEMHERU*-Ancient Egyptian Book of Enlightenment

Summary: Adoration of what is affirmed

Nuk   **pu**   **Asar**
I-am   that   Osiris

I identify myself as being one with God and not with any group, or as an animal-human or with a family or with a country, or any ethnic group, or gender; I am one with transcendental and immortal Spirit.

Summary: Affirmation of Spiritual Identity

Neterian Adoration/worship concept

Uash
Worship/magnification
To worship, to magnify

"O behold with thine eye God's plans. Devote thyself to adore God's name. It is God who giveth Souls to millions of forms, and God magnifyeth whosoever magnifyeth God."

-AEP

Neterian Wisdom: How to break through Social and Egoist Conditioning?

- ✓ Living by objective and not subjective truths-understand falseness of ignorance and egoist delusions
- ✓ Living by dispassion about the social and egoist conditionings –rejecting heated personality
- ✓ Living by devotion to those truths through affirmation and worship

Teachings of Amenemopet Chapter 2 V-Turn Away from Negative Experiences, Thoughts, and Feelings that Negatively Condition the Personality

Verse 1.

    1.1.   *Aa   ary   hem   {mdj} {hi} udjay   pa   ban*

    1.2.   <u>Hey actions steering {fig} {force} voyages   that   bad</u>

    1.3.   Listen, as concerns our boat of life, one should steer away from that which is bad.

Verse 2.

    2.1.   *iu   ben   aryu   mi   qednu {mdj} tu-f*

    2.2.   <u>it is   not   acting   like   turn around {fig} to-he</u>

    2.3.   The aforesaid is about not acting like those who are bad, the heated persons; in other words, it means turning around and going another way as opposed to going ahead and joining the heated persons in their bad doings.

EGYPTIAN BOOK OF THE DEAD HIEROGLYPH TRANSLATIONS Vol. 5

Teachings of Amenemopet Chapter 9 XI-EXPOSE ONESELF TO THE GOOD/TRUTH

Verse 14.

14.1. **im an tu k   khenkhennu   f   er   se-djed**
14.2. refrain/renounce/give up your going close to him for   causing conversation
14.3. Also, do not allow yourself to go close to them/do not approach them to start up a conversation.

Verse 15.

15.1. **su udja   {mdj} nest   rush   but   en   her   pet{a}   k**
15.2. cause vitality   tongue yours   take care   abominable person to personality heavenly yours
15.3. Instead, act in a manner that will be beneficial for you, increasing your vitality by controlling your tongue, the means (mind) by which your feelings and thoughts are expressed in the external world. Take care and watch out because the heated person is an abominable thing to your heavenly personality, the part of you that exists in the astral plane (mind and feelings).

Verse 16.

16.1. **im an tu k   sau   {mdj} {hi} kheru   aah {mdj} qesen   f**
16.2. refrain/renounce/give up your guard/protect words great {fig} bad/evil/injurious he
16.3. Therefore, give up on the ideas of associating with heated people and instead think about guarding and protecting yourself from those who speak great and high sounding words but who are, in fact, negative personalities that mean you harm and are only using high sounding words to gain your confidence only to later take advantage of you and harm you.

Summary:

When a human being falls under the delusion of individuality and the desires of human "beingness", those desires cause the person to focus on and emphasize the human perceptions and individual thoughts, feelings, and desires, that can be experienced in physical life, as real possible sources of fulfillment and abiding happiness. However, since the world is ever changeable and because, therefore, no matter what situation of prosperity is reached by a human being there will always be change externally in the world and or in the mind, causing changes in perceptions, thoughts and or feelings that would render the prosperous conditions incapable of causing more than temporary apparent fulfillment The term "apparent" is used here because something that is apparent is only temporary and fleeting, not eternally abiding, and is, therefore, from the mystical philosophy of Shetaut Neter, would be deemed as illusory. In other words, it is only a conditional manifestation.

So, "magnifying" the illusions leads to amplifying egoism and the individualized prospect for frustration and unhappiness as well as endless, fruitless seeking for fulfillment in the world of time and space as a human being. Meanwhile, there is Divinity in the personality, albeit unknown to the person in question, which sustains either a human being's egoism or their enlightened state of being. Therefore, the path of the temple and the scriptures are geared towards promoting the path towards true satisfaction and spiritual fulfillment that is abiding and eternal, instead of towards that which is transient and fleeting and thus, illusory.

Description and summary.

The following image shows the temple facade with four sitting figures of Ramses II. Looking at the center of the Façade, above the main door, an image can be seen within a square niche containing a standing figure, which appears to be a god composed of a composite human body, hawk head, and sun-disk crown. This is actually one of the spiritual names of Ramses II, as will be seen later. From this vantage point, we are looking from East to West, towards the interior portion of the temple. So we are facing towards the inner shrine of a temple and "from the bottom of the mountain" towards the top.

Image of Temple Façade

The temple of Amun-Ra entrance with the presentation of "some" tied up prisoners facing east-towards Ra

Description and summary.

In the next image, we are facing the Eastern Horizon. On the left and right can be seen images of prisoners that are being made to face towards the east. The east is where the sun rises. The sun is a manifestation of the god Ra. In other words, they are being presented to the divinity as the sun rises in the eastern Horizon. Also, the image and the niche on the top of the facade faces towards the east. Therefore, the spiritual name of Ramses II, *User-Maat-Ra,* on the eastern facing wall of the façade of the temple, faces his namesake in the Eastern Horizon; they face each other and as if come eye to eye in Communion together at dawn and throughout the first half of the day.

EGYPTIAN BOOK OF THE DEAD HIEROGLYPH TRANSLATIONS Vol. 5

Façade Wisdom USER-MAAT-RA Facing Ra

EGYPTIAN BOOK OF THE DEAD HIEROGLYPH TRANSLATIONS Vol. 5

Close-up of the Façade Recessed Compartment, Containing a Raised Relief Image of the God Ra-Herakty being adored by Two Male Figures, one on each side.

User - Ra - Maat

Description and summary.

In the following image, some close-ups of the Facade niche image containing the name of Ramses II which is User-Maat-Ra are provided. The image, below, shows the traditional cartouche format in which the name is usually written. The composite presentation shows that the god Ra is the prominent focus of the spiritual name of Ramses II. In this context, it means that the higher identity of Ramses II, as a human, is of the Divine. Thus, here on the temple Facade, we can see a foreshadowing of what is worked out in detail within the experience and teaching of the temple. In a final context what is presented on the Facade is a projection of the workings of the inner portions of a temple. So this is to be seen, looking from inside the temple to the inside, as a presentation of the final outcome of the production of the temple, a spiritually realized personality. This feature will be made clearer as we engage the study of the temple wisdom.

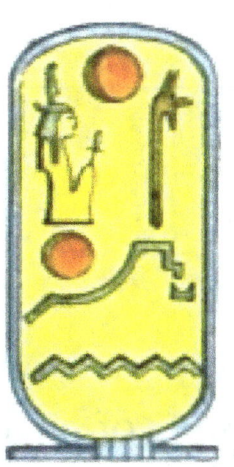

EGYPTIAN BOOK OF THE DEAD HIEROGLYPH TRANSLATIONS Vol. 5

Translation of the Hieroglyphs

	 ***User*** Power/Dominion	The same name as depicted in the traditional "cartouche" format:  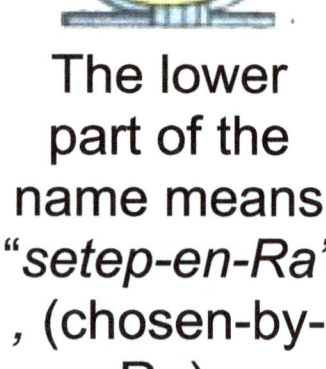 The lower part of the name means "*setep-en-Ra*", (chosen-by-Ra).
	 ***Maat*** Goddess of Justice, truth, order	
	***Ra***  Creator-Spirit	

EGYPTIAN BOOK OF THE DEAD HIEROGLYPH TRANSLATIONS Vol. 5

Amun-Ra (combining Ra-Herakty and Amun)

FORMS OF AMUN-RA

Image of Amun-Ra	Transliteration Col. 1	Translation Col. 1	Contextual Translation Col. 1
	Amun-Ra *Ankh* *her* *pet* *Neteru*	Hidden-Creator-Spirit living personality heaven gods goddesses	This is the living Hidden-Creator-Spirit, the personality of the heaven and the gods and goddesses.

EGYPTIAN BOOK OF THE DEAD HIEROGLYPH TRANSLATIONS Vol. 5

Description and summary.

The following images are all from the great hypostyle hall of the Temple of Amun Ra. The eight massive columns, with the images of Ramses, are depicted in the form of a human being with royal emblems and regalia. The number 8 is special to the temple teaching as will be learned from the study of the upcoming translated panels. A "Royal Person" is a member of a class of personalities that is qualified to tread the spiritual path of the temple and be allowed to enter into specific sections of the temple to receive the temple teaching. Those persons could be classified as being part of the Royal class or as part of the clergy class. Nevertheless, any such persons, including the priests and priestesses, having this type of access, are to be considered as Royal Personalities since they are traversing the "Royal Road" or path of the temple.

The path begins at the front of the temple in the east, through successive hypostyle halls, and to the inner sanctuary. So the initiate of the temple starts the journey through the temple path, visiting the prescribed sections and partaking in the depicted iconographies, starting from the lowest level of the Temple floor, the façade, leading from there, up the temple mountain to its peak, the sanctuary room, wherein communion with the divinity of the temple is reached, and with that communion, the human being attains spiritual enlightenment, discovering their true identity.

Though smaller than the megalithic façade sitting images of Ramses II, these eight standing images of Ramses attached to the columns within the hypostyle area (see image below), are nevertheless also massive and convey the idea of the awesome, expanded nature of the result of traversing this royal Road from East to West from ignorance to enlightenment and the knowledge of the true identity of Self.

PART 2: Wisdom of Identifying with the Human Being

The image above is of the second hypostyle hall. It should be noted that our nomenclature may be different (reversed) than the numbering system used by traditional Egyptologists. It is based on the tradition of the Holy of Holies being the first area of the Temple that is built representing the mound where creation first came into being. Then everything expands out from there. So when entering from the east, the most outer halls would have been built last. Thus, whereas traditional Egyptologists consider the first room upon entering as the first hypostyle hall, we number in order from the Holy of Holies. Therefore, the first room entered into this Temple is the 2nd Hypostyle Hall.

The first column on the right, as one walks into the temple hypostyle hall, is presented here as a representative sample of all eight columns. The columns represent the perfected Royal Person, Ramses, standing erect with the garb of a Royal Person. The columns are situated facing the central axis of the temple. As such, they represent the inner portion of the Hypostyle Hall and the central axis path from west to east, lower to higher, human to Divine. Surrounding the eight columns, on the walls behind the columned statues, are scenes of Ramses fighting unrighteousness, symbolized by enemy cultures that surrounded Ancient Egypt. Symbolically, Ramses has fought and has beaten those inimical forces and is delivering them, on one side of the temple, to the God Ra and on the other side of the temple to the God Amun. Since other Royal Persons, who historically did not experience war during their reigns, are equally depicted as being in combat, this feature of temple iconography is to be taken figuratively, meaning that it depicts spiritual warriors and not actually physical, historical warriors.

A spiritual warrior is one who fights inimical forces to uphold righteousness. In this temple, the Royal Person is depicted as fighting on a chariot and with bow and arrows. The chariot may be thought of as the positive movement of righteous feeling and ethical conscience; the bow is the empowered mind and the arrows are the directed thoughts striking the targets of inimical thoughts, desires, feelings, and movements. The ultimate spiritual warrior is the god Heru (Horus). His weapon of choice is a spear which he uses to immobilize his greatest foe, the god Set, who represents egoism. So Heru, who represents spiritual aspiration and the Royal Path to enlightenment, the discovery of the one Absolute, transcendental Supreme Being, uses a spear, which symbolizes oneness, to disable the aspect of the personality (Set) that represents scattered-ness, unrighteousness, and untruth that prevents the personality from realizing the higher identity of self beyond ego and egoism. Since every Royal Person is, as well, regarded as an embodiment of Heru, then it signifies that the Royal Person as a temple initiate is the actual metaphoric personality being depicted on the temple walls as an affirmation of their ethical conscience, and also as an example about the spiritual path for other aspiring Royal Persons to understand and follow.

The location of the column, which we will look at in more detail, is given in the map that is included with the image below. There are two vertical inscriptions on either side of each of the Ramses statues. Among the important teachings represented in the column, currently being focused on, is included the notion that Ramses is not a product of a human birth from human parents. Instead, the inscription states emphatically that Ramses is not just the child of God, in a metaphoric sense, but he came physically from the body of God. Among the implications of this statement, this means that Ramses is also a god (Ancient Egyptian term "neter"). Every Royal Person is also regarded as a child of the Divine and not of the physical world or human culture. We also see here the use of the same name that occurred on the temple façade that we looked at earlier. Additionally, Ramses is stated to be a master of action over objects meaning that he has mastered physical reality and physical human being (or "being human"), as well as the fact that he is also proficient in the temple mysteries and the sacrificial offerings protocols and procedures of the temple. In other words, he is not only a human personality but he has employed his life towards being a Royal Person on a spiritual Road to enlightenment by becoming versed in the temple mysteries.

The Temple of Amun-Ra hypostyle hall #2

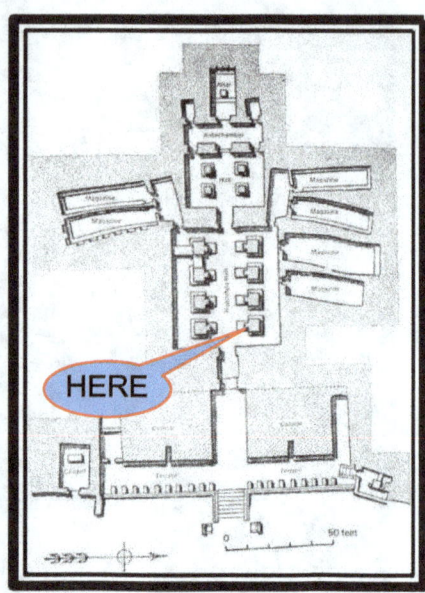

**For anyone interested in in a more detailed discourse on the extensive Wisdom teachings and philosophical implications introduced in this volume, follow the link to view the live presentations given by Dr. Ashby that cover the slides contained in this book as well as the extended commentary on the translated texts by Dr. Ashby presented by him at the December 2019 Neterian conference. This includes access to the 360 Degree Temple Web Site

[https://www.asarucollege.org/2019conference/]

EGYPTIAN BOOK OF THE DEAD HIEROGLYPH TRANSLATIONS Vol. 5

Panel -#1 Honoring the Human Royal Person
360 Degree Web site Location #3

PANEL 1 Hypostyle Hall #2 Colonnade Statue Ramses East side Col. 1	Transliteration Col. 1	Translation Col. 1	Contextual Translation Col. 1
	Sa Ra	Child of the Creator-Spirit	This is the child of the Creator-Spirit, one who came from the body of the Creator Spirit and who is beloved by the Creator-Spirit.
	En Chat F mery	Of Body His Beloved	
	F Neb chau	He Lord risings	This Royal person is the sovereign over risings. This is the second royal name of the Royal Person, "One who is the child of, who came from the body of Ra, the Creator Spirit, and who is beloved by Amun, the hidden witnessing Spirit Self."
	(Rame-ses-Amun-mery)	(Hidden Witnessing Spirit Beloved Creator Spirit-Child of)	
	Ra-Herakty	Creator-Spirit of two horizons	This Royal Person is beloved by the Creator-Spirit of the two Horizons and who is Lord of Heaven.
	Neb Pet	Lord Heaven	
	mery	beloved	

EGYPTIAN BOOK OF THE DEAD HIEROGLYPH TRANSLATIONS Vol. 5

Hypostyle Hall #2 Colonnade Statue Ramses West side Col. 1	Transliteration Col. 1	Translation Col. 1	Contextual Translation Col. 1
	Nesu-bity *Neb Tawy* *Neb* *ari* *chetu* (User-Maat-Ra-Setep-en-Ra) *Amun-Ra* *Neb Nestu Tawy* *mery*	Sovereign Upper-lower Egypt Lord Two-Lands Lord action objects (Dominion-truth-Creator Spirit-chosen-by-Creator Spirit) Hidden-Creator-Spirit Lord Thrones Two-lands beloved	This is the sovereign of Upper and Lower Egypt, the Lord of the two lands of Egypt; the Lord of action, doing things and commanding objects and sacrificial ritual supplies. This is the first royal name of the Royal Person, "One who exercises dominion backed by the righteousness of the Creator Spirit and who is chosen by that Creator Spirit." This Royal Person is beloved by the Hidden-Creator-Spirit, who is the Lord over the thrones of the Two-Lands.

EGYPTIAN BOOK OF THE DEAD HIEROGLYPH TRANSLATIONS Vol. 5

PRESENTATION OF PRISONERS TO THE DIVINE FAMILY
Temple Location: Hypostyle Hall #2 south-west wall, 360° web site Location #3

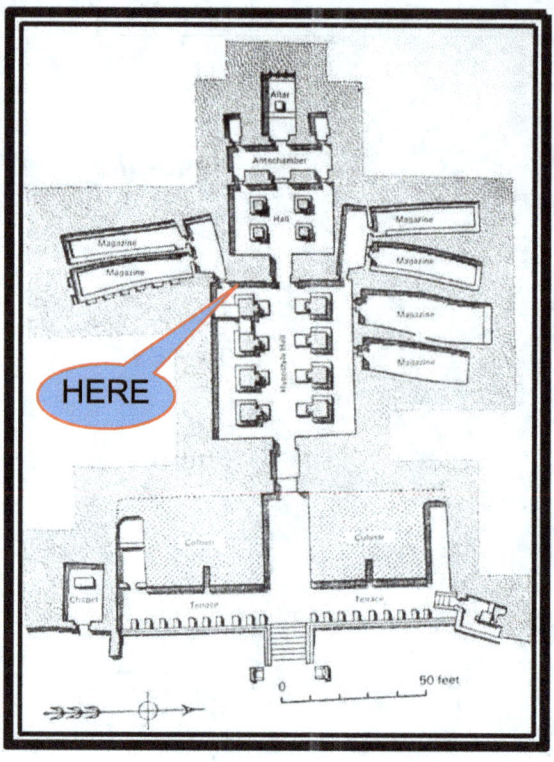

Deliverance of Prisoners to Amun and Family

Description & Summary

The image above is found in the southwestern wall of the second-hypostyle hall of the temple of Amun-Ra. It is a concluding depiction of the presentation of captured southern prisoners (depicted on the hypostyle south wall) to the Trinity of the God, Amun, and his family, his son, the god Khonsu, and his consort/wife, goddess Mut.

This scene is the final section of a series that is on the southern wall of the temple hypostyle hall, which is on the left side of the picture. This is how the image looked in the spring of the year 2019. This image is important for the present study, of mystic identity, since it is depicting a transition from the concentration on the physical personality to now introducing the assimilation of that physicality into the nature of the gods and goddesses.

The following set of images shows the same panel, depicted above from the year 2019, of the southwestern wall of the hypostyle hall along with the same depiction as drawn, in color, by early explorers of the 19th century. This provides a stunning example of the colorful aspect of the temple iconography, which complements the experience of the messages conveyed through the panels and the ambiance of the temple environment.

EGYPTIAN BOOK OF THE DEAD HIEROGLYPH TRANSLATIONS Vol. 5

The text that will be translated contains the speeches or the words that relate to each personality of the Trinity that is being depicted below. The first personality just in front of Ramses, with blue skin color, is the god Amun-Ra. In typical Ancient Egyptian religious fashion, wherein there is reciprocation between the divinity and worshiper, the God is receiving the offering which represents the capturing of inimical forces (in the form of prisoners of war) that are contradictory to truth and order, which is called **Maat**. Having received this offering the God reciprocates firstly by stating that he is the one who is the source of the spiritual valor and spiritual strength of the Royal Person who has brought the offering. As a boon, he grants the Dominion to that Royal Person over the lands and those who dwell on them. In verse 5 the God also states something momentous, that he has granted to the Royal Person their time of conscious awareness. Conscious awareness is the idea of existence as a conscious being as opposed to existence as a life form that is incapable of higher cognitive functions or an inert object in time and space. Therefore, a human being is endowed with their capacity to manifest consciousness and their ability to exercise cognition and awareness of their existence due to the will of God.

Now, the Trinity that is being depicted here has three personalities, the first being **Amun**, the second being his son **Khonsu**, and the third being goddess **Mut (pronounced, moot).** The remarkable presentation here is that in the place of the child, the son, it is the Royal Person, Ramses II, who has been substituted here. The substitution is qualitative in the sense that the Royal Person is being depicted as a Royal Person in the place where the son of the God sits, but also the Royal Person is being depicted with a disk over the head, which is the typical iconography of the god who is the son of the God Amun. Therefore, this signifies that the intent is to show that the Royal Person, that is, the human being who is the initiate of the temple on the Royal Road, is not to be seen as a mere mortal personality. Rather, the spiritual initiate of the temple is to be understood as being more than just physical and mortal. Specifically, the initiate is to be seen through their higher aspects. That higher aspect relates to the nature of the God that is being related to, in this case, the God Khonsu. The God Khonsu symbolically is represented by the moon (which is also related to the God **Djehuty**).

The sun and the moon are used symbolically in Shetaut Neter to represent Creator Spirit and Mind, respectively. That light from the sun is the light of full consciousness that comes from the God Ra, who manifests the source of the consciousness that comes from Neberdjer, the Absolute, through Amun (witnessing consciousness); that manifestation projects through **Ra** (solar Creator Spirit) and Ra's cosmic mind (the god Djehuty, the Lord of the Eight). That cosmic mind of the Divine reflects, in a limited manner, like the moon, which is the symbol of the human mind. The aforesaid is how the sun and moon symbolism works in Anunian Theurgy. In Wasetian Theurgy, the solar Divinity is Amun and the Lunar Divinity is Khonsu.

The God Khonsu, in addition to representing the lunar reflection of the solar Amun, symbolically also represents the concept of movement whereby the father Amun (witnessing consciousness) witnesses creation through the changing phases of mind (moon=reflected shining consciousness (Amun) that shines through the sun, that reflects on the moon)). Among these phases, the present moon phase relates to the movement towards fullness. That fullness represents the full reflection of light from the sun.

EGYPTIAN BOOK OF THE DEAD HIEROGLYPH TRANSLATIONS Vol. 5

Deliverance of Prisoners to Amun and Family Speech of Amun Col. 1 2 3 4 5	Transliteration Col. 1	Translation Col. 1	Contextual Translation Col. 1
	Medu dje In Amun-Ra **Khenti** **Aptu**	Words spoken By Hidden-Creator-Spirit Foremost Karnak	These words are now being spoken by the divinity known as Hidden-Creator-Spirit. This divinity is the foremost being of the great temple in the city of Thebes.

EGYPTIAN BOOK OF THE DEAD HIEROGLYPH TRANSLATIONS Vol. 5

Deliverance of Prisoners to Amun and Family Speech of Amun Col. 1 2 3 4 5	Transliteration Col. 2	Translation Col. 2	Contextual Translation Col. 2
	Medu dje *Di* *en-en* *k* *qent* *necht* *neb*	Words spoken Given to thee spiritual valor spiritual strength all	He says: I have given to you spiritual valor and spiritual strength, totally, completely.
	Transliteration Col. 3	Translation Col. 3	Contextual Translation Col. 3
	Medu dje *Di* *en-en* *k* *tawiu* *chestu* *nest* *tebty* *k*	Words spoken Given to thee lands foreign throne feet thine	He says: I have given to you the foreign lands along with the thrones, the kings and queens governing those lands to be at the feet of your throne.

--

EGYPTIAN BOOK OF THE DEAD HIEROGLYPH TRANSLATIONS Vol. 5

Deliverance of Prisoners to Amun and Family Speech of Amun Col. 1 2 3 4 5	Transliteration Col. 4	Translation Col. 4	Contextual Translation Col. 4
	Medu dje *Di en-en k*	Words spoken Given to thee	He says: I have granted to you…
	Transliteration Col. 5	Translation Col. 5	Contextual Translation Col. 5
	Aha ra *en Ra*	Time of conscious awareness of Creator-Spirit	…the time of conscious awareness of the Creator-Spirit consciousness.

Deliverance of Prisoners to Amun and Family Speech of R.P. (R to L) Row. 1	Transliteration Row 1	Translation Row 1	Contextual Translation Row 1
	Medu dje in) Ramesu-Amun-mery (Di en-en k ankh was neb	Words spoken By Ramses Given to thee life flow all	These words are now being spoken by the Royal Person,) Child of the Creator-Spirit, beloved by the Divinity of Witnessing Consciousness, now identifying as Khonsu(. I have given to you all life and all power.

--

Deliverance of Prisoners to Amun and Family Speech of Mut (L to R) Col. 1 2 3	Transliteration Col. 1	Translation Col. 1	Contextual Translation Col. 1
	Medu dje In	Words spoken By	These words are now being spoken by the Goddess known as "Mother Vulture," the great goddess of the Asher region (of Thebes.)
	Mut	Mother vulture	
	Ur	Great	
	Neb	all	
	Asher(u)	Asher region (of Waset)	

Deliverance of Prisoners to Amun and Family Speech of Mut (L to R) Col. 1 2 3	Transliteration Col. 2	Translation Col. 2	Contextual Translation Col. 2
	(Asher)ru	Asher region	Indeed, she is the mistress of and Queen Mother of Karnak, the Temple of the Thrones" in the city of Thebes.
	Neb	Mistress	
	Henut	Queen-mother	
	Aptu	Karnak	
	Transliteration Col.3	Translation Col. 3	Contextual Translation Col.3
	Di *en-en* *k* *heh* *im* *Sed*	Given to thee eternity form-of Sed festival	She says: I have granted you an eternity in the form of Sed festival periods for you to be as a reigning monarch.

EGYPTIAN BOOK OF THE DEAD HIEROGLYPH TRANSLATIONS Vol. 5

Description & Summary

The third personality on the panel is the goddess **Mut** (moot). In receipt of the offering being given by the Royal Person, she reciprocates by granting eternal existence. Metaphorically, the concept of **Sed** festivals means the renewal of Pharaonic reign. Therefore, this grant by the goddess is a form of figurative, speech, an allegorical statement signifying that the Royal nature of the human being is now to be recognized as everlasting. Of course, this idea does not relate to remaining on earth, as a human monarch literally, as even in ancient times there were no human kings or queens who lived more than the natural lifespan of a healthy human, which can be into their 80s, 90s or early 100's, etc. Therefore, this statement was never meant to relate to the physical personality or the physical aspect of human existence. Rather, it always related to the nature of spirit being that is the essence of the human. In this context, the hall scene represents the idea that the spiritual work of rounding up inimical forces is to be seen as allegorical as well. Those inimical forces are not to be seen as physical human beings or cultures, but rather as negative thoughts feelings ideas, and unrighteousness in the heart that damage human psychological and social culture and the capacity to realize the higher, eternal nature of the soul. In other words, the practice of the spiritual discipline of doing the ethical work and making the devotional offerings to the divine leads to the discovery of the underlying eternal spiritual nature of the human personality. In order for the spiritual work to become effective, that spiritual work is to be done with an understanding of the philosophy that has been conveyed by the temple related to the higher identity of the human being.

Sebayt, that mystical philosophy or **sebait**, as it is called in Ancient Egyptian texts, is the wisdom philosophy imparted by the priests and priestesses to the Royal Persons of the temple. It is also contained in spiritual texts such as the *Egyptian Book Of The Dead*. Thus, if the spiritual philosophy were to be correctly understood, and if it were to be properly implemented in day-to-day life along with its devotional offerings to the divine, the personality would be cleansed from the negative inimical forces that control and degrade the personality Those same forces are the factors that cause ignorance in the mind and lead to unethical behavior, the disregard of ethics and ill will towards others and towards nature as well as towards oneself, thereby degrading human existence and leading to spiritual ignorance, suffering and frustrations of life. This teaching, related to the philosophy of Ancient Egypt also termed "Egyptian Mysteries", is being espoused through the texts, iconographies, and architecture of the temple. It is the wisdom that is being explained in the commentaries, throughout this volume, and in other volumes, brought forth by Dr. Muata Ashby. In this context, the depictions of the temple are models/ prototypes/ archetypes and templates for qualified human Royal Persons (initiates) to activate to elevate human consciousness from the level of a mortal human to that of the immortal divine.

EGYPTIAN BOOK OF THE DEAD HIEROGLYPH TRANSLATIONS Vol. 5

360 Degree Temple Web Site

**For anyone interested in in a more detailed discourse on the extensive Wisdom teachings and philosophical implications introduced in this volume, follow the link to view the live presentations given by Dr. Ashby that cover the slides contained in this book as well as the extended commentary on the translated texts by Dr. Ashby presented by him at the December 2019 Neterian conference. This includes access to the 360 Degree Temple Web Site

[https://www.asarucollege.org/2019conference/]

EGYPTIAN BOOK OF THE DEAD HIEROGLYPH TRANSLATIONS Vol. 5

PRESENTATION OF RAMSES AS UPHOLDER OF TRUTH AND ETHICAL CONSCIENCE
Temple Location: Hypostyle Hall #2 south-west wall, 360º web site Location #3

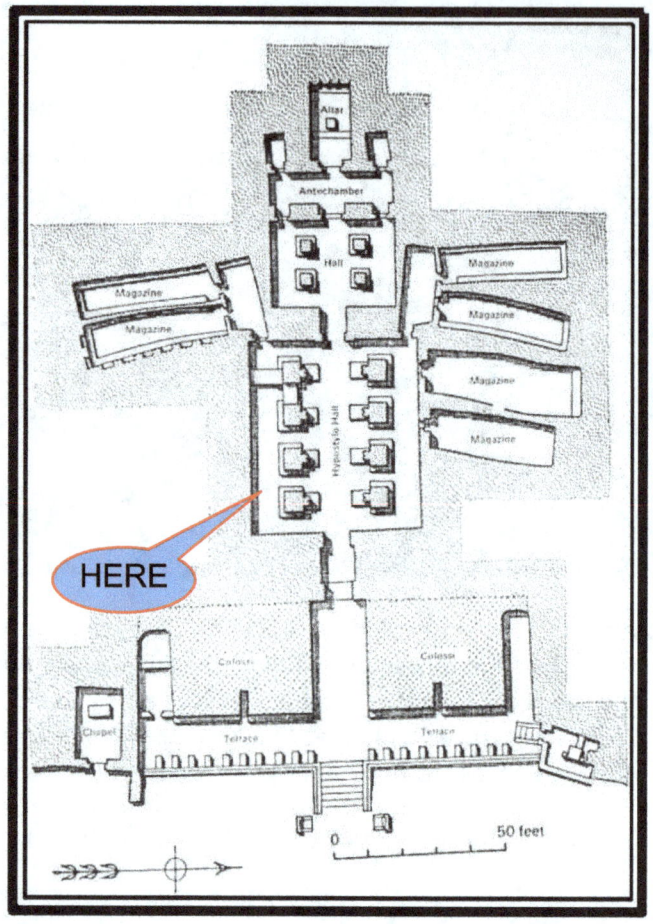

Description and summary

On the next two pages the current day image of the Royal Person, in this case, Ramses, is being presented showing how he upheld the concept of righteousness and truth, Maat, by confronting those inimical forces as a warrior on a chariot. The bow and arrow are the projections of righteous thoughts and feelings countering the negative forces; the chariot is the movement that carries the personality forward, with dynamism, spiritual strength and spiritual valor to confront unrighteousness. In this way, a Royal Person is to face the wayward, inimical forces of life, egoism, hatred, anxiety, lust, jealousy, envy, greed, etc. in order to suppress and then sublimate those negative forces, as symbolized by their delivery, all tied up, to the God. The following image is of the same panel, in the temple, but also drawn and painted by early explorers of the early 19th century.

EGYPTIAN BOOK OF THE DEAD HIEROGLYPH TRANSLATIONS Vol. 5

EGYPTIAN BOOK OF THE DEAD HIEROGLYPH TRANSLATIONS Vol. 5

EGYPTIAN BOOK OF THE DEAD HIEROGLYPH TRANSLATIONS Vol. 5

Meeting the God Ptah and Receiving the Emblems of Royal Personhood
360 Degree Web Page Location #8, Temple Location Vestibule #2

EGYPTIAN BOOK OF THE DEAD HIEROGLYPH TRANSLATIONS Vol. 5

Description and summary

"The lips of the wise are as the doors of a cabinet; no sooner are they opened, but treasures are poured out before you. Like unto trees of gold arranged in beds of silver, are wise sentences uttered in due season."

-Ancient Egyptian Proverb

The following image (left) is found in vestibule number two of the Temple of Amun-Ra. It depicts the Royal Person making offerings to the God Ptah, who is sitting in his shrine. Ptah is the third member of the great cosmic Trinity Amun-Ra-Ptah. He represents the aspects of the ability that manifests physicality, in other words, he symbolizes the physical creation, the physical universe. Therefore, it is fitting that we find Ptah in this panel where the reciprocation to the Royal Person is in the form of the granting of the emblems of Royal Personhood. Those emblems include the crook and the flail which are the classical emblems of Ancient Egyptian sovereignty. In this manner, the God gives his approval of the Royal Person as being a legitimate Royal Person due to the work of upholding ethical conscience and making devotional offerings both of which purify the personality and bring the human aspect of personality closer to divine awareness. In this panel, we find, just above the two hands of the Royal Person, the two Pro-forma spiritual names and titles of the Royal Person.

The term "pro forma" relates to the part of a transaction for a contract or a statement that is obligatory and necessary; in other words "standard". This is why it is found on virtually all the panels as they already relate to the same Royal Person who is the sponsor of this particular temple. Other temples sponsored by other Royal Persons would depict the pro forma names of those persons. The other aspects of the panel, the iconography, the hieroglyphic texts, contain the more specific and special aspects of iconography and text that go beyond the pro forma formulas and adoration statements. In way of analogy, this idea of the pro forma and non-pro-forma aspects of the panel depictions may be likened to silver and gold, respectively. There is an Ancient Egyptian Proverb that speaks of the words of wise as trees of gold in beds of silver. In this analogy, the silver refers to the pro forma aspects that must be there in the temple process that includes the devotional and ethically conscious life of the Royal Person. The gold aspects refer to the special allusions, beyond the standard elements; they are the special teachings, special iconographies, and special ritual approaches by a Royal Person who engages in and discovers, their spiritual identity, as being not only human or as a god and goddess, but moving further to realize their own nature as one with the supreme divine.

The text goes on to identify the nature of the God Ptah as being the architect of creation and then proceeds to make a momentous statement of the relationship between the god and the Royal Person. That relationship is revealed to be of parent and child. Going further, the relationship is one of parent and child where the child is loved. Then the God proceeds to grant certain boons to the Royal Person. The boons include the emblems of Royal Personhood and also some further important aspects of divinity. The God grants power, verticality, and dual life (two ankhs), that is, eternal life with dual consciousness, having the capacity of upright conscience that means wakefulness as opposed to death; it means life in the physical form, the apparent reality, as well as life beyond physicality. Those grants are to be experienced through the effect of a special ceremonial knife/sword instrument, a scimitar.

The scimitar is a ceremonial instrument, a sword that is used for cutting away unrighteousness from the personality. The same term, scimitar, is used for the chepesh object that is used in the opening the mouth ritual for the Royal Person. In Ancient Egyptian mystic wisdom, the term "Opening the mouth" relates, symbolically, to opening /expanding the mind, which is, expanding conscious awareness. This object also relates to a constellation in the northern hemisphere that points to the North Pole which symbolizes uninterrupted unobstructed and perennial light which symbolizes awaken consciousness for spiritual enlightenment. The nature of this special instrument involves the practice of certain disciplines, obtaining certain levels of purity and progressing on the spiritual path of Royal Personhood in the temple that leads to experiencing the effect of the boons (power verticality and eternal life with dual consciousness. These experiences are foundations to pursue the opening of the mouth, which means expanding conscious awareness beyond human limitations, expanding to discover the nature of transcendental Spirit Being that lies beyond the mundane worldly human form of awareness.

EGYPTIAN BOOK OF THE DEAD HIEROGLYPH TRANSLATIONS Vol. 5

EGYPTIAN BOOK OF THE DEAD HIEROGLYPH TRANSLATIONS Vol. 5

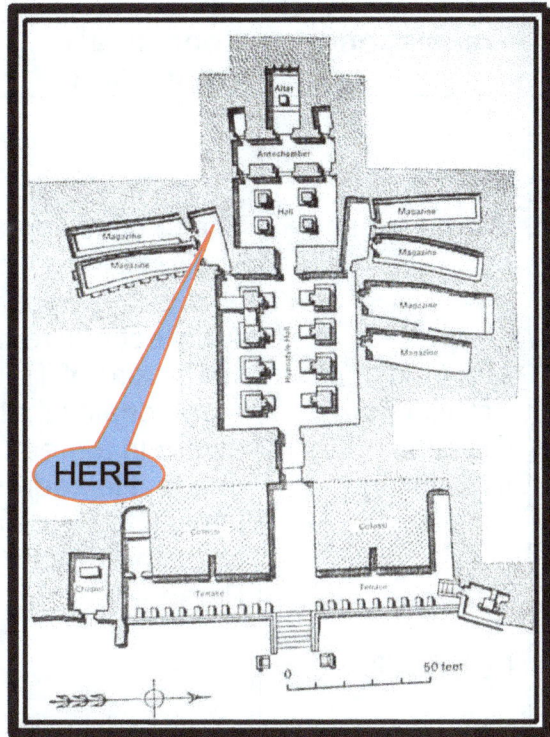

Text of Right Royal Aspect of same Royal Person	Transliteration	Translation	Contextual Translation
Col. 1 1st main Pro-forma spiritual name of Ramses	**Neb tawy** (U̲S̲E̲R̲-M̲A̲A̲T̲-R̲A̲-S̲E̲T̲E̲P̲-E̲N̲-R̲A̲)	Lord Two lands (Power of the truth of the Creator Spirit and chosen by the Creator Spirit)	The Royal Person, Ramses, is Lord of the Two Lands and goes by the name: "One who exercises dominion backed by the righteousness of the Creator Spirit and who is chosen by that Creator Spirit."
Col. 2 2nd main Pro-forma spiritual name of Ramses	**neb chau** (A̲M̲U̲N̲ M̲E̲R̲Y̲ R̲A̲-M̲E̲S̲U̲)	Lord Risings/thrones (Hidden Witnessing Spirit Beloved Creator Spirit-Child of)	This is the second royal name of the Royal Person, as Lord over crowns and therefore an emperor, known as "One who the child is, who came from the body of Ra, the Creator Spirit, and who is beloved by Amun, the hidden witnessing Spirit Self."

EGYPTIAN BOOK OF THE DEAD HIEROGLYPH TRANSLATIONS Vol. 5

Col. 1	Transliteration	Translation	Contextual Translation
	Medu dje in	Words spoken by	These next words are spoken by the God who is known as the Architect of Creation. He is Lord of Truth and a personality that dwells in a great abode. He addresses himself to his beloved child, the Royal Person.
	Ptah	The God Architect of Creation	
	{Neter}	{a Divinity}	
	Neb	Lord	
	Maat	Truth	
	her	Personality	
	aset-per	abode	
	ur	great	
	en	to	
	sa	son	
	F	his	
	mery	beloved	
	F	him	
--			

EGYPTIAN BOOK OF THE DEAD HIEROGLYPH TRANSLATIONS Vol. 5

Col. 2	Transliteration	Translation	Contextual Translation
	(A M U N / M E R Y / R A - / M E S U)	(Ramses(born of Ra)-Amun-Beloved)	This R.P. goes by the name Ramses (child of Ra)-beloved of Amun(Divinity of Witnessing Consciousness). Here, take what I am granting for yourself.
	seshep	receive-this	
	en	for	
	k	yourself	

--

EGYPTIAN BOOK OF THE DEAD HIEROGLYPH TRANSLATIONS Vol. 5

Col. 3	Transliteration	Translation	Contextual Translation
	Heka nekaku *cha* *k* {Vignette} *was* *djed* *ankhy*	Crook Flail crown thine {Vignette description} power(flow) verticality dual-life	(Take…) the crook and flail; the crook is an affirmation of your legitimacy as being an heir to the throne of God, it is an emblem of rulership symbolizing your capacity to be a shepherd of men and women; and take the flail your authority, sowing the capacity to exert discipline on yourself… ======= {Vignette description} Ptah holds the scepter of power and the Djed symbol of Osirian verticality symbolizing the awakening of the higher psycho-spiritual consciousness centers (eastern chakras) bringing spiritual enlightenment (vertical movement to Spirit) and holds two ankh amulets, one for the human existence and one representing the life everlasting in Spirit (dual life, meaning eternal life with dual consciousness, having the capacity of upright conscience that means wakefulness as opposed to death, and life in the physical apparent reality as well as life beyond physicality.

EGYPTIAN BOOK OF THE DEAD HIEROGLYPH TRANSLATIONS Vol. 5

Col. 4	Transliteration	Translation	Contextual Translation
(relief image)	*im* *chepeshu*	through scimitars	…via the ceremonial scimitar, the force by which victory is attained on earth and in Spirit. In this way, having received the crook and flail, by becoming a Royal Person on the royal road of spiritual enlightenment prescribed by Shetaut Neter, acting with Maat and opposing untruth in life, offering truth to the Divine, Amun-Ra, along with your coolness and love, this will open the way for your generative power to forge a path that your offering to Amun will cut away obstacles for you leading to the polestar of non-dual higher consciousness-stable enlightenment. Step #1 Qualify to be a Royal Person Step #2 Receive the stamp of approval from Ptah Step #3 then the offerings to Amun (prisoners of unrighteousness) will bear fruit in the form of spiritual success: ✓ LISTENING ✓ REFLECTION ✓ CONCENTRATION ✓ MEDITATION

EGYPTIAN BOOK OF THE DEAD HIEROGLYPH TRANSLATIONS Vol. 5

Delivering Prisoners to the God Amun
360⁰ Web Page Location #3, Temple Location Hypostyle #2

Description and summary

The next image occurs in the main hypostyle hall. It depicts the Royal Person in an active stance holding prisoners in front of the god **Amun**. Earlier, we discussed the spiritual significance of this scene of the offering of the prisoners to the Divinities. Our focus here will be the scimitar and its connection to the philosophy of the Chepesh/ and attaining Nehast, spiritual Enlightenment. Notice that the God Amun is holding a scimitar ceremonial instrument. This signifies that the spiritual work of ethical conscience, that is, the capturing of the inimical forces and delivering those to the divinity constitutes a major act of service that legitimizes the Royal Person and makes them worthy to receive those emblems of Royal Personhood, and also activates the boons granted that lead to spiritual enlightenment. The next image that follows is of the same panel, but in color, as drawn by the early European explorers who discovered the temple in the early 19th century before photography was invented.

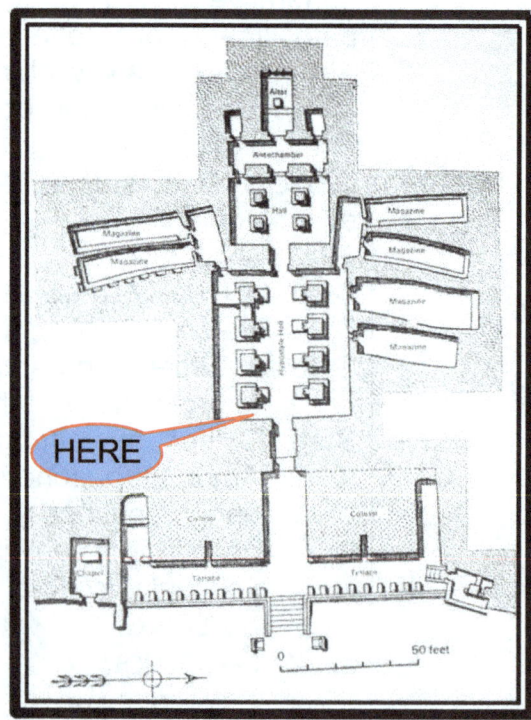

EGYPTIAN BOOK OF THE DEAD HIEROGLYPH TRANSLATIONS Vol. 5

EGYPTIAN BOOK OF THE DEAD HIEROGLYPH TRANSLATIONS Vol. 5

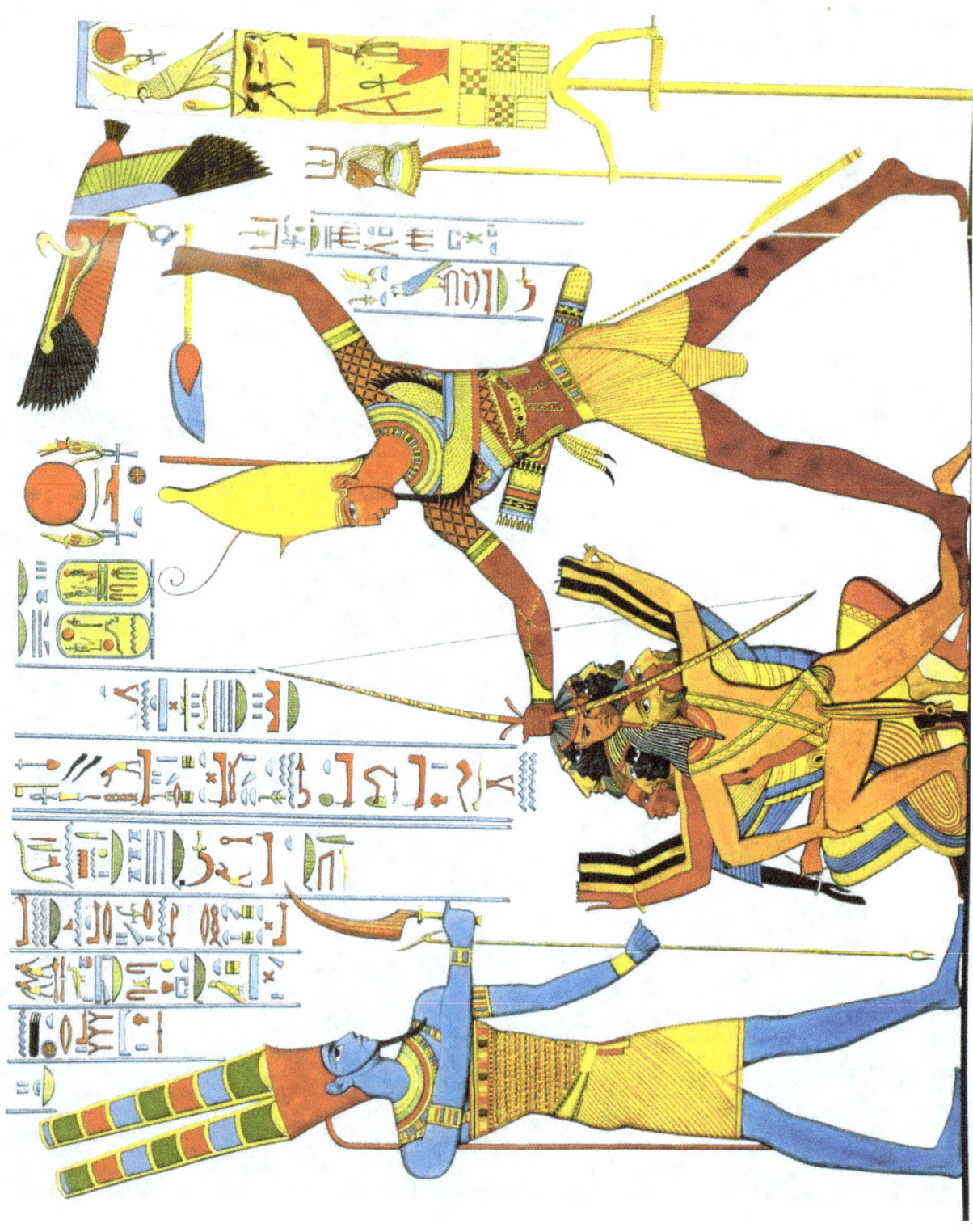

EGYPTIAN BOOK OF THE DEAD HIEROGLYPH TRANSLATIONS Vol. 5

Description and summary

The following hieroglyphic terms are given here to further explain the concept behind the scimitar or Chepesh. It relates to the mystery about the northern constellations, and an astronomical mythic ritual process that was part of the Ancient Kemetic spiritual tradition. It relates to mystic teachings that refer to the North Pole area where certain stars, called **Akhemu Seku,** that never go below the horizon and rise up above the horizon, are found. Those stars are referred to as imperishable stars because their capacity to shine is not obstructed from view because they do not go below the horizon; they can always be viewed in the night sky. They are also known as pole stars. The stars that do go below the horizon and emerge later after several hours are therefore absent from view part of the night; therefore, they are referred to as perishable stars or **Akhemu Urdu**. Philosophically, in the tradition of Shetaut Neter, this constellation philosophy of perishable and imperishable stars relates to the context of understanding human consciousness as something fluctuating as opposed to continuous, respectively. The human mind is not continuously aware. There are times when the human being is asleep, when a human being is awake, or when the human being is asleep and dreaming. Those three states are states of fluctuation of human consciousness, and they are symptoms of unstable or fluctuating conscious awareness (perishable). The desired state of advanced human existence is the attaining of the level of awareness that is continuous and not subject to fluctuations. That state of higher consciousness (imperishable) is referred to as **nehast,** or spiritual enlightenment. These two states of human conscious awareness, perishable or imperishable, relate to the teaching given by the Ancient Egyptian sage Amenemopet in his wisdom texts. In that text, he relates these two kinds of conscious awareness as relating to states of the human personality as being heated (perishable) or silent (imperishable). The following section contains some definitions about the teaching of the imperishable stars as well as the role the Great Pyramid played in these teachings on the Mystical Constellations, and also, verses from the teachings of Ancient Egyptian sage **Amenemopet** from chapter 4 of his Wisdom Text scripture that provide additional insights into this topic.

How to meet the Criteria of Being Recognized as a Royal Person and Receiving the approval of Ptah, the God of the Earth Plane and Physical Creation and the Granting of the Royal Person Status in the form of the Heka, Nekaku and Chepesh/scimitar

Answer: For those who are qualified, the Khepesh leads to **Akhemu Seku**-Enlightenment. For those who are not it leads to reincarnation.

Akhemu Urdu - never resting stars (always visible going below and then rising above the horizon) - setting. [Heated Personalities] – <u>unstable</u> conscious awareness.

Akhemu Seku - never setting stars (that do not go below the horizon and rise from behind the horizon)– imperishable [Silent/cool personalities]-<u>stable</u> conscious awareness.

The Great Pyramid of Egypt with the Mystical Constellations (view from the East). (below)

The image below shows extended lines from shafts in the Great Pyramid at Giza in Egypt. One of the shafts points towards the north pole, which is surrounded by the same constellations (including the chepesh, that constitute the imperishable stars, thus relating the structure to the same concept of "imperishableness" or immortality. Viewed from the south, the northern shaft leading from the main chamber in the great pyramid (far right) points to the point in space where there is no movement.

EGYPTIAN BOOK OF THE DEAD HIEROGLYPH TRANSLATIONS Vol. 5

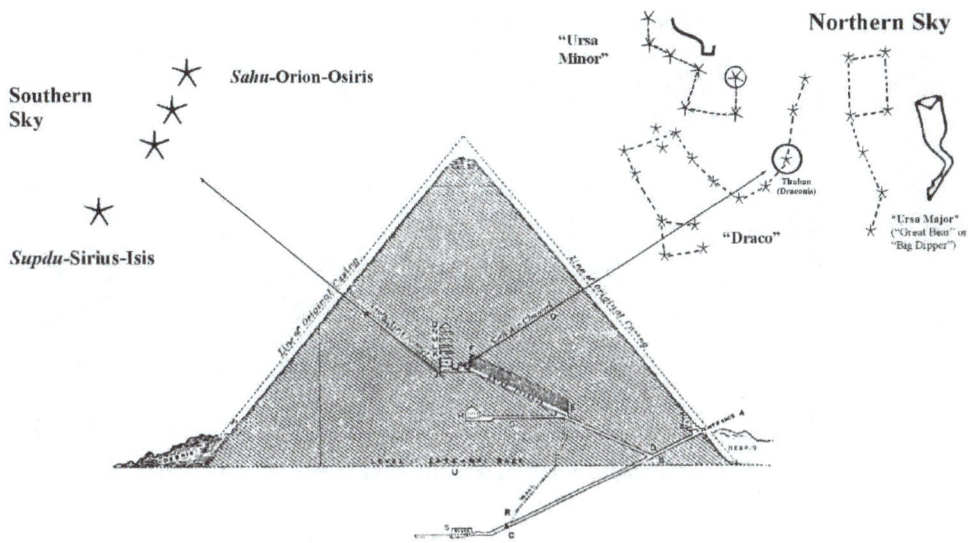

(below) The Great Pyramid of Egypt with the Mystical Constellations (view from the South).

    A simulated time-lapse photo (above) of the northern sky produces a circular motion and starlight appears as streaks across the background of the darkness of outer space. The closer one moves towards the pole the stars appear to "move" less, which is in smaller circles until at the very center there is no movement at all. This center is, of course, an abstract point that transcends time and space.

EGYPTIAN BOOK OF THE DEAD HIEROGLYPH TRANSLATIONS Vol. 5

The changing nature of the "Pole Star" indicates that the philosophy related to the "imperishable" stars is not a physical location but rather a mystical one. The abode that is the goal of all souls is not in the stars but rather in that place where no changes or fluctuations occur, the Absolute.

Teachings of Amenemopet Chapter 4

Verse 1.

          er   pa   shemm   {khet}{cheft} en   Neter het

1.2. <u>As for that heated person   {fire}{enemy} to   Divinity temple</u>

1.3. As concerns those heated people, when they go to the temple...

Verse 2.

    2.1 *su mi   shatu.   red   {mdj} im   chenty   per*

    2.2. <u>his like trees   growing   {fig} in advancing-inside building</u>

    2.3. ...to them it is like a tree going inside the temple, which is a covered building; so those people, like the trees, who do not gain illumination from the sun or rain, in the same way, those people do not get the benefit of the illumination from the Divine, that the temple has to offer.

Verse 7.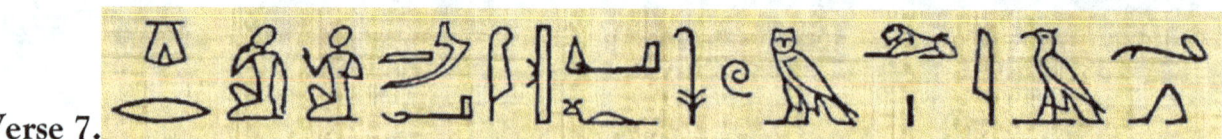

    7.1.   *ger   a   maa {mdj} di-f   su   im   raaa*

    7.2.   <u>silent   truly {fig} gives-he his through leaving</u>

    7.3.   The ones who are truly silent, they give their answer/response to the heated ones in the form of being remote, distant isolated/secluded/apart/aloof/withdrawn/reserved/inaccessible, detached...

Verse 3.

    3.1.   *su*   *mi*   *shatu*   *red*   *im*   *tihentu*
    3.2.   his   like   trees   growing   in   water and   {lands}

    3.3.   ...to the silent they are like a tree growing in a place with plenty of water and fertile earth and open to the sky so they grow to the fullness of their capacity.

Summary of the Ancient Egyptian Wisdom Text Teachings of Sage Amenemopet instructs:

MAIN QUALIFICATIONS OF A ROYAL PERSON INCLUDE:

- ✓ Silent(cool) personality, (not heated), dispassionate, level-headed
- ✓ Ethical conscience, straying away from wrongdoers, living by the truth
- ✓ Devotion to God with reverence for sages and others on the spiritual path with the desire for enlightenment.

Awareness on the path of life as opposed to living unconsciously; Awareness of the Transcendental Divine as the foundation of life

EGYPTIAN BOOK OF THE DEAD HIEROGLYPH TRANSLATIONS Vol. 5

LIVING MANIFESTATION OF THE DIVINE, a Royal Person (the human accepting and honoring the higher expression of one's own human being, the becoming of a Royal Person. Temple of Amun-Ra at Abu Simbel –[location Branch #4-east wall]

Adorations of the Royal Person to him/herself as a LIVING MANIFESTATION OF THE DIVINE
360⁰ Web Page Location, Temple Location Branch #4

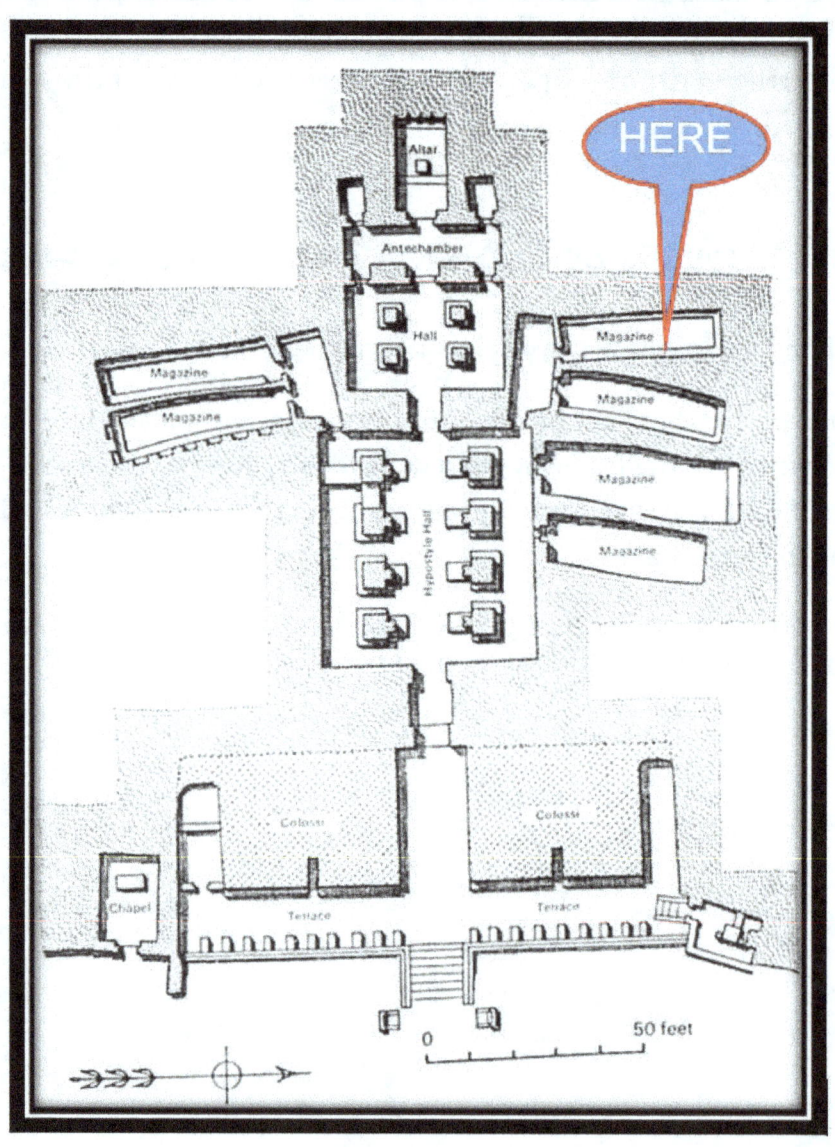

Panel 1.5-Adorations of the Royal Person to him/herself as a

Description and summary

This particular image (above) was taken from a panel that can be seen in branch number four of the temple. This panel includes some pro forma elements that we've seen before as well as a special, non-pro-forma, important philosophical teaching.

That important non-pro-forma term and teaching is called **Ankh-Neter-Nefer** or "the living manifestation of the Divine". We have seen how, in the easternmost parts of the temple, that the Royal Person has been designated with having the name of the Royal Person encircled by an elongated oval Shen symbol (called "cartouche, by the French). In this context, the definition is: "an ornamented tablet of stone wood, or metal destined to receive an inscription" or 'royal rings'. The Ancient Egyptians named this **Shenu** and the root of the term is related to the Ancient Egyptian word "**Shen**" or eternity. Some descriptions regard the word cartouche as being originated in the cartridges used by the French army to hold munitions.

The cartouches contain the two main spiritual names of the Royal Person. Here the Royal Person is kneeling with offerings in both hands and facing a divinity. The hieroglyphic text is informing us that the sitting figure is a living manifestation of the divine. The key to understanding the significance of this naming nomenclature is that the term used to refer to a Royal Person, in Ancient Egyptian iconography and philosophy, is: "Neter Nefer" or "Good God". The term good God is a mythic and metaphorical statement about the practical as well as a deeper reality of the identity of the Royal Person. The Royal Person is someone who is in a position to provide sustenance, the necessary condition for life to continue and flourish. They have the power to take certain actions that promote life and well-being to their community and country, acts akin to the Divine that sustains Creation.

The new term added to this naming nomenclature, the hieroglyph *ankh*, signifies that now the Royal Person is not being referred to as a "Good God" metaphorically but rather as a living manifestation of God literally. Therefore, the identity of the person sitting on the throne on the left side of the picture is not of a divinity in ordinary terms. Rather it is a manifestation, in perceptible time and space, of the higher divine aspect of the Royal Person that is doing the worshiping. Therefore, we are being alerted to the progressive development of the idea of the Royal Person or Initiate. We are to realize that the Royal Person or Initiate is more than human and actually human as well as superhuman. In this manner, as the Royal Person worships their own higher nature they are able to recognize and realize through devotional interest, attention, and wisdom, the higher nature of their own existence. In this manner, the visual aspects of the depiction of the iconography, the hieroglyphic texts, and the wisdom contained in the iconography can impact the person who witnesses, who gazes at the panels. Therefore, the panels are not images of static ideas or occurrences. Rather, the panels are images of spiritual fact that when understood with the earlier aforementioned wisdom allow an onlooker, who is the temple initiate, or any given Royal Person who is qualified, to partake in this ongoing scene of worship of their own Higher Self.

Thus, it is not absolutely necessary to travel to Egypt to gain this experience even though the presence at the very location of this panel or a large (mural-sized) photograph of the panel (as was done during the presentation of this study at the 2019 Shetaut Neter (Neterian) Conference in Florida USA) would help to enhance the feeling and attentive aspect of an initiate's spiritual practice. What is important is to live in accordance with and then realize the wisdom behind the iconography and text of the panels in order to partake in/with the experience being depicted; that is, realizing that one is that Royal Person who is being depicted. Having done so, the temple initiate may contemplate on an extended basis, the wisdom contained in the iconography that relates about their own living divine manifestation that they are, have been, and always will be.

This is an important aspect of the spiritual process of the temple promoting the evolution of the advancement of self-identity of the temple initiate. The significance of the statement ("the living manifestation of the Divine") by the Ancient Egyptian priests and priestesses is that they are stating unequivocally that the human person, who thought they were individuals and created separate or different entities, are being defined here now as manifestations and not as created beings. In this context, a manifestation is not a separate, distinct "created thing" but rather an expression, an appearance of the original. And as such, a manifestation of the original is not something different from the original but indeed an aspect or angle, a perspective, a viewpoint of the original pre-existing entity. Thus, human "beingness" is not objectified as objects having apparent independent existence; doing so would assign the "beingness", that is, the non-corporeal (spiritual) aspect of a person, which sustains their temporary physical manifestation as a human person, to a status equal to any otherworldly objects in Creation. This statement negates the existence of the human ego and egoism (separate, distinct "created thing") as human delusions. The human is essentially God and not a lowly, mortal human animal.

"Gods and goddesses are immortal men and women, and men and women are mortal gods and goddesses."

-Ancient Egyptian proverbial wisdom

EGYPTIAN BOOK OF THE DEAD HIEROGLYPH TRANSLATIONS Vol. 5

Adorations of the Royal Person to him/herself as a Royal Person (the human accepting and honoring the higher expression of one's own human being, the becoming of a Royal Person. (Left side panel detail)

EGYPTIAN BOOK OF THE DEAD HIEROGLYPH TRANSLATIONS Vol. 5

Adorations of the Royal Person to him/herself as a Royal Person (the human accepting and honoring the higher expression of one's own human being, the becoming of a Royal Person. (Right side panel detail)

EGYPTIAN BOOK OF THE DEAD HIEROGLYPH TRANSLATIONS Vol. 5

Text of Left Royal Aspect of same Royal Person			Text of Right Royal Aspect of same Royal Person	
Col. 3	2	1	Col. 1	2

Text of Right Royal Aspect of same Royal Person	Transliteration	Translation	Contextual Translation
Col. 1 1st main Pro-forma spiritual name of Ramses	(USER-MAAT-RA-SETEP-EN-RA)	(Power of the truth of the Creator Spirit and chosen by the Creator Spirit)	The Royal Person, Ramses, goes by the name: "One who exercises dominion backed by the righteousness of the Creator Spirit and who is chosen by that Creator Spirit."
Col. 2 2nd main Pro-forma spiritual name of Ramses	(AMUN MERY RA-MESU)	(Hidden Witnessing Spirit Beloved Creator Spirit-Child of)	This is the second royal name of the Royal Person, "One who is the child, who came from the body of Ra, the Creator Spirit, and who is beloved by Amun, the hidden witnessing Spirit Self."
--			

Text of Left Royal Aspect of same Royal Person				
Col. 6	5	4	3	2	1

Text of Left, Royal Aspect of same Royal Person	Transliteration	Translation	Contextual Translation
Col. 1	**Neb** **tawy** **neb** **chau**	Lord Two lands Lord Risings/thrones	This is the Royal Person, the Lord of the Two Lands as well as Lord over crowns and therefore an emperor.
Col. 2	**Ankh-Neter-nefer neb-tawy**	Living-Divinity-beautiful Lord of two lands, Lord…	This is the beautiful living embodiment of the Divine. It is Lord of the two lands of Upper and Lower Egypt (duality).
Col. 3	**Neb ari chetu {medj}**	Lord action objects {figurative}	This is the Lord of action, doing things, and commanding objects and sacrificial ritual supplies.
Col. 4	**Neb chepesh**	Lord strength war	This is the Lord of strength and warfare, generation.
Col. 5	(damaged)	(damaged)	(damaged)

--

EGYPTIAN BOOK OF THE DEAD HIEROGLYPH TRANSLATIONS Vol. 5

Description and summary

On the left side of the image, there are some hieroglyphic texts (see below). The term written there is called "sa ankh" or "protective life-force".

    The idea given by this term is that of a protective life force energy consciousness that is transmitted from its source, the Supreme Being, the divine, to the Royal Person. Actually, the wisdom about the protective life force that is found in the other Ancient Egyptian texts talks about the fact that this special life force comes originally from the Creator Spirit, the God Ra. It is transmitted through the gods and goddesses of his creation, which are the cosmic forces that course through the creation. By doing this service of upholding ethical conscience and doing the devotional work that helps the human being turn their awareness towards the divine, this special energy consciousness protective life force is drawn from its source (the God Ra). Additionally, the texts talk about the fact that this special protective life force energy consciousness is necessary for being able to "discover" and "understand" the nature of the Creator Spirit. In other words, it is a kind of divine grace that is extended from the divine reaching out to humans who are qualified to make the approach to the divine so as to have their consciousness opened.

    Thus, in consideration of the iconography and text, the positioning of the hieroglyphs of the protective life-force energy-consciousness and the positioning of the characters with the Royal Person making the offering and the living Divine manifestation of the Royal Person receiving the offering, and understanding the nature of their relationship as being human worshiper and divine Higher Self of that same human, it can be discerned that the "living divine manifestation of the human Royal Person" has the capacity to transmit that Sa Ankh, that protective life force, to the human Royal Person. In other words, one's own higher self has the capacity to transmit this special energy consciousness to one's own human aspect allowing it to evolve spiritually. Therefore, since the Divine is within the human, that aspect of the human, when accessed, can serve the function of transmitting the Sa Ankh, the protective life-force energy consciousness that opens the mind and expands conscious awareness of the Divine in the human being. This internal, direct access, to the protective life-force energy consciousness of immortal, transcendental Spirit, is opened by the devotion to the Divine along with the increasing understanding about the nature of oneself as being a manifestation of the Divine.

Sa-ankh

Text of Left, Royal Aspect of same Royal Person Col. 6　　5　4	Transliteration Col. 6	Translation Col. 6	Contextual Translation Col. 6
	Sa ankh	Protective life-force energy consciousness	This occurrence (the viewing of this panel with an understanding of the mystery (**mystic wisdom**) and feeling as being the protagonist participant) of this ritual, making offerings to one's Higher, Divine Self, provides a protective life-force <u>***energy/consciousness***</u> originated from Ra/Heru through gods and goddesses and their Divine Manifestations to the Royal Person that sustains life and allows conscious awareness of the Divine.

--

SA-ANKH "Divine Protective Energy-Consciousness"

Appears in Ancient Egyptian scriptures since the time of the Pyramid Texts (old Kingdom period).
Comes from Ra/Heru (Creator-Spirit)
Purpose:
- Sustains conscious awareness of humans and gods and goddesses
- To enliven the personality and make it possible for the human to understand the nature of the Divine (Enlightenment)

Can be transmitted to humans through gods and goddesses via:
- adoration/devotion of gods/goddesses
- embraces by/with gods/goddesses,
- laying on of hands by the gods and goddesses
- offering to and discovering one's own Divine nature that is also connected to Ra, the Creator Spirit.

Requires:
- ✓ wisdom-understanding of spiritual being turning (attention) towards the Divinity conscious-awareness
- ✓ devotional offering
- ✓ Reciprocation by Divinity that is elicited by the attention and offerings given to the Divine.

Image from Karnak Temple

EGYPTIAN BOOK OF THE DEAD HIEROGLYPH TRANSLATIONS Vol. 5

Panel of Identification with Gods and Goddesses
360° Location Branch #2

Description and summary

The next panel that will be studied, that conveys deep insight into the nature of the human spiritual identity, comes from branch number two of the temple. Actually, this is a dual-panel study. It is created in the context of what we refer to as the holographic convergence.

Definition of a Holographic Convergence in the context discovered by Dr. Muata Ashby:

A holographic convergence means that, for example, if there are two images on opposite (and sometimes the same) temple walls and if one were to visualize these two identical images coming off the walls and converging in the center of the room, and especially if the initiate is standing in the center where they converge, it would lead to a focusing of the thought and feeling the energy of the cosmic principles depicted and or talked about in the panel being looked at. Many people have visited the Ancient Egyptian Temples and have seen but not noticed or experienced these areas of "Holographic Convergences" which are quite interesting and powerful aspects of Ancient Egyptian architecture and spiritual teaching. Having the understanding of the holographic convergence feature of the Temple, along with its philosophical intent, and with the iconographical and metaphysical mystery insights gained from the hieroglyphic texts, affords an opportunity to partake (be connected) with the architecture, and not just understand the teaching being put forth by the Temple priests and priestesses. A sensitive person is also able to feel it, when passing through spaces that, if seen and understood, project visual images that evoke feelings, thoughts, and energies in the viewer and thereby allow them to experience what the images and spaces are projecting as well. That capacity will intensify the experience as well as provide a greater opportunity to allow the teaching to go beyond intellectual levels to deeper understanding and enlightenment.

The holographic convergence concept includes a "projection matrix". In this matrix, the wisdom, feeling, and energy of the first panel "projects" (moves, propels, transfers) to another panel. This movement can signify a deeper understanding to be seen in the successive panel or it could refer to a progression of the developments of the first panel or it could, as well, signify the transference of the energies, ideas, principles or feelings evoked by the first panel to the second. Still, another possibility is that the convergence signifies the exchange of positions of the personalities in both panels, and additionally could include the idea that the personalities on both are mirror images of each other or images showing different aspects of the same personality or theme. These are some of the main concepts behind the "projective" qualities of the holographic convergence feature of the panels in the Ancient Egyptian temples.

EGYPTIAN BOOK OF THE DEAD HIEROGLYPH TRANSLATIONS Vol. 5

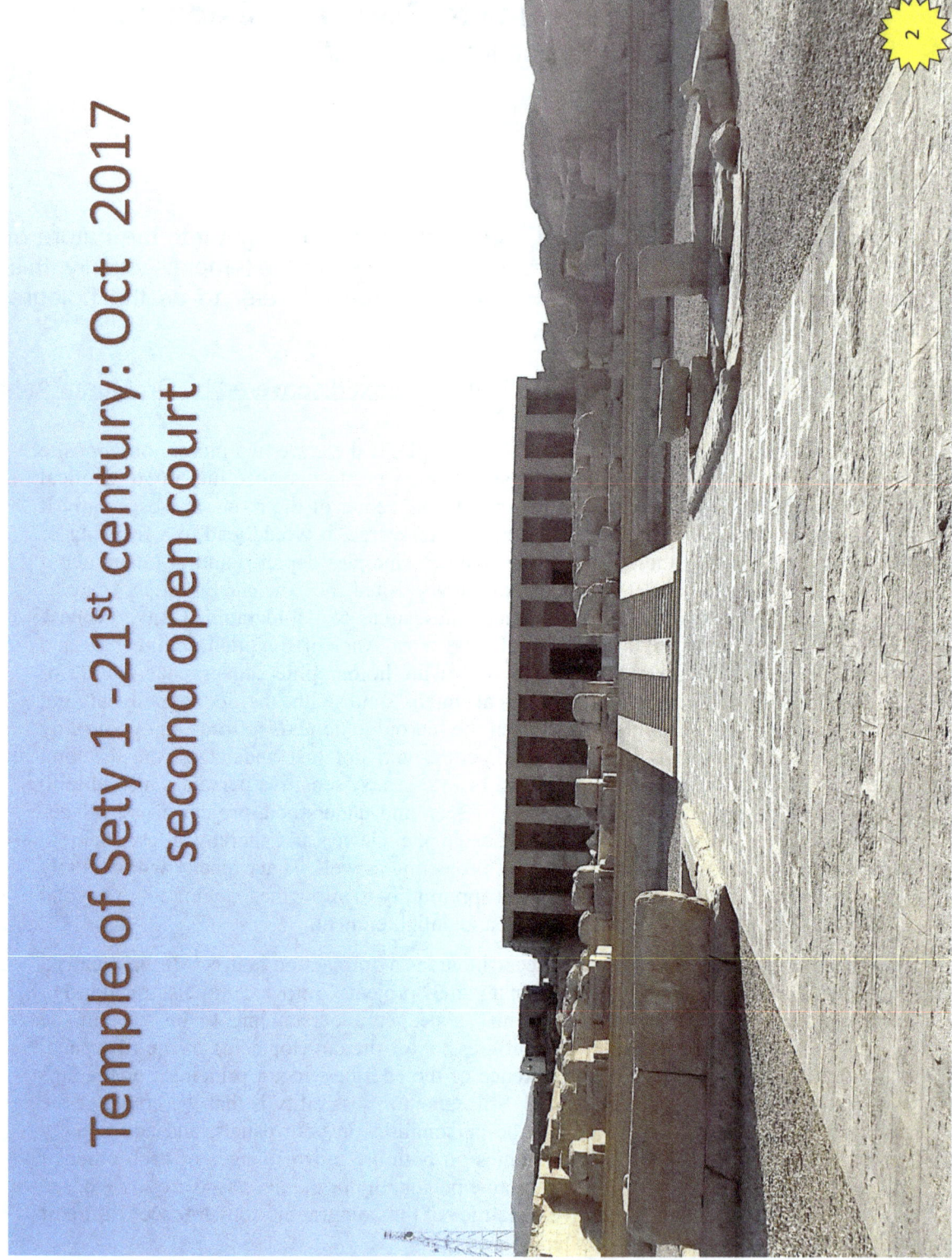

Temple of Sety 1 - 21st century: Oct 2017 second open court

Temple of Asar (Osiris) at Abydos

EGYPTIAN BOOK OF THE DEAD HIEROGLYPH TRANSLATIONS Vol. 5

Example of a "Holographic Convergence in the Ancient Egyptian Temples:

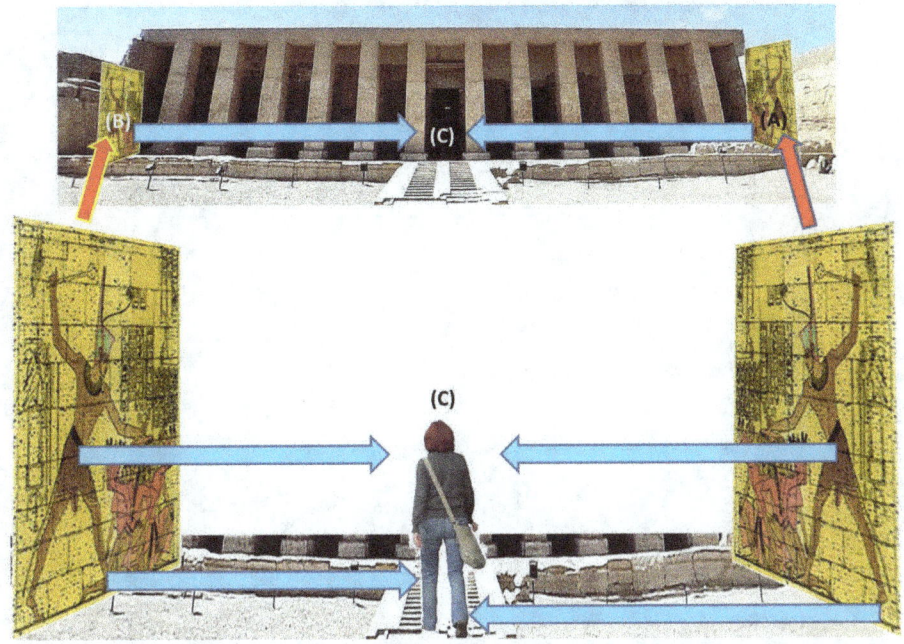

Temple of Asar Façade highlighting the Holographic convergences of (A) north and (B) south walls and the central standing spot (C) where they converge

Above- Two panels on the north and south sides of the façade portico, from the temple of Osiris at Abydos, face each other with matching characters and actions, forming a holographic convergence at the center axis of the temple when a person walking in the center, reaches the top of the steps.

The dual panels, that form a "holographic convergence" in the Temple of Amun-Ra(see below), are viewed by entering branch number two of the temple which has the entrance facing from south to north. Looking from south to north, when turning to the right wall on the east side of the room the first image can be seen above the white arrow. Looking to the left, on this west side of the branch, the second image can be seen above the second white arrow. The Temple incorporates a directional matrix (context in which the directions that the iconographies are facing are related to the physical/architectural orientation of the temple) which is based on cardinal points as well as the East-West path of the sun-disk (east to west). The temple directional matrix is a subtle indication of sequences and thematic movements through the temple that is embedded in the iconography and texts of the panels and also relative to their placement locations. It assists in the readings of the panels and in understanding their sequence as well as their interrelations and contexts. In this case (Temple of Amun-Ra) the temple directional movement is from East to West and North to South. Therefore, we begin by looking at the panel that is on the right side which is the East and then we move to look at the panel on the left side which is on the West.

EGYPTIAN BOOK OF THE DEAD HIEROGLYPH TRANSLATIONS Vol. 5

EGYPTIAN BOOK OF THE DEAD HIEROGLYPH TRANSLATIONS Vol. 5

Location Branch #2 looking South to North

360⁰ Web Page Location, Temple Location Branch #2

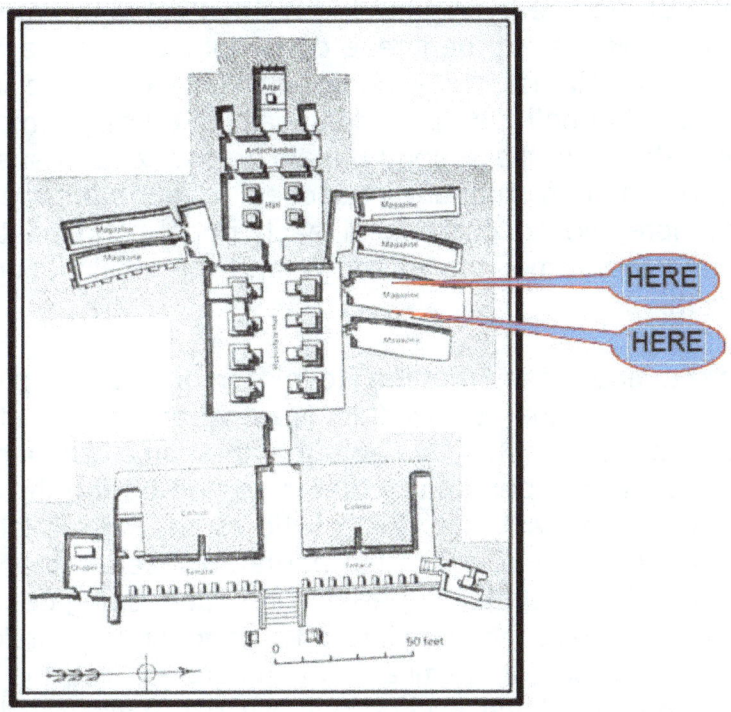

Note: The following description and summary applied to the following images.

The holographic convergence indicates that these two panels are related in a projective format meaning that panel number one (on the right side) projects (moves to, brings its message to, etc.) into panel number two (left side). Panel number one depicts another offering scene whereby the Royal Person is kneeling and making offerings towards another personality that is seated on the throne. As we have seen, in virtually all cases, these panels include offerings, which can be considered as a Pro-forma aspect, a standard, required, customary and important factor, of the iconography. The particular items being offered are not considered as Pro-forma aspects as the specific offerings do not occur in every panel. So, the concept/philosophy of offering is standard and required while the specific offering being offered is non-standard and depending on the theme of the panel. Other Pro-forma aspects include the factor of looking towards divinity from a kneeling position and the divine aspect depicted as sitting on a throne, atop a pedestal that has a sloping wedged on one side, making it the symbol of truth (Ma'at). The factor of the regular presence of worship and offerings and the dual spiritual names of the Royal Person can be considered as Pro-forma aspects of the iconography and texts. The specific and particular texts, teachings, and unusual descriptions or nomenclatures for the personalities are some of the non-pro-forma aspects of the presentations.

EGYPTIAN BOOK OF THE DEAD HIEROGLYPH TRANSLATIONS Vol. 5

The inscription states that the personality on the throne is the divinity who is the Lord of the "City of the Eight". That description fits only one divinity and that is the God Djehuty (Thoth/Hermes). This God is the City of the Eight, the scribe of the gods and goddesses, the mind of the Creator Spirit, and his symbol is the moon and particularly also the crescent moon. However, the image does not look like the typical iconography associated with the God. Rather, the iconography is akin to the iconography of the Royal Person as pictured in both panels. Additionally, the images match in terms of the occurrence in the hall (both are the second panels on east and west sides), both contain corresponding spiritual names that are supposed to appear together (in the same panel); importantly, here they occur one in each panel. The postures of the sitting personalities are both the same; the offerings and the designations of the kneeling personality also match.

Therefore, we are to understand that the Royal Person is worshiping their own higher self which has this divinity (Higher Self) within. Now, when we look at the second panel, on the west side (2B) of the room/hall, we note that the same personalities are depicted, however, here we see that the personality that is seated on the throne, though looking the same as the one on the east side (2A) of the room, here is labeled as being the Royal Person and the designation is with the name enclosed in the cartouche. In other words, this signifies that in panel 2B the personality that is being described as sitting on the throne is a circumscribed personality. The cartouche encircles the name and therefore the name is enclosed, it is limited, circumscribed. Yet, the panel combination is indicating that the human Royal Person actually has divinity within. This particular divinity, the Lord of the eight, who is also the moon and the mind, is an important development in the human capacity as opposed to ordinary animal existence, which does not have access to high intellectual capacity and cognition. Therefore, the advancing Royal Person, having this higher capacity of intellect, which this Ibis headed god also symbolizes, is consequently equipped to advance towards understanding the nature of spirit-being and thereby attain spiritual enlightenment. In this panel, we see the usage of the term *sa ankh* - protective life force energy consciousness that is transmitted by divinity and which is necessary for discovering and understanding the ultimate divine. Again, the approach of a spiritual aspirant to the panels of the temple with the understanding of its mystery teaching, its holographic interrelationships, its spatial directional matrices along with having purity of heart and devotional feelings towards the divine allows the human being to understand the nature of spirit-being and their relationship to it such that the human is able to discover their higher identity. As such, the personality that has been able to make this approach to the temple and its panels will draw the divine grace as well as protection of the personality such that they are able to experience the nature of true life and not just existing on earth, as mortal personalities, with ignorance of their true nature, only for a limited time followed by death.

(panel 2A , Panel 2B)

Importantly, the concept of Ankh-Neter-Nefer or "The Good Living Manifestation of the Divine" is also used in both of these panels (2A and 2B) but here they are used to refer not to the personality in the seated posture but rather to the kneeling personality, the human Royal Person. From this, we may take away the idea that the human Royal Person has divinity within them and that Divinity is the source of the Living Divine that manifests through them. Additionally, that same "Good Living Manifestation of the Divine" is the entity that resides in the higher self-identity, the god/goddess identity of the Royal Person. So, the human level is Divine and the god/goddess level of experience is a higher manifestation of the same Divine.

East wall-Looking South to North

EGYPTIAN BOOK OF THE DEAD HIEROGLYPH TRANSLATIONS Vol. 5

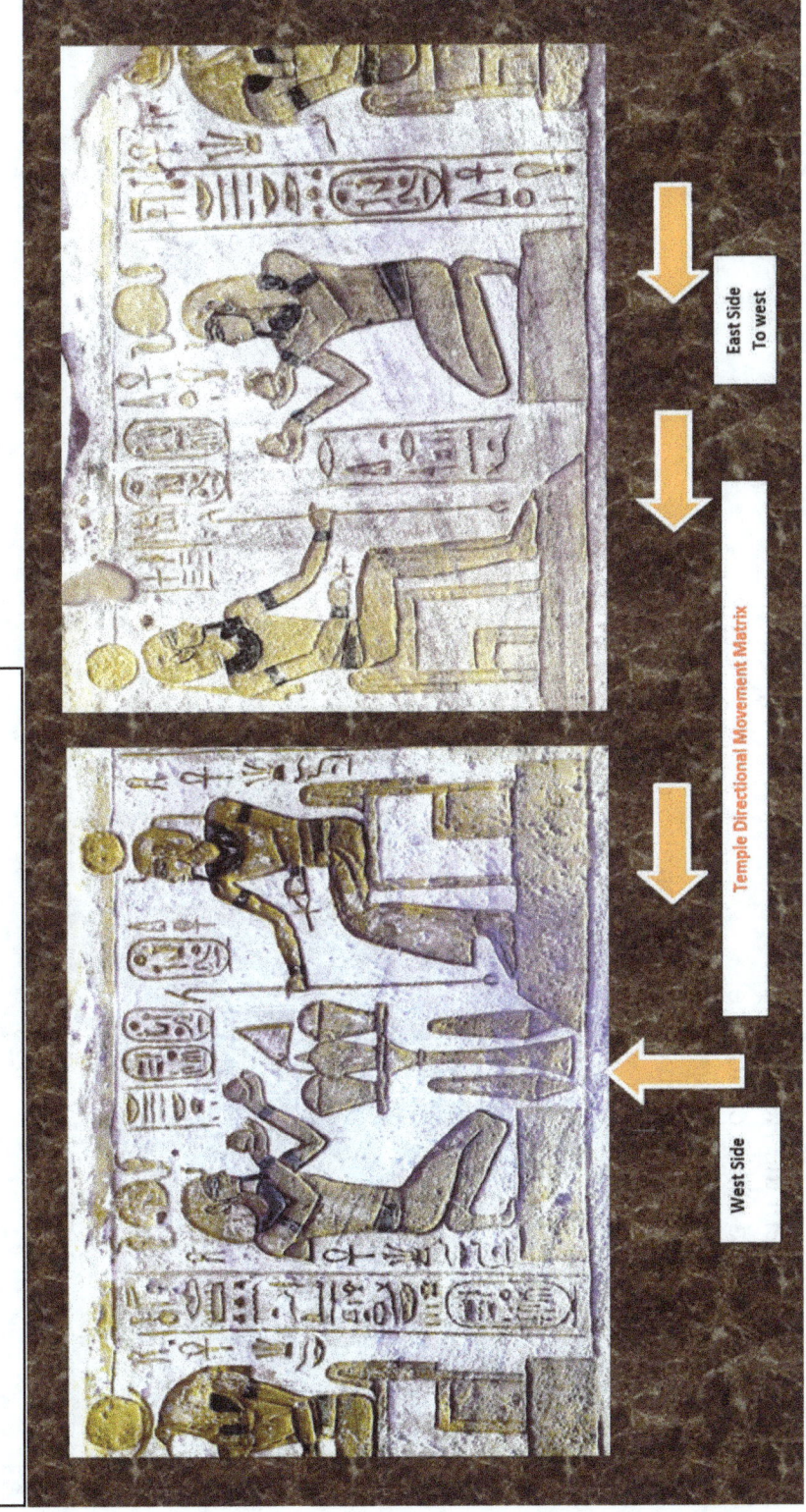

Panels 2-a, 2b: Trilinear Translation of Temple of Amun-Ra Abu Simbel–Panel (Branch #2) complementary holographic panels depicting worship of the Divine within the Royal Person

EGYPTIAN BOOK OF THE DEAD HIEROGLYPH TRANSLATIONS Vol. 5

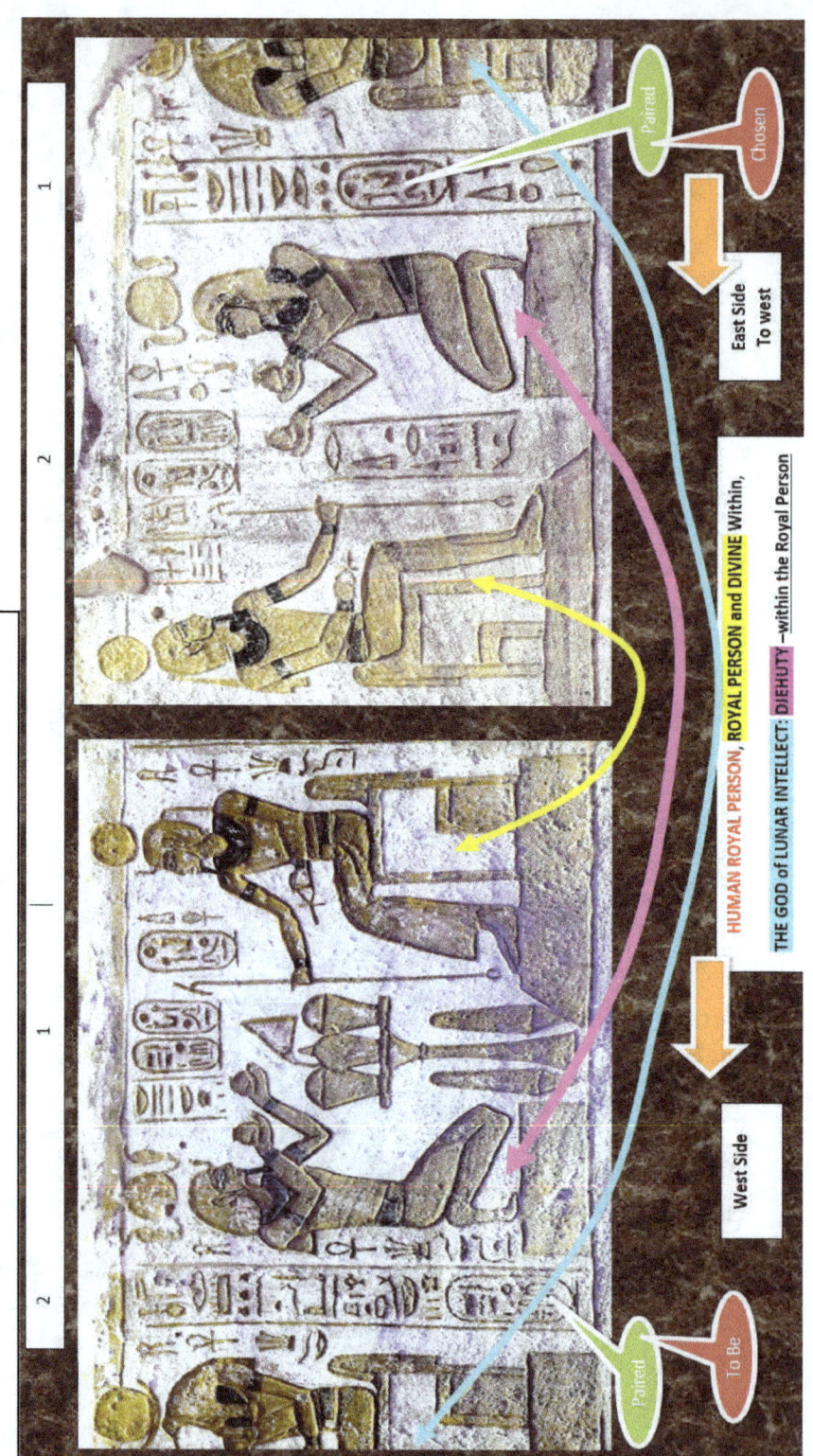

Two Keys to discern the Royal Person:
1-Proforma names within cartouche,
2-Royal designation as a noble Royal Person
The two personalities on each panel are correlated (paired).

EGYPTIAN BOOK OF THE DEAD HIEROGLYPH TRANSLATIONS Vol. 5

Panel #2b on south side of Branch #2

North to South

EGYPTIAN BOOK OF THE DEAD HIEROGLYPH TRANSLATIONS Vol. 5

Panel #2a on west side of Branch #2
South to North

Forms of Lord (God) Djehuty-God of the Moon, Intellect, Serpent Power and Writing

The God Djehuty as Ibis Headed Man as the scribe of the gods and goddesses, controller of the dual serpentine life force, and below as the baboon god of wisdom.

Below, the God Djehuty who cleanses the Eye of Heru and the Eye of Hetheru (Hathor)

EGYPTIAN BOOK OF THE DEAD HIEROGLYPH TRANSLATIONS Vol. 5

The offering of the Royal person to himself in the form of a God PANEL #1
Col.   2   1   3   4   5   6

7

--

The offering of the Royal person to himself in the form of a God				PANEL #1
Col.	2 1	3	4	5

Column	Transliteration	Translation	Contextual Translation
1-Text of R.P as Djehuty	*Sheps*	Noble, spiritually exalted	This is the spiritually exalted being…
2-Text of R.P as Djehuty	*im Khemenu*	within city-of-eight	In the city of the eight, where the God Djehuty, High Intellect, resides.
3-Text of R.P	(User-Maat-Ra-Setep-en-Ra)	Power/dominion righteousness/truth-chosen-by-Creator Spirit	This the first of the royal names of the Royal Person, known as: "One who exercises dominion backed by the righteousness of the Creator Spirit and who is chosen by that Creator Spirit."
4-Text of R.P	(AMUN MERY RA-MESU)	(Hidden Witnessing Spirit Beloved Creator Spirit-Child of)	This is the second royal name of the Royal Person, "One who is the child, who came from the body of Ra, the Creator Spirit, and who is beloved by Amun, the hidden witnessing Spirit Self."
5-Text of R.P	*Di ankh mi-Ra*	Gives life like-Creator-Spirit	Gives life as the God, the Creator

EGYPTIAN BOOK OF THE DEAD HIEROGLYPH TRANSLATIONS Vol. 5

6-Rubric Text	Transliteration	Translation	Contextual Translation
	Ankh-Neter-nefer	Living-Divinity-beautiful	This is the beautiful living embodiment of the Divine. It is Lord of the two lands of Upper and Lower Egypt (duality) and Lord of action, doing things and commanding objects and sacrificial ritual supplies. This is one of the royal names of the Royal Person, known as: "One who exercises dominion backed by the righteousness of the Creator Spirit and who is chosen by that Creator Spirit." This personality gives life like Ra gives life.
	Neb Tawy	Lord of two lands, Lord	
	Neb Ari chet	Lord action objects	
	(<u>User-Maat-Ra-Setep-en-Ra</u>)	(Power/dominion righteousness/truth -chosen-by-Creator Spirit)	
	Di ankh	Gives life	
	mi-Ra	like-Creator-Spirit	

--

Column #7	Transliteration	Translation	Contextual Translation
	erdit	Giving	This is the giving of a wine offering to my father.
	irp(dmg)	wine	
	en	to	
	tef	father	

The Offering of the Royal person to himself in the form of a Royal Person PANEL #2

Col. 1　2　　　　　3　4　5　6　7　　　　8

EGYPTIAN BOOK OF THE DEAD HIEROGLYPH TRANSLATIONS Vol. 5

The offering of the Royal person to himself in the form of a Royal Person Col. 1		Transliteration Col. 1	Translation Col. 1	Contextual Translation Col. 1
		ankh Neter nefer ary menu en atef di en her nest f per neb chau Ramesu-Amun-mery	Living divinity beneficent Action/deed monument to father giving to person throne his building Lord Risings/thrones Ramses- Amun- Beloved	This Living Divinity (Royal Person), who is beneficent and beautiful, has made this monument for his father (Amun-Ra), who has given to the R.P. their throne in his palace. The R.P. is the Lord of risings, like the sun ever dawning, and like an emperor, Lord over many crowns of minor kings. This R.P. goes by the name Ramses (child of Ra)-beloved of Amun(Divinity of Witnessing Consciousness).

EGYPTIAN BOOK OF THE DEAD HIEROGLYPH TRANSLATIONS Vol. 5

Col. 2 The offering of the Royal person to himself in the form of a Royal Person (corresponding to the opposite side of the panel)		Transliteration	Translation	Contextual Translation
		Sa	Protection	This ritual occurrence leads to the divine protective energy consciousness for the Royal Person; their body parts will have life essence, and therefore safety, from death, forever.
		Ankh	Life	
		Ha	Body	
		F	His	
		djeta	forever	

--

The offering of the Royal person to himself in the form of a Royal Person Col. 3		Transliteration	Translation	Contextual Translation
		Neb	Lord	This is the Royal Person, the Lord of the Two Lands as well as Lord over crowns and therefore an emperor.
		tawy	Two lands	
		Neb	Lord	
		Chau	Risings/thrones	

	Col. 4 Pro-forma Royal Titles of the Royal		Transliteration	Translation	Contextual Translation
			(AMUN MERY RA-MESU)	Amun Beloved Ra-Child/born of	This is one of the royal names of the Royal Person, known as: "One who is the child, who came from the body of Ra, the Creator Spirit, and who is beloved by Amun, the hidden witnessing Spirit Self."
	Col. 5 Pro-forma Royal Titles of the kneeling Royal Person	**REFERRING TO kneeling R.P.	Transliteration	Translation	Contextual Translation
			(User-Maat-Ra-Se-tep-en-Ra)	Power/dominion righteousness/truth-chosen-by-Creator Spirit	This is one of the royal names of the Royal Person, known as: "One who exercises dominion backed by the righteousness of the Creator Spirit and who is chosen by that Creator Spirit."

EGYPTIAN BOOK OF THE DEAD HIEROGLYPH TRANSLATIONS Vol. 5

Col. 6 Royal Titles of the Royal Person being worshipped on the throne	***REFERRING TO DIVINE ESSENCE OF R.P.	Transliteration	Translation	Contextual Translation
		(User-Maat-Ra-Se-tep-en-Ra)	Power/dominion righteousness/truth-chosen-by-Creator Spirit	

Col. 7 The action of the Royal Person being worshipped on the throne	Transliteration	Translation	Contextual Translation
	Di	Give	This Royal Divine aspect of the Royal Person, infused with purified intellect, gives life.
	Ankh	life	

Col. 8 Result of the Worship, a holographic text corresponding to the opposite sides of the panel.	Transliteration	Translation	Contextual Translation
	Sa	Protection	This ritual occurrence leads to the divine protective energy consciousness for the Royal Person; their body parts will have life essence, and therefore safety, from death, forever.
	Ankh	Life	
	Ha	Body parts	
	F	His	
	djeta	forever	

Description and summary

The following images, originally presented during the 2017 Neterian conference, by Dr. Ashby, show the condition of one of the temples that are located in the district called Hermopolis, by the Greeks and known to the Ancient Egyptians as "Khemmenu", the city of the Eight. The number eight refers to the eight gods and goddesses who are in the company of the Lord of the Eight. They are directed by their Lord, to do the work of sustaining creation.

The Lord of the Eight is the cosmic mind empowered by the Creator Spirit (god Ra). One of the designations of Lord Djehuty, the Lord of the City of the Eight, is "**ab Ra**" or heart of Ra. Thus he is the mind (**ab**) of the Creator Spirit. As the cosmic mind, he directs the events of creation and also sustains the minds of conscious beings. He also invented the hieroglyphic text and recorded the wisdom of his Lord the creator so that it might be available to be imparted to those with the capacity to understand and make use of it, i.e. the Royal Persons.

Insights Into the Concept of the "City of the Eight (FROM 2017 Neterian Conference)

NAMES OF KHEMENU		
	Khemenu	City of the eight; the domain of Djehuty
	Khemenu	8 Gods and Goddesses of the Company of Gods and Goddesses of Djehuty
	Khemenu	8 Gods and Goddesses of the Company of Gods and Goddesses of Djehuty
	Khemenu	8 Gods and Goddesses of the Company of Gods and Goddesses of Djehuty

EGYPTIAN BOOK OF THE DEAD HIEROGLYPH TRANSLATIONS Vol. 5

Description and summary

This chart shows a listing of the eight gods and goddesses, which represent principles of duality that sustain creation and that are managed by the Lord of the Eight. Each god/goddess principle represents four principles in a context of polarity, thus producing eight principles. That polarity sustains the differentiations of Creation and the energies within it that cause elements to combine, move, and sustain life.

8 Cosmic Principles of Khemenu and their Implications

	Male	Female
Nunu	Principle of Undifferentiated Consciousness	Undifferentiated Consciousness as a manifestation in time and space
Hehu	Principle of Ether/space	Ether/space as a manifestation in time and space
Kekui/Kekyu	Principle of Duality	Duality operating as light and dark manifestation in time and space
Gereh	Principle of silence-stillness	as a manifestation in time and space

Question:
What would happen if the 8 cosmic forces of **_Khemenu_** that emanate from the mind of **_Djehuty_** (Cosmic Mind), which is supported by Creator-Spirit Consciousness {Ra}), were to become open/unconfined/free/unsealed?

Answer: they dissolve into uncreated/un-manifest existence which is **_Neberdjer-_undifferentiated and transcendental absolute.** *This issue will be explored further in the next section.*

Summary

The last god and goddess of the company of the Lord of the eight, in the chart above, contain an important term, Gereh, the principle of silence and stillness, that is seen elsewhere in Ancient Egyptian wisdom. In the Ancient Egyptian wisdom texts of the Sage Amenemopet, he concentrates his teaching on two aspects of human personality. One of those aspects is called **shemm** or heated and the other aspect is **ger** or silent. These two terms were previously discussed in the section above called: "**Meeting the God Ptah and Receiving the Emblems of Royal Personhood**" Which presented the scripture titled Teachings of Amenemopet Chapter 4.

In order to have a deeper understanding of the significance of these panels, and their allusion to the Lord of the Eight, we will look at some passages from the Ancient Egyptian Book of the Dead that provide insights into the nature of this Lord as well as the City of the Eight and some metaphysical teachings about what happens to one who is on the spiritual path and succeeds in reaching into the light of spiritual enlightenment. The spiritual journey is likened to the movement through the netherworld which is the experience of astral reality that is above time and space physical worldly existence and then moving through increasingly subtler astral planes. The texts talk about the City of the Eight being opened up as opposed to being closed, as well as the head of a person as being sealed. The text also talks about the eye of Horus as being complete, integrated, in a perfect state. It also talks about the eye of Horus as being complete, integrated, in a perfect state.

Above: Lord Djehuty returning the eye of Horus to Horus, healed and whole.

According to the Ancient Egyptian myth of Asar (Osiris), (Aset) Isis, and Heru (Horus), Horus was in a battle with his uncle over the rulership of Ancient Egypt. During the battle, Horus' eye (of intuitional vision) was damaged but the Lord of the Eight healed it by uttering special words of power based on the wisdom teachings and metaphysical practices that are being discussed here and which are inscribed in the Ancient Egyptian Temples. That eye of Horus represents the higher spiritual vision of the human being that is symbolized as the third eye that resides in the astral forehead, i.e. the spiritual eye. The Scripture goes on to explain that the initiate, having opened up the eight gods and goddesses and having sealed the head, meaning the closing off of perceptions of the senses and thoughts of the mind, the spiritual initiate is able to discover the final spiritual faith which is the realization of the higher nature as being Asar (Osiris). That Osiris, that is their individual soul, is also one with the absolute Transcendental Self, the Universal Soul. Therefore, through this process, there is a realization, to be discovered, that one is not just a mortal limited human being but rather a manifestation of divinity partaking in the soul of the Supreme Divine.

Through the auspices of the Lord Djehuty, the Moon God, who represents the cosmic mind, and enlightened intellect, that sustains the human mind and is accessible to humans who are ethically conscious with purity of heart, one is to understand the nature of Divinity and also the path to realize, beyond intellect, oneself as being one of the gods and goddesses. Thus, the Ancient Egyptian Scripture complements and informs the depth of the temple architecture, iconography, and spiritual philosophy contained in the hieroglyphic text inscriptions of the temple. Therefore, we are seeing the evolution of human conscious awareness from limited human to now being referred to as being in the company of the gods and goddesses, which means discovering existence at the level of the astral plane. In Ancient Egyptian myth and metaphysics, there are three main planes of existence, the physical (Ta), the astral (Pet), and the causal (Duat), the latter two encompassing the netherworld and higher astral planes. Through the journey of the temple, each plane is studied, honored, experienced, and transcended in order to discover the next higher plane until the ultimate existence is discovered wherein the ultimate Divine resides beyond which there is nothing else to be discovered.

Ger-silence-stillness (Teachings of Amenemopet)

EGYPTIAN BOOK OF THE DEAD HIEROGLYPH TRANSLATIONS Vol. 5

PMH Pert em Heru Chapter 8- Making a passage through Amentet and going into the light realizing Osiris Identity and Djehuty identity in enlightened consciousness

Verse 1.

1.1. *Ra   en   uba   {mdj}   Amentet   [Pert]   im   ra Medu Dje in **Asar***
1.2. [chapter of] drilling {fig}   beautiful-west   [going]   into light words spoken by Osiris
1.3. **This is the chapter about piercing / penetrating / making a hole through the region called "beautiful-west", the abode of noble souls in the netherworld; then to go forth into the light of Shining Spirit Consciousness. The following words are being spoken by** the initiate who is called Osiris…

Verse 2.

2.1. *.Any   unnu   unnu   chetem   tep-a   Djehuty   aqer{mdj}   arit*
2.2. Any   open   Hermopolis   sealed   head-mine Hermes   perfect   eye
2.3. …Any, Open is Hermopolis, the city of the moon god of intellect and cosmic consciousness of Creation, and he has sealed my head so that it can no longer function as ordinary humans think and understand, being constricted and ignorant about their true identity and the nature of existence. I have a higher vision of existence since Hermes, my intellect has worked out the perfection of the eye (of Horus) which is the knowledge of my higher existence as an immortal Spirit Being through the eye of…

EGYPTIAN BOOK OF THE DEAD HIEROGLYPH TRANSLATIONS Vol. 5

Verse 3.
- 3.1. *Heru   seshedu   arit   Heru ach{mdj} khakeru   a   im   wept*
- 3.2. Horus   carrying   eye   Horus shine{fig} ornament me   in   forehead
- 3.3. …Horus that Hermes is carrying. My intellect (Hermes) has worked out the perfection of Higher Consciousness, the Eye of Horus, which shines like the moon on the forehead…

Verse 4.
- 4.1. *Ra   atef   Neteru [nuk] Asar puy   nen   amentet   rech*
- 4.2. Creator-Spirit father gods/goddesses [I] Osiris that there   [in]   beautiful-west   knowledge
- 4.3. …of Ra, the Creator-Spirit, who is the father of the gods and goddesses. [I] am Osiris, the same one in the Beautiful West, the final and coveted abode of the enlightened beings. The type of knowledge …

Verse 5.
- 5.1. *en Asar [h][eru] f   tem   f   unen im   an   unen a   im   nuk*
- 5.2. of Osiris day   his ending   his will-exist in not will-exist I within I-am
- 5.3. … that Osiris has is of his daylight, that is to say, of enlightened consciousness; that will be his ending(eschatology), that will be the final resolution of his spiritual journey, ending up within the light. Osiris will exist in the light but I, my non-Osiris conscience, will not exist within the light since my individual self is, in reality, Osiris and I, my ego, does cannot exist in the light. Finally, I am…

Verse 6.
- 6.1. *Yaah   im   Neteru   an   tem   a   aha   ar k   Heru*
- 6.2. Moon-god within   gods/goddesses   ending mine   stands-up for thee Horus
- 6.3. … also the moon god, Hermes/Osiris, within/in the midst of the gods and goddesses, being the brightest among them; one who's cosmic consciousness outshines all the cosmic forces. Since Hermes is a moon god of intellect I am Hermes; since Osiris is the moon, the night time reflection of Ra, the daytime solar illumination of Spirit Conscience, I am also Osiris. That will be the final outcome and ending of my spiritual journey…

EGYPTIAN BOOK OF THE DEAD HIEROGLYPH TRANSLATIONS Vol. 5

Verse 7.

7.1. **ap   f   tu   im   ma   neteru**

7.2. <u>counting he you within behold gods and goddesses</u>

7.3. ...to be counted, by him, as being among the gods and goddesses as one of them.

Description and summary

The below chart entitled: "Wisdom of the moon and the source of human-divine energy consciousness" displays three Ancient Egyptian personalities. The first one on the right side is the Royal Person. In Ancient Egyptian mystic wisdom, the Royal Person is the soul, which is also known as Osiris. In order to have interaction with thoughts of the mind and external objects in time and space, the soul witnesses experiences through the mind. Thus, the moon divinity Djehuty by being within the personality of the Royal Person is the cosmic principle that allows for that process of the experiencing through the mind. Djehuty, the moon God and Cosmic mind, is the divinity or cosmic principle that supports the individual intellects and minds of people. All individual souls have an individual mind that is sustained by Djehuty, the Cosmic Mind. That mind, in turn, is sustained by the Creator Spirit who in mythic terms is represented by the Sun God, Ra, himself an emanation of Neberdjer, (Cosmic Consciousness).

The following analogy is given for conceptualization purposes. Just as the moonlight is a reflection of the sun, so too the cosmic mind divinity, Djehuty, is a reflection of the Creator Spirit. Therefore, the Creator Spirit, Ra, symbolized by the sun, reflects consciousness on the lower level of existence called mind, the moon. Thus, in order to be able to become aware of and understand the nature of Spirit, which is universal, transcendental and infinitely expansive, the soul needs to have access to not just the ordinary individual human mind, but also the nature of cosmic expanded mind by the development of higher intellect. That the expanded cosmic mind is represented by the Lord of the Eight, the God Djehuty.

Now, with this understanding of the relationship of Cosmic Mind, Djehuty, the Lord of the Eight and the Royal Personality, we need to go a step further to discuss the concept of Shu Akhu, which is the light of consciousness that allows those thoughts and experiences of mind to be perceived. In order for the individual soul to have access to conscious awareness, the Creator Spirit imparts a measure of shining spirit consciousness called **Shu-Akhu**. That measure of shining spirit consciousness, Shu Akhu, is what illumines the thoughts in the mind allowing the soul to perceive objects in time and space, through the perceptions of the mind and senses. Those objects include external objects in the world, as well as internal objects in the form of thoughts, perception of internal feelings, memories, desires, etc. In order to obtain higher spiritual advancement and enlightenment, it is necessary to cleanse the egoistic mind, the individual personality, and then access expanded levels of awareness, discovering one's own shining spirit through mental clarity, ethical conscience, and higher spiritual perception beyond body and mind.

From a higher perspective, the analogy of the sun and moon fails to capture the highest notion of the teachings in that the higher realization of enlightened being is not just that of a source and its reflection. The higher analogy would be to think of the sun and its rays. The rays are not reflections, though, when they land on certain materials, they cause the effect of a reflection of the sun as in the case of a reflection of the sun in a pool of water. In this analogy, the reflection is, of course, illusory and the rays are the souls; additionally, the sun is the Spirit. The rays are no different from the sun; they are pieces of the sun and a "piece" of something is the same composition as the thing it came from just as a drop of ocean water is the same as the ocean. If the rays think they are the reflection they are likened to mortal souls in a deluded state. If they turn around and see whence they came, and realize they are the sun then they are likened to persons that have realized their immortal spirit nature.

EGYPTIAN BOOK OF THE DEAD HIEROGLYPH TRANSLATIONS Vol. 5

Wisdom of the Moon and the Source of Human Divine Energy Consciousness		
Ra	*Djehuty* *(Ab-Ra)*[Heart of God]	*Suteny*
Sun	**Moon**	*Royal Person*
Spirit	**Mind**	**Soul**
Source Consciousness	**Reflection Of Consciousness in mind**	**Experience (Conscious Awareness in the human) based on reflected light**
Shu-Akhu (individual ethereal light of consciousness)	**Tat (image)**	**Kheperu (created forms)**

EGYPTIAN BOOK OF THE DEAD HIEROGLYPH TRANSLATIONS Vol. 5

FINAL WISDOM ABOUT THE SOLAR AND LUNAR METAPHOR: Understanding the Philosophy of solar and lunar wisdom and its implications about the nature of the mind as a reflection of Divine consciousness.

QUESTION: Can humans know God with their minds?

- ✓ The Moon-god Djehuty is within the human Royal Person
- ✓ The Moonlight (Djehuty) is reflected Sunlight (Ra)
    - o Therefore moonlight (Djehuty) is a partial reflection of Creator Spirit consciousness (Ra)
- ✓ If Human conscious awareness is based on Lunar Djehuty consciousness
    - o Then human conscious awareness is based on partial/fractional/restricted /incomplete /consciousness.

EXAMPLE: Illumining the Tomb with a polished metal reflector.

- ✓ If one were to explore an ancient tomb, as was done by early explorers in Egypt, but without electricity, it could be done by reflecting light from outside the tomb to the inside using a shiny piece of metal. However, the amount reflected would be limited in amount and the area covered. In this analogy, the Sun is Spirit, and the reflecting medium, the shiny piece of metal, is the reflected lunar illumining power in the mind. What it shines on is perceived in the same mind. But again, what the mind can perceive with its limitations, is incomplete and therefore, by definition, illusory. Therefore, the following conclusions may be drawn.
- ✓ Illumining the tomb with partial reflection cannot illumine the whole tomb just as moonlight (Djehuty) cannot illumine the world as the sun (Ra) can.
    - o Therefore, mind Djehuty (moonlight) cannot be useful in revealing God just as when there is an eclipse the moonlight cannot illumine the sun
- ✓ The mind is useful in gaining
    - o 1-philosophical/ theoretical (epistemological) understanding about the nature of the Transcendental Spirit, Neberdjer (God) and,
    - o 2- what needs to be done to discover Transcendental Spirit, Neberdjer (God) .
- ✓ Having gained an understanding of the philosophy and theory of mind and then having successfully pursued the discovery of the divine means going beyond reflected consciousness to the source of consciousness. This attainment bestows spiritual emancipation from the limitations of mind which are the tunnel through which the soul has learned to understand the world its mind is perceiving.

Part 4- From Identification as a Human to Identification as one of the Gods and Goddesses

Temple Location: Hypostyle Hall #1, south-east wall, 360⁰ web site Location #2

Description and summary

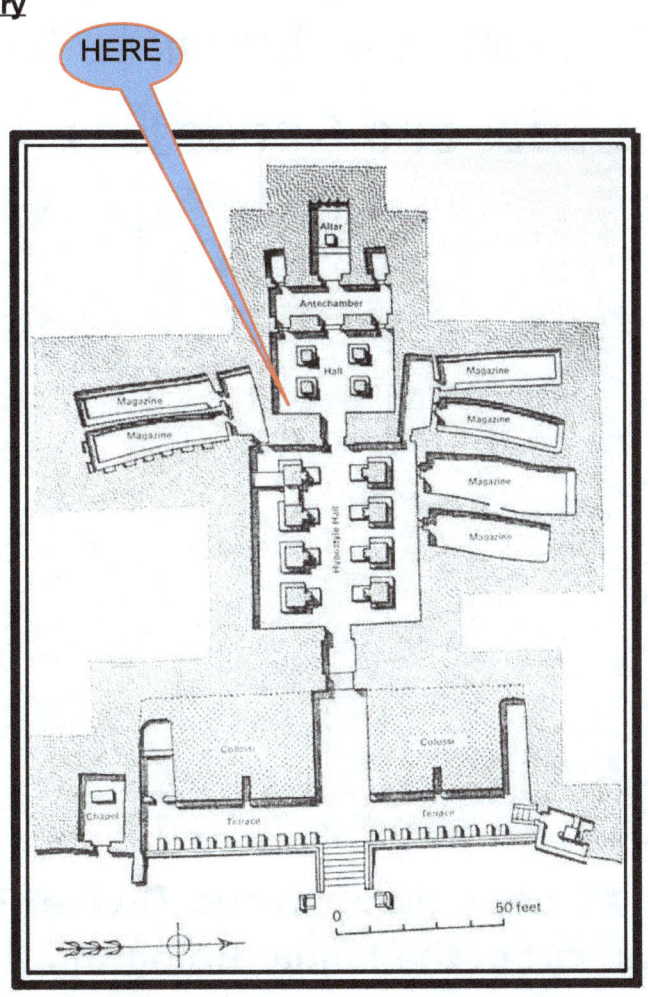

    In hypostyle number two, we saw how the relationship of the human spiritual initiate who enters the temple, discovers Royal Personhood. We saw how the God Ptah, the Architect of Creation presented, and the Royal Person received, the Royal emblems of royal legitimacy. We also saw the introduction of the mystery about having divinity within in the form of the Moon-god, Djehuty. Here we begin to enter the first hypostyle hall where images and text depict the Royal Person worshiping himself or herself along with the divine family. A special aspect of this section of the temple is depicted on the south-eastern wall showing that the Royal Person is worshiping the Trinity that includes him or herself as part of that divine Trinity. The Trinity is composed of the High God (Amun), the child of Amun (Khonsu), and the spouse of the God (Goddess Mut).

In the place where the youth/child of the God and Goddess is to be depicted, the Royal Person is depicted as filling that role. Therefore, the mystery is of realizing the higher nature of human beings which is of the nature of the gods and goddesses and in fact realizing kinship with the gods and goddesses as being one of them, in fact, as shown here, as being interchangeable with them.

From Identification as a Human to Identification as one of the Gods and Goddesses

Hypostyle Hall #1 adorations to the Divine Family with the Royal Person as part of the family Hologram Part 1

The following image, (from the north-eastern wall, directly across from the last image) is essentially a holographic mirror image of the one above. It shows the Royal Person on the far right side of the panel, facing the Trinity on the left. The central personality of this Trinity, in the image above which is on the southeastern wall, is again, the Royal Person in the role of the divine youth, Khonsu, who is a form of the Neter (god) Heru (Horus). We will use this image for our concentrated study of the temple teaching of the Royal Person as part of the family of gods and goddesses at this stage of the temple mystery of Divine Identity.

EGYPTIAN BOOK OF THE DEAD HIEROGLYPH TRANSLATIONS Vol. 5

Panel 3- The Royal Person is Part of the Family of Gods and Goddesses

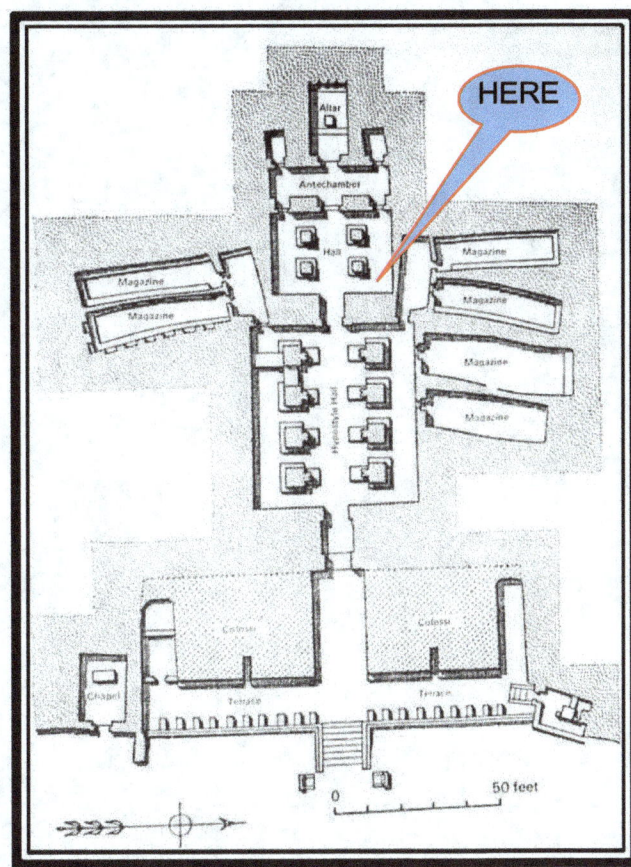

Identification as a member and heir of the Divine Trinity.

EGYPTIAN BOOK OF THE DEAD HIEROGLYPH TRANSLATIONS Vol. 5

Following image: Temple Location: Hypostyle Hall #1, north-east wall, 360⁰ web site Location #2

Adoration and Offering by the Royal Person to the second form of the Divine Trinity. Temple Location: Hypostyle Hall #1, north-east wall, 360 web site Location #2

EGYPTIAN BOOK OF THE DEAD HIEROGLYPH TRANSLATIONS Vol. 5

Following image: Temple Location: Hypostyle Hall #1, north-east wall, 360⁰ web site Location #2

EGYPTIAN BOOK OF THE DEAD HIEROGLYPH TRANSLATIONS Vol. 5

Following image: Temple Location: Hypostyle Hall #1, north-east wall, 360⁰ web site Location #2

EGYPTIAN BOOK OF THE DEAD HIEROGLYPH TRANSLATIONS Vol. 5

Description and summary

We will proceed to look at the divine family panel in <u>Hypostyle Hall #1, on the north-east wall,</u> by examining the iconography and texts in the panel and thereby discovering the mystic wisdom that is being imparted in it. Each section of the text relates to each of the personalities that are being depicted. We will first look at the text of Ramses, the Royal Person, then we will look at the text of the God Amsu (Amun), followed by the text of the Royal Person as a divinity and finally, we will look at the text of goddess Aset (Isis). So, as we see in the complementary panel on the southeastern wall, the trinity represents the Theban family, Amun Ra as the divine father, Khonsu, the divine child, and goddess Mut, the divine mother. However, in this northeastern panel, the trinity is represented by Amsu Min, Khonsu, and the goddess Aset. Thus, there is an expanded understanding of the henotheistic nature of Kamitan Mythic Religion, that the gods and goddesses are cosmic principles and these cosmic principles can represent different aspects or forms of the different neteru (gods) as aspects of each other. Thus, Amsu Min is an aspect of Amun Ra, and the goddess Aset (Isis) is an aspect of goddess Mut. Also, because goddess Aset (Isis) is traditionally associated with the Asarian Trinity of Aset (Isis) as the Divine mother, Heru (Horus) the Divine child, and Asar (Osiris) as the Divine father, goddess Aset's presence in this panel means that the other cosmic principles that are also being represented here are the principles of spiritual aspiration, Heru (Horus), associated with the divine child Khonsu, and also the Asar, the Soul, associated with Amsu Min (Amun).

EGYPTIAN BOOK OF THE DEAD HIEROGLYPH TRANSLATIONS Vol. 5

Text of Isis			Text of Ramses as Khonsu/Heru		Text of Amsu-Min-Asar Col.				Text of Ramses	
Col. 3	2	1	2	1	4	3	2	1	Col. 1	2

Text of Ramses		Transliteration	Translation	Contextual Translation
Column	1	Neb Tawy (USER-MAAT-RA-SETEP-EN-RA)	Lord of Two Lands, Power of the truth of the Creator Spirit and chosen by the Creator Spirit	The Royal Person, Ramses, is the Sovereign over the two lands of upper and lower Egypt, the totality of above and below, he goes by the name: "One who exercises dominion backed by the righteousness of the Creator Spirit and who is chosen by that same Creator Spirit."
Column	2	*Neb chau* (AMUN MERY RA-MESU)	Lord of thrones (Hidden Witnessing Spirit Beloved Creator Spirit-Child of)	This is the second royal name of the Royal Person, "One who is the child, who came from the body of Ra, the Creator Spirit, and who is beloved by Amun, the hidden witnessing Spirit Self."
--				

EGYPTIAN BOOK OF THE DEAD HIEROGLYPH TRANSLATIONS Vol. 5

Description and summary

The next series of texts, from right to left, relate to the God Amun Ra, here in his form or aspect as the Neter (god), Amsu Min. In the text of the God, we are informed about the nature of this divinity who created himself. We're also told that he (The God) is the innermost personality/reality of this temple, which has been caused to be built, by Ramses, the Royal Person. Ramses (on the right side of the panel below) is making an offering of lettuce to the divine Trinity. This offering represents at the same time, the fruits of ethical work, devotional feeling, and a loving attempt to please the divinity, as lettuce is one of his favorite foods. In reciprocation for the efforts of the Royal Person, the God grants the boons of spiritual valor and spiritual strength for success on the spiritual journey.

EGYPTIAN BOOK OF THE DEAD HIEROGLYPH TRANSLATIONS Vol. 5

Text of Isis			Text of Ramses as Khonsu/Heru		Text of Amsu-Min-Asar Col.				Text of Ramses	
Col. 3	2	1	2	1	4	3	2	1	Col. 1	2

Text of Amsu		Transliteration	Translation	Contextual Translation
Column	1	*Medu dje in Amsu-Amun-Ra-ka-mut-f*	Words spoken by Ithyphallic-Hidden-Creator-Spirit-bull-of-mother-his	These words are spoken by the god *Amsu-min,* (Aspect Amun-Ra) known as the Hidden Creator-Spirit with an erect penis, who is the one that brought himself into existence.
Column	2	*Her ab pa per* (AMUN MERY RA-MESU) *Di ankh*	Personality innermost that temple (Hidden Witnessing Creator-Spirit Beloved Creator Spirit-Child of) Gives life	That divinity (Amsu) is the innermost essence of the temple of the Royal Person known by the name: "One who is the child, who came from the body of Ra, the Creator Spirit, and who is beloved by Amun, the hidden witnessing Spirit Self." He is a life-giver.
Column	3	*Di en-en k qen(t) neb*	Given to-thee Spiritual valor	Amsu says: I give to you all spiritual valor.
Column	4	*(di) necht neb*	(given) spiritual strength	Also, I give to you all spiritual strength.

Above- Images From Other Temples: Amun-Ra Ka-mut-f

"Hidden Creator-Spirit Bull-Mother-His"

The High God Creator who Engendered his own Existence"

EGYPTIAN BOOK OF THE DEAD HIEROGLYPH TRANSLATIONS Vol. 5

Description and summary

The next text relates to the Royal Person of this temple, who is **Ramses.** As stated earlier, in this panel, he is being placed in the regular position of the God: Khonsu. In the texts of this panel related to Khonsu, we see one of the pro forma spiritual names. That name is "hidden witnessing creator spirit beloved creator spirit child of". The subtle, but important mystery teaching being given here is the inclusion of the spiritual Name of Ramses where the name or text of Khonsu would ordinarily be placed. The remarkable feature of the use of the name is that it is not enclosed by a cartouche. The absence of the cartouche signifies that the spiritual name, that is, the nature of the Royal Person in this form, in the placement in the position of the divine child/youth, Khonsu, represents an expansion from strictly physical human existence into the nature of the gods and goddesses which is above physical existence. So, instead of being circumscribed, the name of the Royal Person is now being recognized as being uncircumscribed or unbound. Therefore, this teaching represents an exposition of the idea of having expanded existence and along with it expanded conscious awareness of one's deeper essence, one's spiritual identity.

EGYPTIAN BOOK OF THE DEAD HIEROGLYPH TRANSLATIONS Vol. 5

Text of Isis			Text of Ramses as Khonsu/Heru		Text of Amsu-Min-Asar				Text of Ramses	
Col.			Col.		Col.				Col.	
3	2	1	2	1	4	3	2	1	1	2

Text of Ramses		Transliteration	Translation	Contextual Translation
Column	1	*Medu dje in*	Words spoken by	These words are now being spoken by…
Column	2	) AMUN MERY RA- MESU (	{Unbound})-Hidden Witnessing Creator-Spirit Beloved Creator Spirit-Child of-(	… the "unbound" "Un-circumscribed" Royal Person is known by the name: One who is the child, who came from the body of Ra, the Creator Spirit, and who is beloved by Amun, the hidden witnessing Spirit-Self is here recognized as being the divine child, Horus/Khonsu, and member of the dual Divine trinity of Hidden-Creator-Spirit-Bull of-his-mother/Amsu-Min/Asar, Horus/Khonsu and Aset/Isis; Khonsu/ Horus is the offspring of Amsu (Amun)/Asar. In Amun Theurgy he is the "traveler" aspect of Amun and Amun's projection through time and space. In Asarian Theurgy, he in the form of Heru (Horus) represents spiritual aspiration, redemption, and the spiritual victory of the soul over egoism.

Forms of The God Khonsu / Heru, the Divinity whose position is being assumed by the Royal Person

EGYPTIAN BOOK OF THE DEAD HIEROGLYPH TRANSLATIONS Vol. 5

Description and summary

The final text on this panel relates to the goddess *Aset* (Isis). Here she is assuming the position of goddess *Mut*, the counterpart of the God *Amsu (Amun Ra)*, which can be seen on the previous panel on the other side (south) of the hall. We are informed that the goddess is the divine mother and mistress of heaven as well as the Queen Mother of the two lands of upper and Lower Egypt. In reciprocation of this offering by the Royal Person, in addition to the boons being granted by *Amsu*, she is granting the totality of life, verticality, and power. These grants by the goddess are important and momentous because these three items represent the quintessential Ancient Egyptian matrices for experiencing the perfection of human spiritual evolution. *Ankh*, or life principle, represents existence beyond mortality, possessing which added spiritual aspirant will be fully equipped to be successful on the spiritual path. In terms of Ancient Egyptian mystery philosophy, *Verticality* relates to the ability and capacity for vertical spiritual evolution (raising in consciousness) as opposed to horizontal human mortal existence. The power component is the capacity to make effective the verticality that allows abiding existence, which is actually true life, to be discovered and experienced.

EGYPTIAN BOOK OF THE DEAD HIEROGLYPH TRANSLATIONS Vol. 5

Text of Isis Col.			Text of Ramses as Khonsu/Heru		Text of Amsu-Min-Asar Col.				Text of Ramses Col.	
3	2	1	2	1	4	3	2	1	1	2

Text of Isis			Transliteration	Translation	Contextual Translation
Column		1	*Medu dje in Aset urt*	Words spoken by Isis great	These words are now being spoken by Isis great…
Column		2	*Neter Mut nebt pet henut*	Divine mother Mistress Heaven Queen-mother	…Divine Mother goddess, mistress of heaven and Queen Mother…
Column		3	*tawy di – ze ankh-djed-was neb*	Two lands Gives-she Life-verticality-power all	…of the two lands of Upper and Lower Egypt. She gives All Life-Verticality-Power to the Royal Person; this is the fullness of conscious existence, the capacity for rising above time and space and the power to achieve the heights of spiritual experience.

EGYPTIAN BOOK OF THE DEAD HIEROGLYPH TRANSLATIONS Vol. 5

Description and summary

The following images are from the temple of Asar (Osiris), located in Abydos, Egypt. Within this temple exists a panel containing iconography and hieroglyphic texts that give insight into the apparent aberrant depiction of the goddess Aset (Isis) in the temple of Amun-Ra, along with the aspect of Amsu Min, because traditionally she is associated with her trinity portrayed as Asar, Aset, Heru (Horus), rather than with Khonsu, or Amsu Min.

Thus, the appearance of Aset, in the temple of Amun-Ra, would seem to be aberrant because she is usually thought of as being the counterpart of Asar (Osiris). But in this temple, she is being depicted as part of the divine Trinity with the God Amsu (an aspect of Amun) as its head. As stated earlier, she is in the position usually occupied by the counterpart of the God Amun, who is the Goddess Mut. In this temple, the temple of Amun-Ra, we see her being depicted as the counterpart of the God Amun (in the form of Amsu). This apparent anomaly is explained by a panel from the temple of Osiris. Note: the Kemetic and Greek names, Asar, Aset, Heru, and Osiris, Isis, and Horus, respectively, will be used interchangeably.

In the temple of Osiris, the sanctuary has a panel that depicts Osiris in an extended manner. In that panel the God Osiris appears in his characteristic iconographic format (headdress crown of the south, mummy swathings)However, the text of the panel identifies him as being both Horus and Amsu. This depiction, therefore, signals the idea that the God Osiris, who is, in the Ancient Egyptian creation myth, regarded as the universal Soul, is the Absolute Self-manifesting in time and space. In the form manifesting beyond time and space, where there are no forms, the absolute is called **Neberdjer**, the "All-Encompassing Divinity", the Absolute. So, when transcendental Spirit is unmanifest it is referred to as Neberdjer, the Absolute; when manifesting in time and space as the living soul/consciousness in Creation, it is called **Asar** (Osiris). Therefore, we are to understand that what we are seeing in the temple of **Amun-Ra** is actually a depiction of Osiris but in the form of Amsu. Consequently, the Trinity that is depicted in the temple of Amun-Ra is at the same time of **Amun-Mut-Khonsu** and **Asar-Aset-Heru** (Osiris-Isis-Horus). This is an indication of the equivalency of Ancient Egyptian gods and goddesses that, though seeming to be separate and distinct, are actually manifestations of the same *Ultimate Divine* albeit in varied forms and described by varied nomenclatures. In this case, we are to also understand that in this north side of the temple hypostyle hall, the Ancient Egyptian priests and priestesses who directed the creation of the temple, are meaning to mystically infuse the insight and feeling of Isis into the iconography and wisdom of this holographic panel image. As the goddess of intuitional realization, her wisdom relates to the mysteries of transcending the mind and the spiritual practice that incorporates a meditation system applying the serpent power metaphysics that lead to breaking through the illusion of creation and discovering the Transcendental Divine.

For more of the expanded mystic wisdom of goddess Isis go to the books *Mysteries of Isis and Ra* and *African religion volume 4: Asarian Theology* and the book *Serpent Power (all by Dr. Muata Ashby)*.

The Temple of Asar (Osiris)

Insights about The Temple of Amun-Ra from the Temple of Asar

HERE

Panel from the Temple of Osiris(Asar) at Abydos, Egypt. Location: 10 Column Hall Sanctuary East Wall- Amsu-Asar-Heru.

The Royal Person opens a shrine and within there is an image of the God Asar with all typical Asarian iconography.

Temple of Asar Sanctuary East Wall-Amsu-Asar-Heru Col. 1	Transliteration Col. 1	Translation Col. 1	Contextual Translation Col. 1
	Amsu Heru sa Aset	Ithyphallic-Hidden-Creator-Spirit-bull-of-mother-his Horus son Isis	This personality is Amsu/Amun and also Horus the son of Isis
	Transliteration Col. 2	**Translation Col. 2**	**Contextual Translation Col. 2**
	Medu dje in Amsu-Heru Sa Aset Her ab [Het-Men-Maat-Ra] Di En-en K Renpetu Ta tje Suty (damage) (poss. *mi-Ra*)	Words spoken by Ithyphallic-Horus child Isis Innermost reality [House-One-Established-Truth-Creator-Spirit] Given To- thee years earth tied Royalty (damage) (poss. like Ra)	These words are now being spoken by Amsu, the Ithyphallic spiritual redeemer of the soul, the child of Goddess Isis. He is the innermost reality of the temple of the Royal Person known as "One-Established-Truth-Creator-Spirit." I have given to you, who have come to my shrine, many years to be on the earth planet alive as a human, in the capacity of a Royal Person.

EGYPTIAN BOOK OF THE DEAD HIEROGLYPH TRANSLATIONS Vol. 5

Above left: Papyrus depiction of the god Asar(Osiris)

The Divine Family of Amun-Ra, Mut, Khonsu is also the Divine Family: Asar, Aset, and Heru

Description and summary

The three images below are depictions of the divinities that are encompassed into the iconography of the sanctuary panel of the temple of Osiris that we just discussed above, which relates Osiris to Amsu Min and Horus. The deeper meaning of this arrangement by the Ancient Egyptian priests and priestesses is that the divine is manifesting on all planes of experience and notably through these three main forms of spiritual manifestation. As the God Amun/Amsu, the divine is manifesting as the High God who created Itself. With the incorporation of the iconography of Osiris, that same High God manifests as the soul in time and space. The same divinity is manifesting as the Horus or spiritual aspirant that is to become the monarch over time and space, governing in the human world for its parent, the high divinity (Asar [Osiris]).

In a higher context, the iconography and hieroglyphic texts indicate that all of these manifestations of divinity are underlain by the same essential essence of the Transcendental Divine. Therefore, while human existence appears to be separate from the divine as well as separate from other human beings, it's deeper essence is actually common to all. This concept and its realization hold the key to progressing on the path of the Egyptian Mysteries, transcending the lower human limited existence, and attaining the knowledge and experience of the Transcendental Divine.

EGYPTIAN BOOK OF THE DEAD HIEROGLYPH TRANSLATIONS Vol. 5

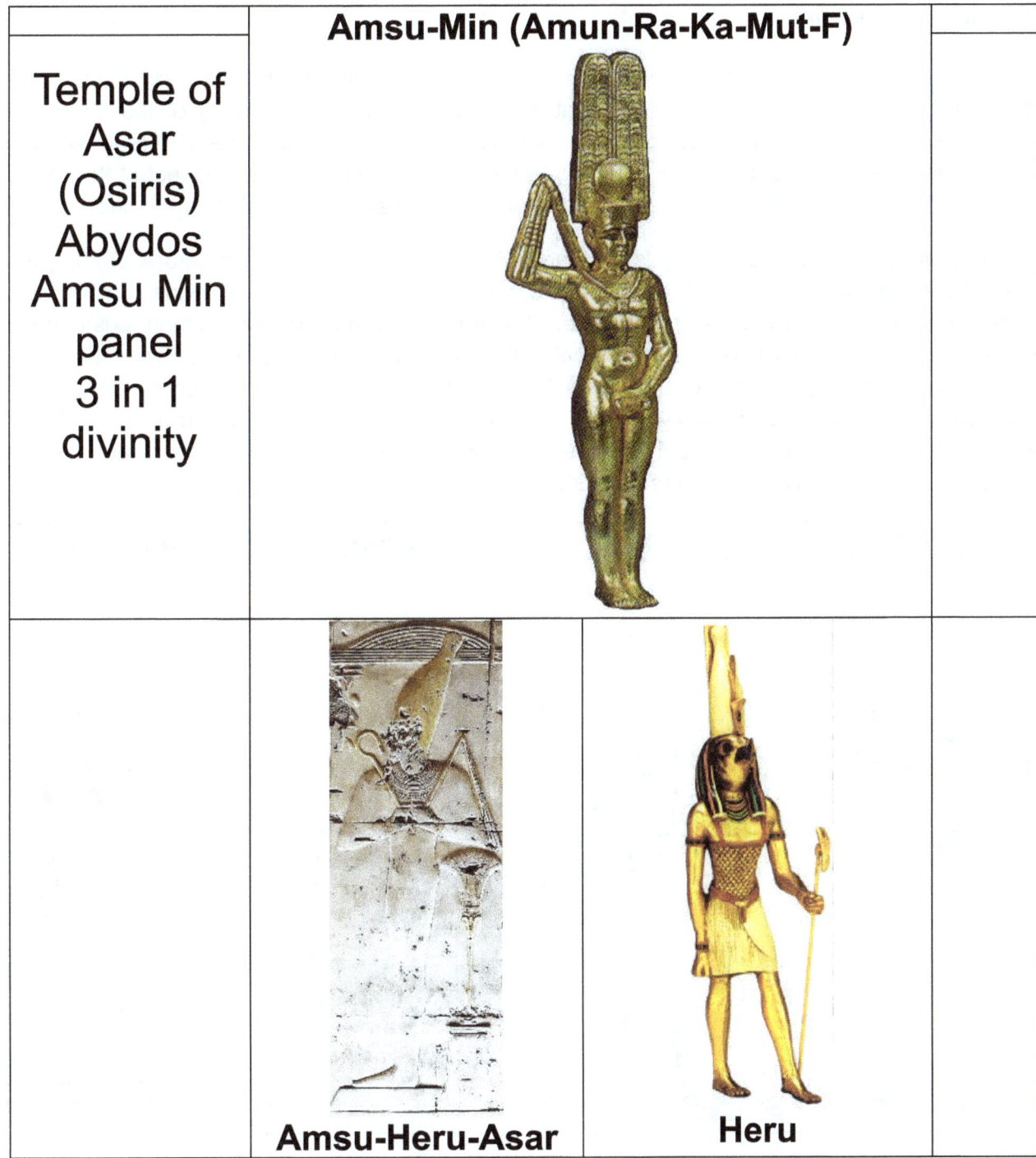

Temple of Asar (Osiris) Abydos Amsu Min panel 3 in 1 divinity

Amsu-Min (Amun-Ra-Ka-Mut-F)

Amsu-Heru-Asar

Heru

EGYPTIAN BOOK OF THE DEAD HIEROGLYPH TRANSLATIONS Vol. 5

Description and summary

Expanding the idea of the underlying essential essence of divinity, the following chart shows the four main manifestations of divinity that are presented in the sanctuary of the temple of Amun-Ra. From left to right we see the God Ptah, the God Amun-Ra, the Royal Person, and the God Ra-Herakty. In accord with the teaching of the temple, each one is an aspect of the divine manifestation; as such there is an aspect of the god Osiris that corresponds to each one.

Therefore, the spiritual journey is not one of transforming into a higher nature. Rather, the task of the spiritual journey is to discover and realize the Transcendental Divine that already, even now, exists on all planes of existence. The problem is that ordinary human existence is usually only exclusively aware of the physical reality and human manifestation based on egoistic notions that are ignorant of the underlying transcendental essence of existence. Hence, the process is to grow beyond strictly human awareness and adopt the perspective of a Royal Person and then to elevate through succeeding higher levels of experience culminating in the discovery of the Transcendental Absolute Divine.

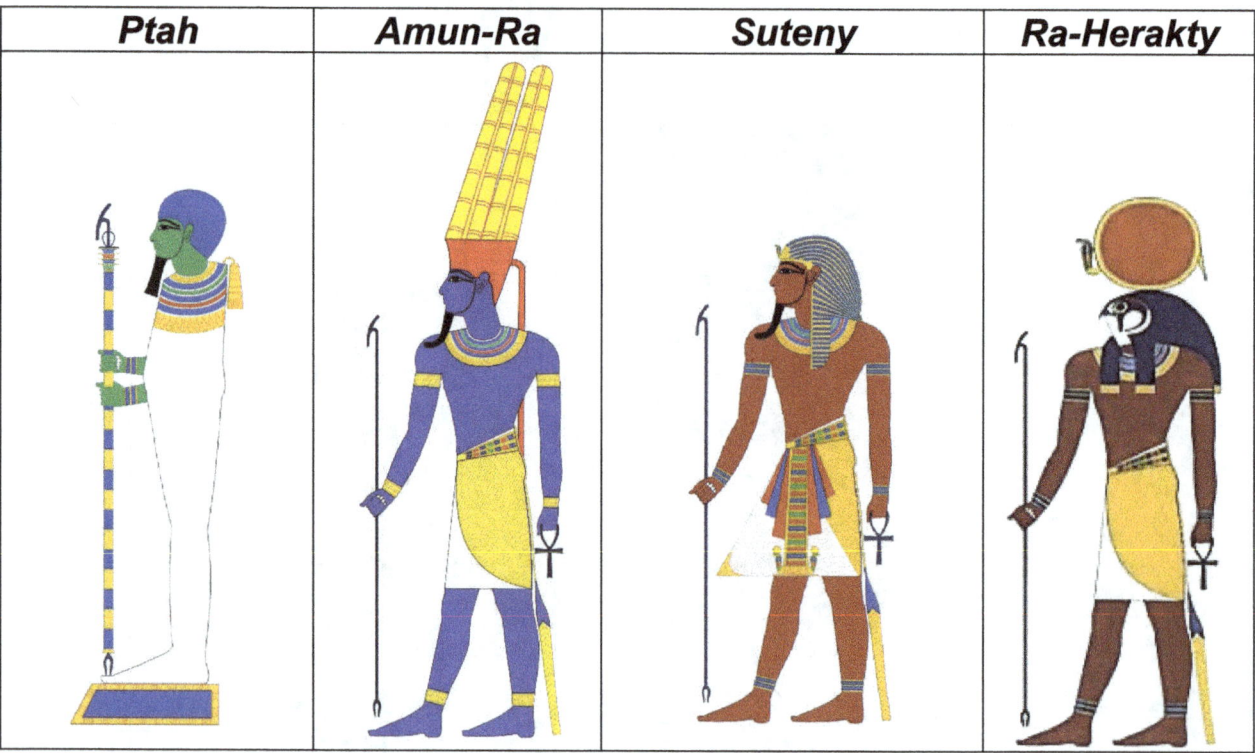

EGYPTIAN BOOK OF THE DEAD HIEROGLYPH TRANSLATIONS Vol. 5

Asar (Osiris) is behind all aspects of the Cosmic Divinities and the Royal Person

Ptah	Amun-Ra	Suteny	Ra-Herakty
Ptah-ZokkarAsar	Amsu-Heru-Asar	Asar - Heru *Asar and Heru are aspects of each other	Asar-Zokkar

Panel #4- The human Royal Person is the Great Divinity—[location Vestibule #2]

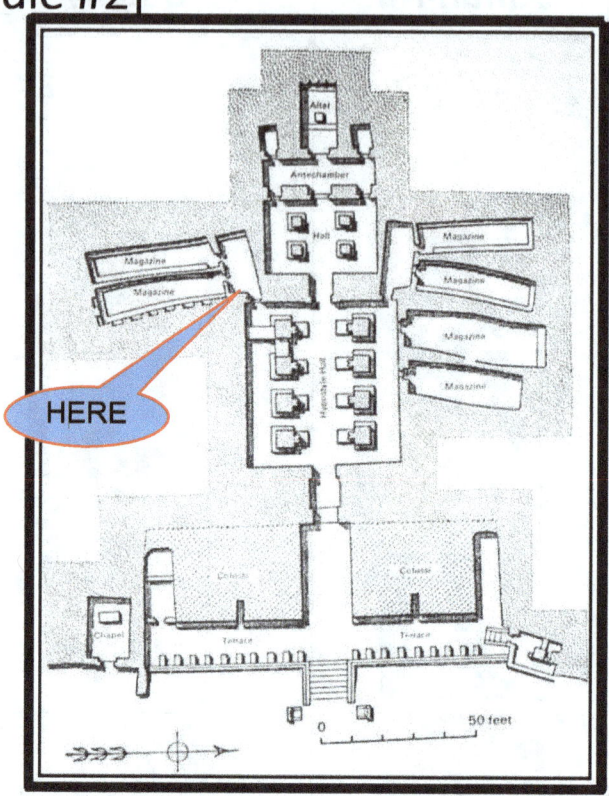

Description and summary

The following panel from the temple of Amun-Ra is located in vestibule number two. This panel will provide an additional nuance into the Ancient Egyptian concept of spiritual identity. In this panel we see the Royal Person, Ramses, making an offering, which he is holding in both hands. He is facing a seated figure on an elevated throne. The inscriptions of the panel identify each personality as being the Royal Person. Both names are encircled by a cartouche and they are matching names to the two spiritual names of the Royal Person (assigning one of the names to each personality depicted-as in the holographic panels #2A-B above, where the two names occurred, one in each panel). In this panel, the names are apportioned on to each personality in the same panel. However, the seated figure has been placed on a higher position in terms of elevation, relative to the Royal Person, who in this case is standing; additionally, the seated figure has a further designation beyond the circumscribed name. This gives us an indication that the name of the seated person being circumscribed, means that we are looking philosophically at the image of the Royal Person, seated on the throne, but at a higher level and in divine form. Therefore, this panel is depicting the worship of one's Higher Self as a God or Goddess, but the text shows an additional special designation of this aspect of one's own divinity.

EGYPTIAN BOOK OF THE DEAD HIEROGLYPH TRANSLATIONS Vol. 5

EGYPTIAN BOOK OF THE DEAD HIEROGLYPH TRANSLATIONS Vol. 5

Description and summary cont.

The text occurs in two groups, the one on the right related to the human Royal Person and the second on the left referring to the higher aspect of the Royal Person. Columns 1, 2, and 3 contain pro forma aspects of the Royal Person titles that we had seen previously. The special highlight here is that the two royal names occur in a single form for each personality and therefore match to represent one being depicted here as two. Therefore there is a human physical aspect and also there is a high divinity aspect of the human as well.

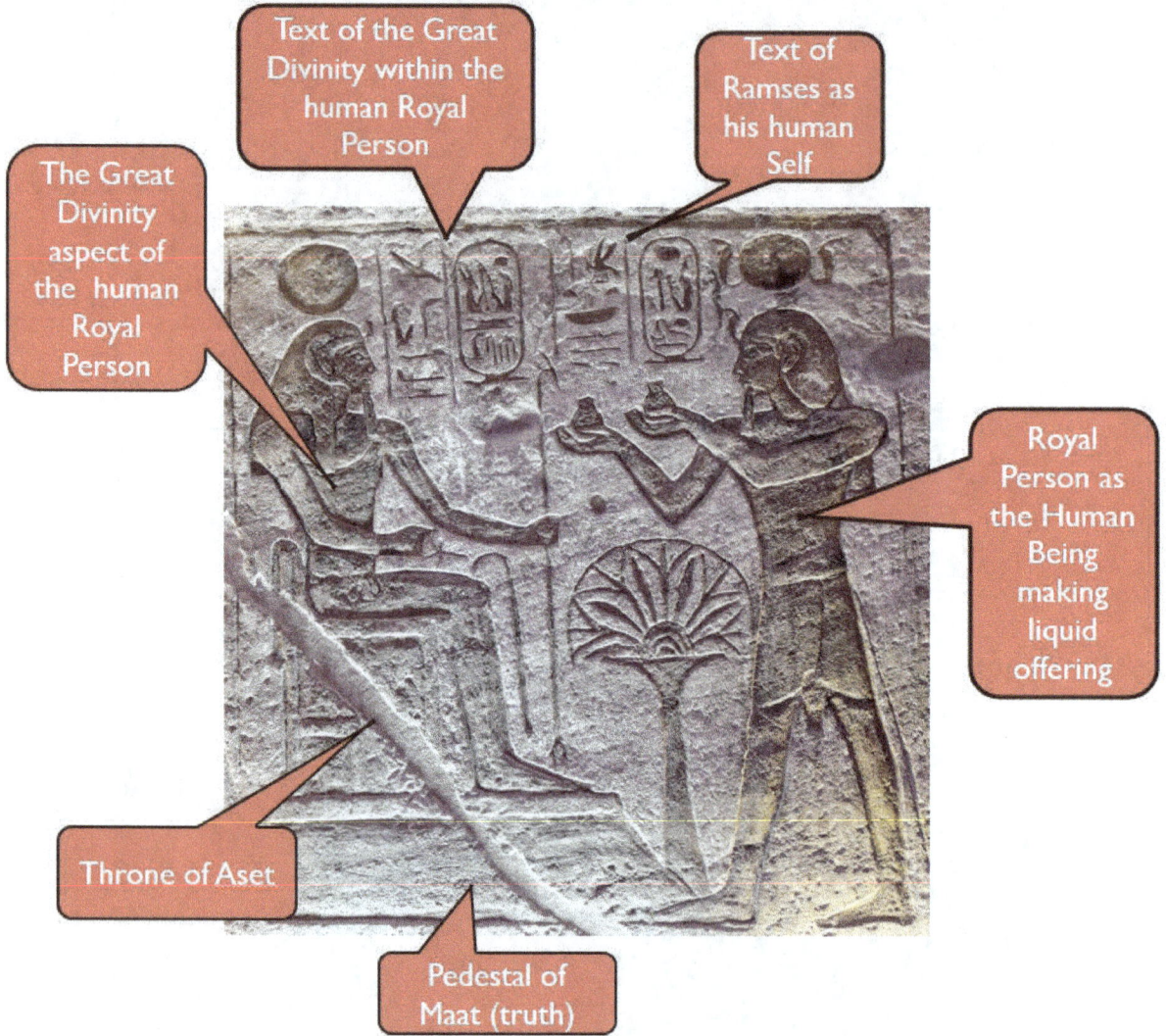

The key teaching presented in this panel occurs in column number four. Column number four identifies the higher self of the Royal Person not only as a God or Goddess but rather as "the Divinity Great". Additionally, the scroll is used here, signifying that this is a figurative/abstract statement; thus we are speaking of the mystic aspect of the human Royal Person. The term "the" and the term "great" are specific epithets that describe the divine nature that rises above ordinary God or Goddess status. The use of the word "the" signifies a specific designation as opposed to "a" as in a god, signifies a reference to The Divinity instead of "any" given divinity in general. In other words, the great divinity is the source of the gods and goddesses. This concept of a high God as being the source of the lesser gods and goddesses is called henotheism in religious studies terminology. Therefore, we understand that beyond the physical nature and limited capacity of the human there are divine aspects within the human. We earlier saw one of those aspects in the form of the Moon-god but in reality, the human soul being an expression of the absolute transcendental divine is actually the source of all divine manifestations of the personality in time and space. This, the deeper mystery that a human being is to discover, with the help of the temple spiritual practices, is the path of becoming aware of the higher nature of being in the form of gods and goddesses (cosmic forces of Creation) and rising above even that level to discover one's identity as the great divinity itself.

Panel 4 - The human Royal Person is the Great Divinity

Text of R.P. aspect as Great Divinity		Text of R.P. aspect as human sovereign	
Column 4	3	1	2

Text of R.P. aspect as human sovereign	Transliteration	Translation	Contextual Translation
Column 1	*Nesu bity neb tawy*	Sovereign Upper-lower Egypt; Lord Two-Lands	This is the sovereign of Upper and Lower Egypt, the Lord of the two lands of Egypt
Column 2 **Note: Matching "circumscribed" Royal Names for the same person**	(USER-MAAT-RA-SETEP-EN-RA)	(Power of the truth of the Creator Spirit and chosen by the Creator Spirit)	The "Circumscribed" Royal Person, Ramses, who goes by the name: "One who exercises dominion backed by the righteousness of the Creator Spirit and who is chosen by that Creator Spirit."
Column 3 **Note: Matching "circumscribed" Royal Names for the same person**	(AMUN MERY RA-MESU)	(Hidden Witnessing Spirit Beloved Creator Spirit-Child of)	This is the second "Circumscribed" royal name of the Royal Person, "One who is the child, who came from the body of Ra, the Creator Spirit, and who is beloved by Amun, the hidden witnessing Spirit Self."
Column 4	*Pa Neter aah {mdj}*	The Divinity Great {fig}	Who is the Great Divinity, and figuratively, The Great Divine aspect of this human Royal Person

A final note on Panel #4

A legitimate interpretation of the finding of the two proforma spiritual names, that are used to determine the single Royal Person, being separated and ascribed, one to each personality in the panel (human Royal Person and Higher Self of the Royal Person as The Great Divinity) is that: The "human Royal Person and their higher being, the Higher Self as the Great Divinity, are great being "The Great Divinity together with the Human". In other words, the apportionment of the two royal names as such, signifying that each half of the naming nomenclature being assigned one to the higher and one lower self, but intrinsically belonging originally to the human is showing an underlying unity of higher and lower or SEMA TAWY, or EGYPTIAN YOGA.

Therefore, the naming nomenclature rule of having two special spiritual names is a subtle reference to one of the names referring to human being and the other referring to being THE Divinity, which the human being actually is, innately, at the same time.

EGYPTIAN BOOK OF THE DEAD HIEROGLYPH TRANSLATIONS Vol. 5

Panel #5 The Royal Person is the Unbound Higher Self of His/Her own existence AND their own parent. 360 Location-Temple Location Branch #5

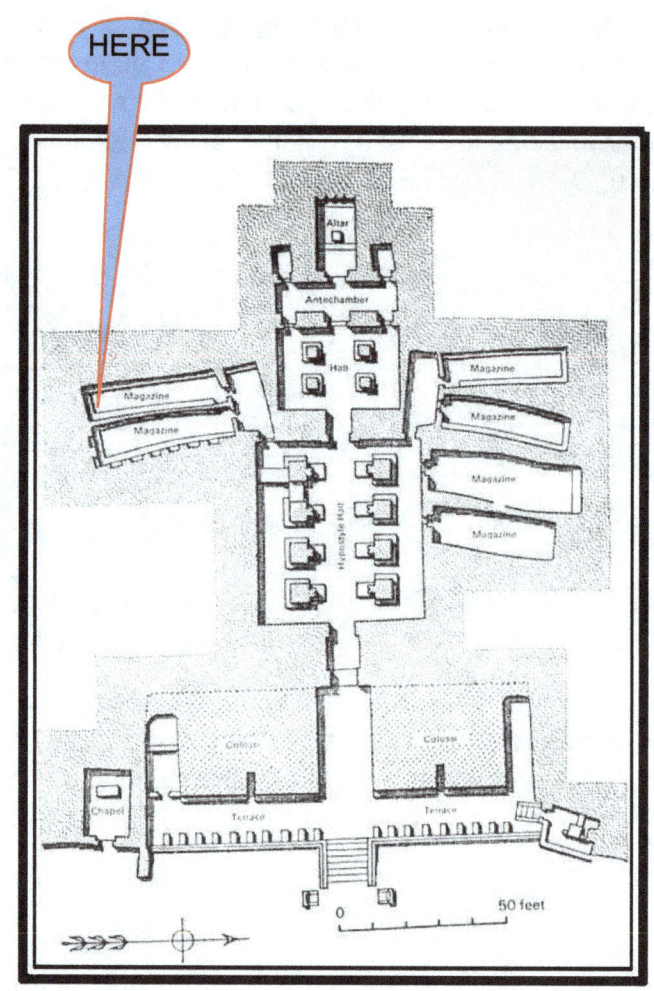

Description and summary

The following panel that will be discussed in the study of the temple wisdom of divine identity is designated as panel number five. It is entitled "The Royal Person is the Unbound Higher Self of His/Her own existence AND their own parent". This panel can be found in branch number five of the temple. It depicts the Royal Person kneeling in front of the city seated figure on a throne representing, again, their own higher self as divine. This panel uses the concept of spiritual identity called "uncircumscribed" or "unbound". The terms "uncircumscribed " or "unbound" refer to the idea of being uncontained that is indicated by the occurrence of the spiritual name without being encircled by a cartouche. In this panel, we also see the concept of protective life force, energy consciousness as well as another new designation of the Royal Person's higher self as being the parent of the same Royal Person. Therefore, just as the high God Amsu, is the "bull of his mother", meaning one who engendered himself, so too the Royal Person is to understand that their existence did not start with physical human birth and or by accident of chance. Rather, their existence is of the nature of immortality, of spirit and therefore beyond time and space and beyond human existence altogether, while being authored by one's own soul. Therefore, the human experience is of a nature of a temporary dream, an association of spirit with the mind and senses as well as the concept of individuality for a temporary period, while the soul is timeless. Yet, as the temple teaching indicates, the higher nature of human beings transcends, but also includes, the experience of human being or we might say, it transcends being exclusively tied to and aware of only human existence.

EGYPTIAN BOOK OF THE DEAD HIEROGLYPH TRANSLATIONS Vol. 5

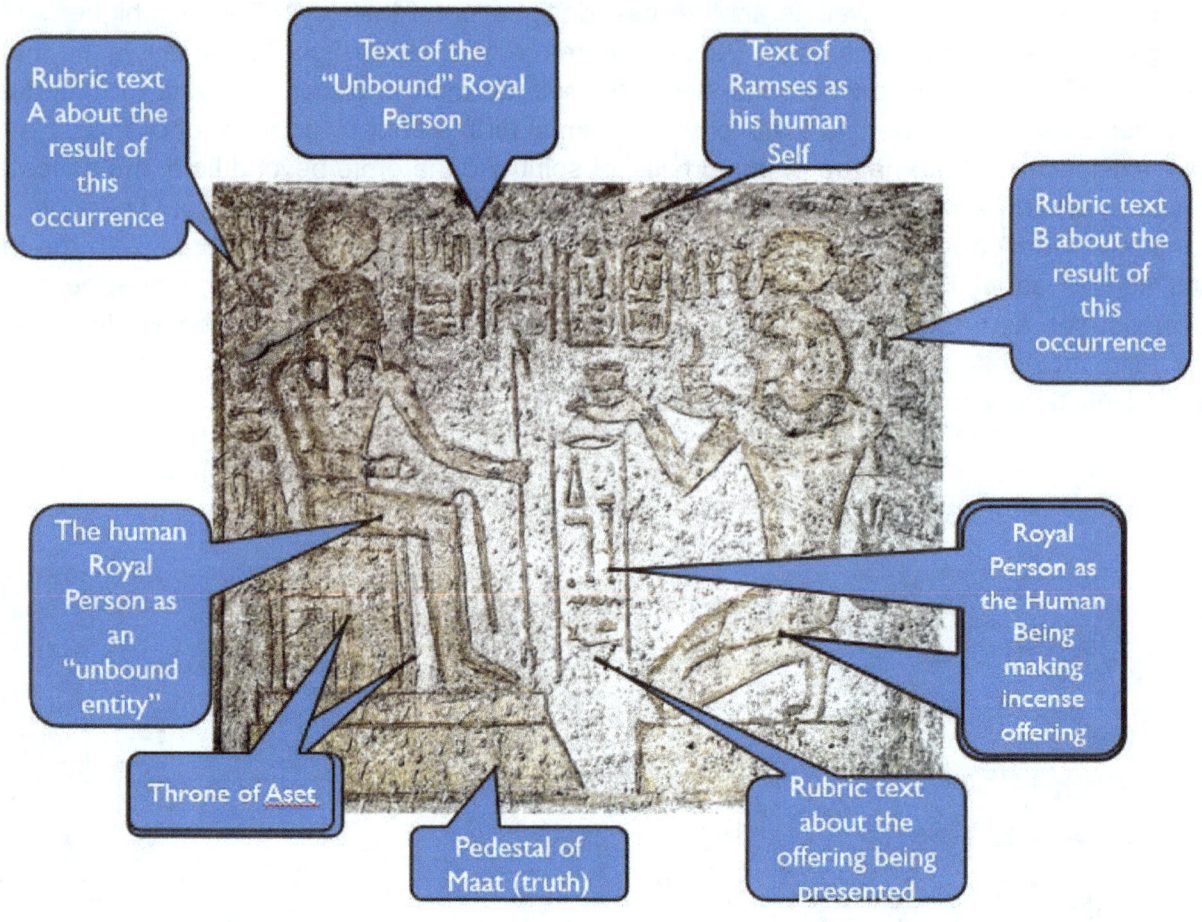

EGYPTIAN BOOK OF THE DEAD HIEROGLYPH TRANSLATIONS Vol. 5

Description and summary

Though it may be difficult to see, this panel has seven columns of text. Columns 1 and 2 and 3 relate to the Royal Person, on the right side of the panel. Columns 4 and 5 relate to the higher manifestation of the Divine Self. In columns one and two we see the pro forma spiritual names of the Royal Person. And, in number five we see the name designation of the higher Divine Self of the Royal Person. Columns number two and number five contain the same name. Therefore, we are to understand that the Royal Person is facing their own higher Divine Self, which is unbound and therefore is a manifestation of expanded consciousness beyond the restrictive encircling of the cartouche.

EGYPTIAN BOOK OF THE DEAD HIEROGLYPH TRANSLATIONS Vol. 5

Panel 5 The Royal Person is also an Unbound Entity who is their own Parent

Text of Ramses (R.P.) aspect as Unbound Entity		Text of Ramses (R.P.) aspect as human sovereign	
Col. 6 5 4 1		2 3 7	

	Transliteration	Translation	Contextual Translation
Column 1 "circumscribed" Royal Names	(USER-MAAT-RA-SETEP-EN-RA)	(Power of the truth of the Creator Spirit and chosen by the Creator Spirit)	The Royal Person, Ramses, goes by the name: "One who exercises dominion backed by the righteousness of the Creator Spirit and who is chosen by that Creator Spirit."
Column 2 Note: Matching column 5 "circumscribed" Royal Names for the same person	(AMUN MERY RA-MESU)	(Hidden Witnessing Spirit Beloved Creator Spirit-Child of)	This is the second royal name of the Royal Person, "One who is the child, who came from the body of Ra, the Creator Spirit, and who is beloved by Amun, the hidden witnessing Spirit Self."
Column 3	Di ankh	Gives life	He is a life-giver
Column 4	Medu dje in	Words spoken by	These words are now being spoken by (this text identifies who this personality is)
Column 5 Note: Matching column 2	(Ra)messu-Amun-mery {Uncircumscribed/ Unbound name}	Hidden Witnessing Spirit Beloved Creator Spirit-Child of	"One who is the child, who came from the body of Ra, the Creator Spirit, and who is beloved by Amun, the hidden witnessing Spirit Self."

EGYPTIAN BOOK OF THE DEAD HIEROGLYPH TRANSLATIONS Vol. 5

Column 6 – Rubric A	Transliteration	Translation	Contextual Translation
	Sa	Protection	The occurrence (the viewing of this panel with the understanding of the mystery and feeling as being the protagonist participant) of this ritual, by a temple initiate, provides a protective life-force ***energy/consciousness*** originated from Ra/Heru through the gods and goddesses and their Divine Manifestations to the Royal Person that sustains life and allows conscious awareness of the Divine. *All like Ra, the Creator-Spirit, the source of the Protective Life-force.
	ankh	Life-force	
	hau	Body(parts)	
		all	
	Neb	Creator-Spirit	
	Ra		
	mi	like	

EGYPTIAN BOOK OF THE DEAD HIEROGLYPH TRANSLATIONS Vol. 5

Column 7 – Rubric B	Transliteration	Translation	Contextual Translation
	Sa	Protection	This occurrence (the viewing of this panel with the understanding of the mystery and feeling as being the protagonist participant) of this ritual provides a protection and energy sustenance of all the body parts of the human Royal Person.
	ha	Body (parts)	
	f	his	
	neb	all	

EGYPTIAN BOOK OF THE DEAD HIEROGLYPH TRANSLATIONS Vol. 5

Adoration by the human Royal Person to THE GREAT DIVINITY who is also Horus/Ra, the Royal Person's own Higher Self" –[location Branch #1]

Description and summary

The following image in Branch #1 below is designated as panel six "Adoration by the human Royal Person to The Great Divinity who is also the God who is the Royal Person's Higher Self." This image is found in branch number one of the temple. In this panel, the Royal Person is depicted kneeling in front of the image of the divine in the form of a hawk wearing a sun-disk. The divine entity being depicted is later described as Horus, even as he is wearing solar iconography as does the God Ra (they are aspects of each other). However, the naming nomenclature of this entity makes use of the second spiritual name of the Royal Person. Therefore, the human Royal Person on the left of the panel is facing his own Higher Self in the form of Horus/Ra. In the Asarian Resurrection myth, Horus defeated Set, his uncle, and redeemed his father, Osiris so that he could be at peace, and fully restored to rulership in the astral plane, the plane of the gods and goddesses that is above the physical plane, and Horus rules over the physical plane as a manifestation of his father Osiris. In this way, the Royal Person is referred to as Horus since they are doing the work of battling against the unrighteousness of egoism to realize the truth of their own being and at the same time redeeming their own soul (Osiris). The successful completion of that work means redeeming Osiris, their soul, within themselves, and restoring it to its rightful place as the master and recognized, effective ruler of the Royal Person's identity, thereby transcending the human and royal designations.

A further remarkable aspect of this panel, which introduces a new insight into the nature of Ancient Egyptian spiritual identity wisdom, is that the entity being worshiped while being recognized as a higher form of the Royal Person, namely Horus/Ra, that higher self-designation, also contains an epithet that we saw earlier, by including the term "PA-NETER-AAH" or The Great Divinity. Therefore, we are to additionally understand that the Higher Self of a human being is the nature of the sun god, the Creator Spirit, manifesting as the solar hawk. Heru (Horus) the solar hawk, is the son of Osiris and Isis and the one who defeated the unrighteous egoistic personality, represented by the god Set, who killed Osiris and usurped his throne. Osiris is the soul, and the god Set is the symbolic representation of egoism in the personality, and Isis represents the Akhu, the shining spirit intuitional wisdom aspect of the personality. Osiris, Set, and Isis are all locked into a divine drama that depicts the journey of the soul through time and space existence along with its interactions and relations with personalities of other human and divine beings as well as the interactions of those divine qualities as the qualities of the human psyche. This divine drama is playing out in the different aspects of the personality of the Royal Person and throughout their life. But, just as the God Horus defeated the god Set and thereby redeemed his father Osiris at the behest of his mother Isis, in the same way, the Royal Person assumes that character or shall we say, discovers that aspect of personality, Heru, the heroism within himself/herself, so as to successfully tread the path of life and of the temple.

Another special and remarkable feature of this panel is the inclusion of an offering that has important significance for spiritual evolution. The offering is designated as **Qeb**. Qeb means the libation with water and highlights the coolness (temperature) of water. The extended meaning of the term is that which is opposite to **Shemm**, which is heat and used to designate the heated personality, as was discussed above from the teachings of Sage Amenemopet. The shemm or heated personality is a personality that is agitated, rough, quick to anger, distracted, greedy, prideful, restless, devoted to acquiring worldly possessions, and concerns with worldly desires as opposed to turning towards the divine with a calm mind, inner peace and devotion. The details of this distinction were made clear in the Ancient Egyptian wisdom texts by the Ancient Egyptian sage Amenemopet (Amun-em-het). Therefore, this panel is giving specific instructions about the nature of the Higher Self of the Royal Person as well as the important feature of human character to be cultivated and brought before the Divinity as part of the libation offering, that is, making the approach to the Divinity having cultivated a silent, cool personality in order to have success on the spiritual path.

EGYPTIAN BOOK OF THE DEAD HIEROGLYPH TRANSLATIONS Vol. 5

Panel #6: Adoration by the human Royal Person to THE GREAT DIVINITY who is also Horus/Ra who is the Royal Person's own Higher Self"
Temple Location: Branch #1, 360 web site Location Branch #1

EGYPTIAN BOOK OF THE DEAD HIEROGLYPH TRANSLATIONS Vol. 5

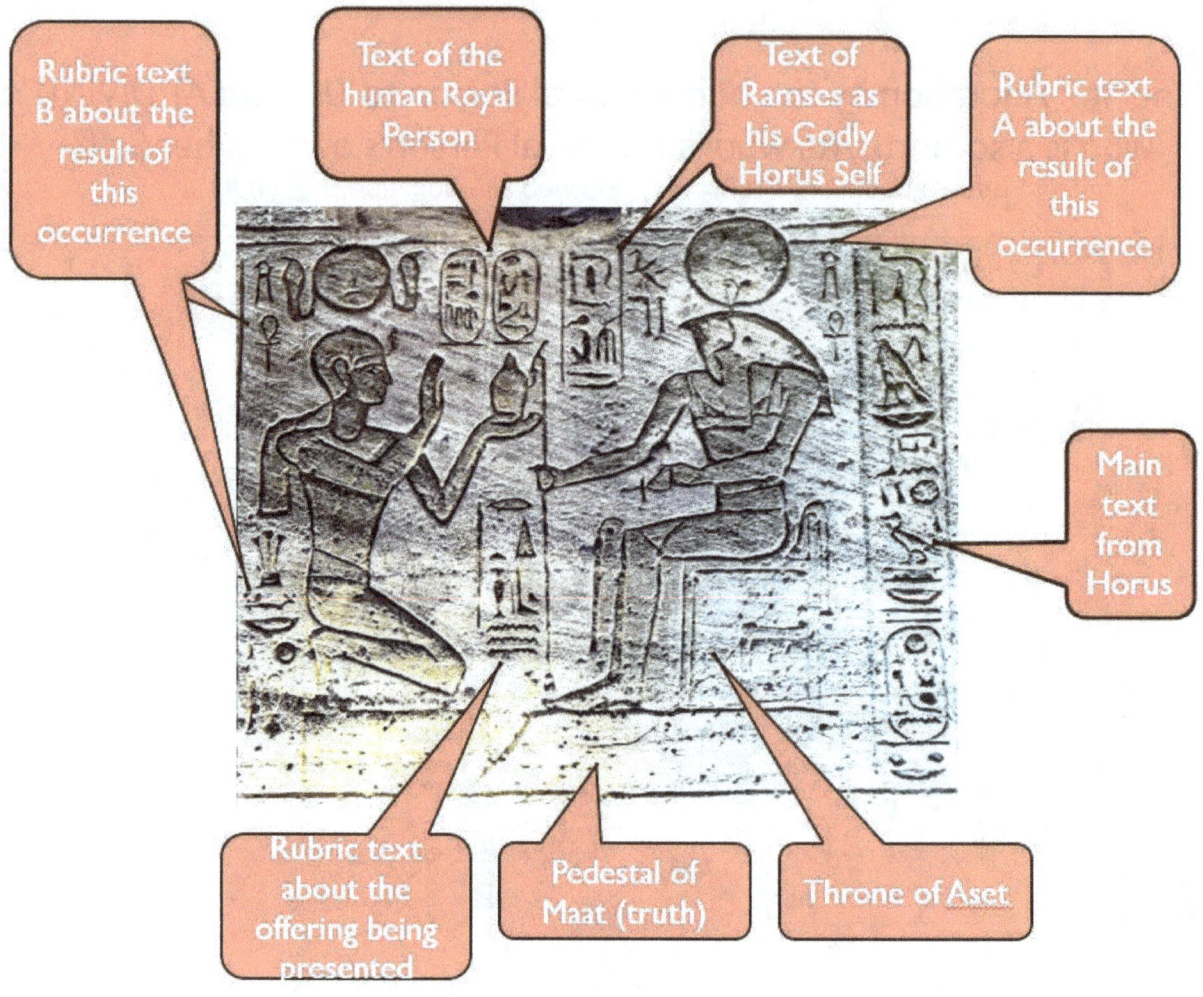

EGYPTIAN BOOK OF THE DEAD HIEROGLYPH TRANSLATIONS Vol. 5

Text of Left Royal Aspect of same Royal Person	Text of Great Divinity Horus Aspect of Royal Person
Col. 6 2 1 3 4	7 5

Panel 6- The HUMAN R.P. is the UNBOUND SELF AND THE GREAT DIVINITY

Verse 3. The approach with Coolness offering

Trilinear Translation of Panel 6 Adoration of One's Higher Self, the Great Divinity Horus

Text of Right Royal Aspect of same Royal Person	Transliteration	Translation	Contextual Translation
Col. 1 1st main proforma spiritual name of Ramses	(USER-MAAT-RA-SETEP-EN-RA)	Power of the truth of the Creator Spirit and chosen by the Creator Spirit	The Royal Person, Ramses, whose first spiritual name is "One who exercises dominion backed by the righteousness of the Creator Spirit and who is chosen by that Creator Spirit."
Col. 2 2nd main proforma spiritual name of Ramses	(AMUN MERY RA-MESU)	(Hidden Witnessing Spirit Beloved Creator Spirit-Child of)	This is the second royal name of the Royal Person, "One who is the child, who came from the body of Ra, the Creator Spirit, and who is beloved by Amun, the hidden witnessing Spirit Self."
Col. 3 4	3-Medu dje in }-Rameses-{	Words spoken {Unbound})-Hidden Witnessing Creator-Spirit Beloved Creator Spirit-Child of-(	These words are now being "spoken" by the "unbound" Royal Person known by the name: "One who is the child, who came from the body of Ra, the Creator Spirit, and who is beloved by Amun, the hidden witnessing Spirit Self"...
	4-pa Neter aah	The Great Divinity	...who is at the same time also the Great Divinity

Col. 5	Transliteration	Translation	Contextual Translation
(hieroglyph column image)	*Medu dje*	Words spoken	These words are spoken by the aspect of Horus who is of *Beheny*, Nubia (present-day Wadi Halfa). He directs his speech to his beloved son, the Sovereign of the Two Lands, The Royal Person who goes by the name: "One who exercises dominion backed by the righteousness of the Creator Spirit and who is chosen by that Creator Spirit."
	in	By	
	Heru[Ra]	Horus	
	Neb	Lord	
	Beheny	Beheny-city	
	Sa	Son	
	Mery	Beloved	
	Neb	Lord	
	Tawy	Two-lands	
	(USER-MAAT-RA-SETEP-EN-RA!)	(Power of the truth of the Creator Spirit and chosen by the Creator Spirit)	
	(damaged) *neb*	(damaged) all	

EGYPTIAN BOOK OF THE DEAD HIEROGLYPH TRANSLATIONS Vol. 5

Wādī Ḥalfā town is in the extreme northern Sudan area. It lies on the east bank of the Nile River 6 miles (10 km) below the Second Cataract, just south of the current Egyptian border with Nubia. Located within ancient Nubia, the town and its environs are rich in antiquities. The ruins of Buhen—an Egyptian colony of the Middle Kingdom period that existed until Roman times—lie across the river. A terminus of both railway and steamship lines, Wādī Ḥalfā is an agricultural and commercial center serving both Egypt and Sudan. In the 1970s it was the focus of archaeological activities to save Egyptian monuments from inundation by Lake Nasser (the reservoir formed above the Aswan High Dam), a fate that part of the town shared. Its populace was relocated at New Halfa to the southeast near Kassala town. WRITTEN BY: The Editors of Encyclopedia Britannica.

EGYPTIAN BOOK OF THE DEAD HIEROGLYPH TRANSLATIONS Vol. 5

Col. 6-7	Transliteration	Translation	Contextual Translation
	Sa	Protection	This is a lifeguard, protection for the body parts of the living body of the Royal Person in such a manner so as for them to be like the body of the Creator-Spirit, i.e. golden(effulgent).
	Ankh	Life	
	Ha	Body	
	F	His	
	Neb	Lord	
	Ra	Creator-Spirit	
	mi	like	

--

Col. 8	Transliteration	Translation	Contextual Translation
	Erdit	Giving/offering	The occurrence of this offering means the Royal Person is bringing the coolness of the personality, silence, stillness, and contentment, in the presence of the Divine, as opposed to the heated nature of egoism and mental agitation. Note: ref. Teachings of Amenemopet.
	Qeb	coolness	
	{moo}	{water}	

WISDOM OF AMENEMOPET & TEACHING OF TEMPLE OF AMUN-RA

Shemm = Heated hearted person (From the Teachings of Sage Amenemopet)

Ger = silent hearted person (From the Teachings of Sage Amenemopet)

Qeb from Temple of Amun-Ra

Verse 2. Definition of **Qeb** = Cool hearted person –the opposite of **Shemm** (Heat)

Verse 4. <u>Therefore-</u> the Neterian terms **Ger** and **Qeb** are compatible & complementary.

The term **qeb** (coolness), which is used in the temple of Amun-Ra is thus related to the term **ger** (silent), which is used in the Ancient Egyptian wisdom text of sage Amenemopet. And the term is also the opposite of the term **Shemm** that is used in the Ancient Egyptian wisdom text of sage Amenemopet. Therefore, the wisdom being imparted by the temple (with the term **Qeb**) is using a different term that, nevertheless, has the same significance as the term used in the Ancient Egyptian wisdom text (**Ger**). This compatibility allows us to gain reciprocal insights into the two apparently different sources of wisdom (wisdom text and temple), meaning that the temple architecture, iconography, and hieroglyphic texts can inform our understanding of the wisdom texts and vice versa. This compatibility, being the case, also allows us to confirm, and reinforce the intent of the teachings and the means for their application.

# Panel #8-- The Human Royal Person is the Living Manifestation of the UNBOUND SELF and the GREAT DIVINITY–[360⁰ Location, Temple Location Branch #4]

Description and summary

The next panel, see below for image, designated as number eight, entitled the human Royal Person is the living manifestation of self and the great divinity contains, as if, an accumulation of the Royal Person's higher self titles that have been seen so far. In other words, in this panel, we'll see most of the designations or epithets of the Higher Self of the Royal Person in previous panels, but here we will see them all together in one panel. Therefore, this panel, with its summary inclusion of most of the designations, will be important for the advancing study of the concept of Ancient Egyptian spiritual identity. The panel is composed of, as we have seen before in previous panels, the human Royal Person with pro forma circumscribed spiritual names and that personality is facing another personality who is sitting on a throne. An important aspect of the throne is that it is set, again, on a pedestal that is the symbol of the goddess of truth, order, and righteousness: the goddess Maat. Additionally, the throne of the sitting personality is, again, placing that personality on a higher elevation relative to the Royal Person, thus, signaling that the personality on the pedestal is a "higher truth," relative to the lower personality carrying out the worship ritual. Though the panel has been damaged and displays much deterioration, it is still possible to discern its parameters. The Higher Self of the Royal Person is being referred to as the living manifestation of the Divine. Additionally, the same Higher Self of the Royal Person has received the naming nomenclature of the second spiritual name of the Royal Person, but here that name is uncircumscribed.

The other important designation of the Higher Self of the Royal Person is the recognition, by the Royal Person who is kneeling, that this Higher Self f that is, their own higher aspect of being, is actually their own parent. In other words, the Royal Person making the offering is recognizing this personality, seated on the throne, as the great divinity, as well as the living manifestation of the Royal Person on earth. That same personality seated on the throne is being recognized by the human Royal Person, who is kneeling, as being their own parent, their own source of being, as well as their very own self. Again, the significance of this is the recognition by a spiritual initiate that they are sustained by and are the authors of their own coming into being in human form, and therefore they are also the authors of their destiny and fate while living as human beings on earth. The implications of these statements and the realization of their applications have far-reaching consequences for the life of a human being as they relate to discovering the nature of one's own Higher Self, which is the higher mystery of life that is the goal of human existence. The exploration of these themes via spiritual, intellectual, and theoretical studies, through devotional work as is depicted in the panels, and the cultivation of a personality that is conducive to inner self-discovery is our primary means to successfully traverse the path of the temple.

EGYPTIAN BOOK OF THE DEAD HIEROGLYPH TRANSLATIONS Vol. 5

EGYPTIAN BOOK OF THE DEAD HIEROGLYPH TRANSLATIONS Vol. 5

EGYPTIAN BOOK OF THE DEAD HIEROGLYPH TRANSLATIONS Vol. 5

EGYPTIAN BOOK OF THE DEAD HIEROGLYPH TRANSLATIONS Vol. 5

Identification of the Royal Person with the Unbound Higher Self

Text of Royal Person Ramses			Text of Royal Person as Ramses Unbound		
Col. 3	2	1	Col. 4	5	6

Column	Transliteration	Translation	Contextual Translation
1	*Neb tawy neb chau*	Lord Two lands Lord Risings/thrones	This is the Royal Person, the Lord of the Two Lands as well as Lord over crowns and therefore an emperor.
2	(USER-MAAT-RA-SETEP-EN-RA)	Power of the truth of the Creator Spirit and chosen by the Creator Spirit	The Royal Person, Ramses, goes by the name: "One who exercises dominion backed by the righteousness of the Creator Spirit and who is chosen by that Creator Spirit."
3	(AMUN MERY RA-MESU)	(Hidden Witnessing Spirit Beloved [of] Creator Spirit-Child)	This is the second royal name of the Royal Person, "One who is the child, who came from the body of Ra, the Creator Spirit, and who is beloved by Amun, the hidden witnessing Spirit Self."

--

EGYPTIAN BOOK OF THE DEAD HIEROGLYPH TRANSLATIONS Vol. 5

Text of Royal Person Ramses			Text of Royal Person as Ramses Unbound		
Col. 3	2	1	Col. 4	5	6

Column	Transliteration	Translation	Contextual Translation
4	**Ankh-Neter-nefer neb-tawy neb**	Living-Divinity-beautiful Lord of two lands, Lord…	This is the beautiful living embodiment/manifestation of the Divine. It is Lord of the two lands of Upper and Lower Egypt (duality) and Lord of…
5	**Ari chetu**	… action Offering objects	… of action, and of offering objects, doing things and commanding objects, and sacrificial ritual supplies.
6	**Ramess Pa Neter aah**	Child of Ra the divinity great	It is none other than Ramses THE GREAT DIVINITY

--

EGYPTIAN BOOK OF THE DEAD HIEROGLYPH TRANSLATIONS Vol. 5

Text of the Offering	Transliteration	Translation	Contextual Translation
	erdit	Giving	This is the giving of wine as an offering to my father, who is my Higher Self that begot myself. **(self-begotten)**
	irp(dmg)	wine	
	en	to	
	tef	father	On the table: a bottle of wine, flowers, stalks of romaine lettuce

EGYPTIAN BOOK OF THE DEAD HIEROGLYPH TRANSLATIONS Vol. 5

Wine Offering from Holographic Panel in Branch #2 (for visibility)

(Included here for comparison to Panel #8)

PART 3: Wisdom of Identifying with the Unified Cosmic

Panel 9-Temple Sanctuary: Amun- Ra Ptah Ramesu–[location Sanctuary] Note-Amun Ra Ptah on Façade

360^0 Web site Location #7, Temple Location: Sanctuary

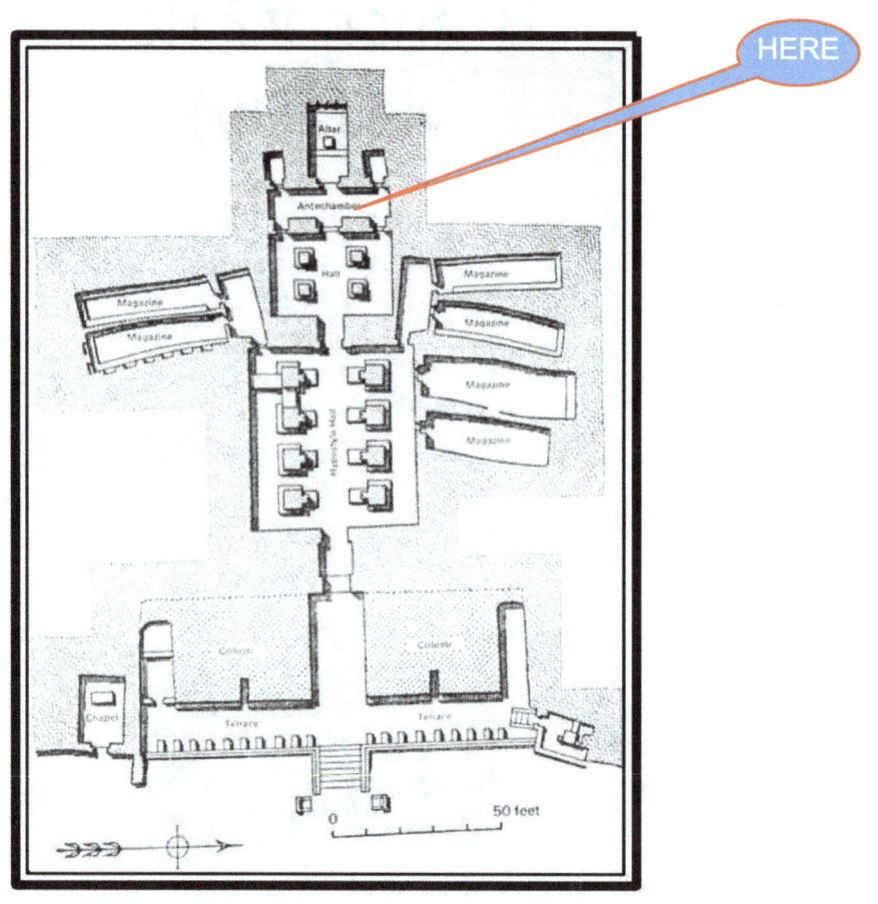

EGYPTIAN BOOK OF THE DEAD HIEROGLYPH TRANSLATIONS Vol. 5

Antechamber and entrance to the Sanctuary of the Temple of Amun-Ra at Abu Simbel

Description and summary

With the following section of the temple to be studied, the sanctuary (Holy of Holies), we move into the next level of spiritual mystic identity which is the cosmic level. For this study, we will enter the sanctuary of the temple. Before entering the sanctuary, we take note of the purposely formatted panel iconography on the entrance facade wall. The wall with the entrance door to the sanctuary has two inscriptions/panels, one on either side of the door. The one on the left contains the divine in the form of the God Amun and the one on the right contains the iconography of the God Ptah. This set up leaves us with the center position of divinity being occupied by Ra, the third divinity in the composite cosmic Trinity of **Amun-Ra-Ptah**. Therefore, this indicates that the divinity being highlighted in the sanctuary is the combined form of Amun-Ra, and more specifically, the dynamic aspect of the solar divinity, Ra-Herakty. Thus, it is fitting that the temple is architecturally setup to allow sunlight to enter all the way into the inner sanctuary but not shine on the panels that are on either side of the entrance to the sanctuary.

Related to this iconography, it is important to understand that this cosmic Trinity represents the triune aspects of time and space conscious-awareness. Time and space conscious-awareness is afforded by the capacity to be aware and to witness events, thoughts, or feelings; this is represented by the god Amun. Secondly, time and space conscious-awareness requires the capacity of having a medium with which that awareness can interact with something other than itself, which is mind; this is represented by the god Ra. The third aspect that is required is the objects to be aware of; this is represented by the god Ptah. In this way, the Trinity of conscious awareness in time and space is composed of Amun, <u>witnessing consciousness (awareness), Ra, mind, and Ptah, objects</u>.

It should be noted that Amun, in this role as witnessing consciousness as part of the Cosmic Trinity of Amun, Ra, Ptah, is different from the role of Amun-Ra as the High God of Waset-Thebes, in ancient Kemet. In the latter case, Amun as the High God, head of Theban Theology, is equated with Neberdjer, all-encompassing Divinity, or the Absolute Soul. This concept holds for any god/goddesses (neteru) of any of the main Theological traditions (e.g. Ra or Ptah). In the Memphite tradition, the god Ptah assumed the role of the High God, and would also be equated with or would be recognized as being a direct time and space projection of Neberdjer, all-encompassing Divinity or the Absolute Soul. The same would go for the goddess traditions. She would be the High God, head of her theological tradition, and in her tradition, would also be equated with or would be recognized as being a direct time and space projection of Neberdjer, all-encompassing Divinity or the Absolute Soul. So, here, as part of the Trinity, Amun, Ra, and Ptah are expressing a specific limited time and space expression of the deeper Transcendental Neberdjer consciousness; so, as part of the Trinity Amun-Ra-Ptah, Amun signifies the witnessing consciousness (awareness) aspect of Neberdjer.

Amun Witnessing Consciousness Subject   **Ra Mind**   **Ptah Objects**

With this setup, the witnessing consciousness awareness subject is able to become aware of objects and through the mind, interact with those objects. This forms the basis of time and space conscious-awareness that a human being is able to tap into, albeit in a limited manner, so as to perceive themselves as a subject with their mind interacting with objects in time and space externally in the world outside as well as internally in the mental world of thoughts, feelings, desires, memories, etc. The problem for human beings is that when they access this limited form of time and space awareness, they develop the erroneous ideas that they are actually knowing something real and abiding. Furthermore, they also erroneously believe, that what they can know with the limited mind and senses is all there is to be known or can be known or all that needs to be known. They also develop the erroneous idea that they are the individual ego that is witnessing and experiencing as a real and abiding subject, as an actual and abiding entity. We have seen throughout the study of the panels that the individual human subject is not an individual at all. Rather, the individual Royal Person has a Higher Self that is their own higher aspect of being of which their human aspect is only a manifestation, albeit limited, mortal, and fleeting, but nevertheless, not abiding and therefore not the final reality of the personality.

Therefore, the task of spiritual evolution is to discover the nature of this Cosmic Trinity of Amun, Ra, and Ptah, and to realize their nature within oneself so as to perceive how objects (Ptah) have arisen through mental perception (Ra) by the cosmic witnessing self (Amun), the

EGYPTIAN BOOK OF THE DEAD HIEROGLYPH TRANSLATIONS Vol. 5

Higher Self that is above the human ego and the true subject of the personality. Having accomplished these realizations, then the task is to explore the depth of this cosmic subject that rests beyond objects of perception and the limited mind so as to expand conscious awareness and discover the existence of transcendental, Absolute Being that is the source of the Trinity. That source is referred to by the term "Neberdjer", the all-encompassing divinity. That all-encompassing divinity, meaning that which is eternal and infinite, manifests as that which is temporal as well as subjective and objective within creation. At the heart of creation, its soul, that same all-encompassing divinity manifests as the soul of all that is manifest. The name of that soul is Osiris. Thus, the soul of the human being is Osiris (Asar) and Osiris is also the expanded nature of spirit-being as the absolute all-encompassing divinity, so the Soul, Osiris, and the Absolute (Neberdjer) are one and the same. This great mystery teaching is the height of the glory of Ancient Egyptian wisdom and mystic philosophy, which is to be studied, practiced, and perfected by the avid spiritual aspirant, i.e. the Royal Person of any temple.

Notice that, in the Amun panel on the left of the entrance to the sanctuary with the seated figures (center), the standing personality, the Royal person, Ramses, is facing from left to right. This translates to a south to north movement, as concerns the Temple Directional Movement Matrix. In that matrix setup, movement from east to west signifies dissolution, going from Creation to an un-created state, from external expansion to external contraction (but with internal expansion in consciousness),. Movement from north to south signifies progress towards the source, towards sustenance and provisioning, nourishment, etc. Movement from south to north signifies spiritual evolutionary progress towards growing and becoming established in the gains of the previous movements. The movement from west to east is a movement expressing creation, the coming into being from the un-manifest to the manifested Creation of objects and time and space, which expands virtually endlessly.

In the case of the sanctuary wall/façade, the movement matrix subtly positions Amun in the south, and Ptah (Ptah Panel on the right side of the entrance), who represents Creation and physicality, in the north. This, the source of Creative sustenance of the south, as with the Nile River, that begins in the south and brings life to the north of the country of Egypt, becomes coagulated/coalesced and solidified as well as firmly established, in the north.

SPECIAL STUDY OF AMUN-RA-PTAH-From Papyrus Salt

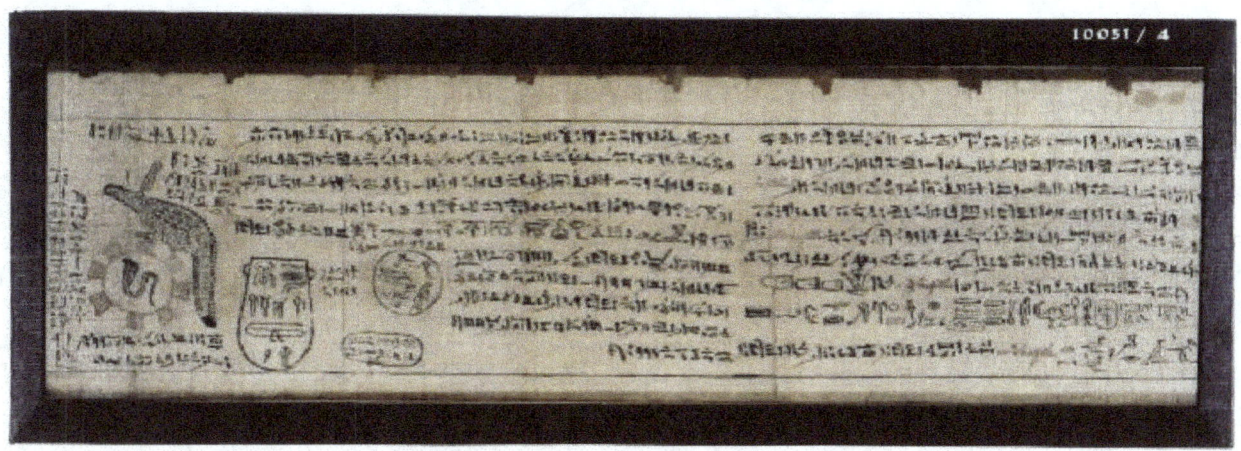

Above: Section from Papyrus Salt

Description and summary

In order to gain a further and deeper understanding of the concept of the Trinity, Amun-Ra-Ptah, we will engage a study of a vignette of an Ancient Egyptian papyrus that provides some insights. That papyrus is called papyrus salt. It contains a special vignette that provides insights into the configuration of the cosmic divine principles that compose the Cosmic Trinity depicted anthropomorphically in the temple of Amun-Ra. Starting at the center of the vignette, a standing figure of the God Osiris is found.

EGYPTIAN BOOK OF THE DEAD HIEROGLYPH TRANSLATIONS Vol. 5

Configuration of Cosmic Divine Principles from Papyrus Salt

Vignette of Amun-Ra-Ptah and Asar (Osiris) from Papyrus Salt

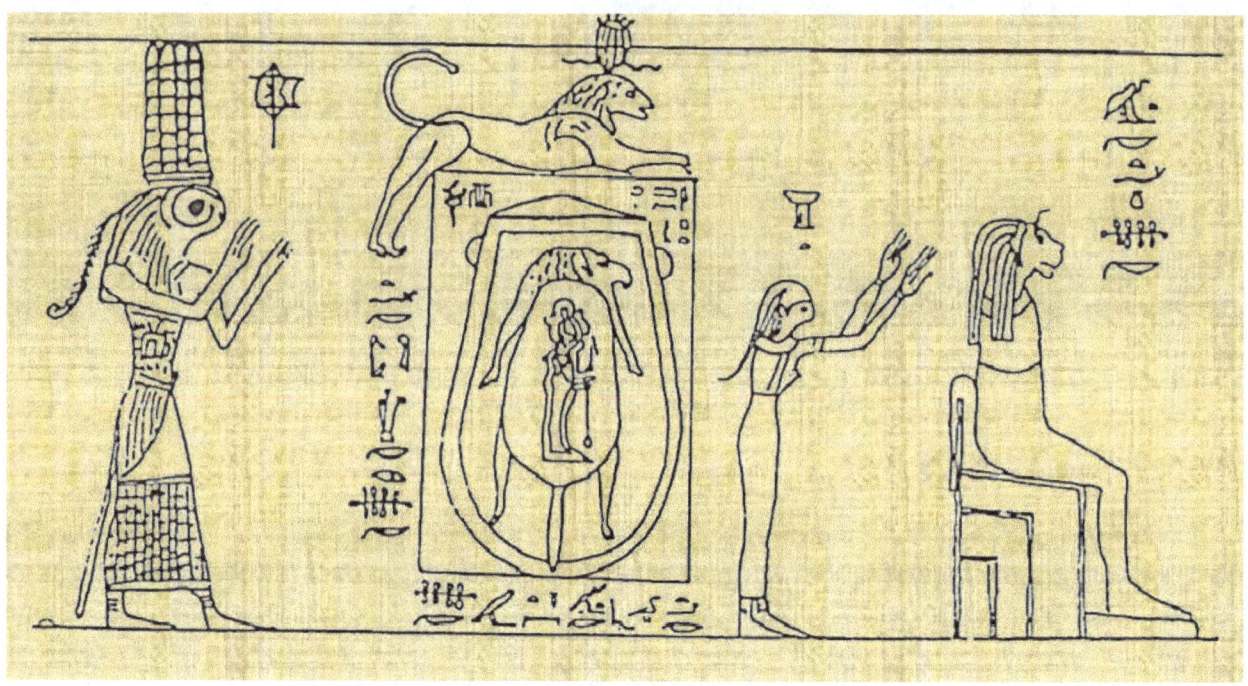

    The following chart highlights the sections of the center of the vignette. Each corner of the vignette or side that contains text has been highlighted (below) with its own color. The essential figure of Osiris is at the center and contained within a coffin and that coffin is contained within an outer coffin in the form of an egg or a cocoon. Within the square section of the vignette, on the outer enclosure, the names of the Trinity (Amun-Ra-Ptah) and the name of Asar (Osiris) are inscribed. Therefore, we are to understand that these are the innermost aspects of divinity. On the outside of the square section of the outer enclosure, the hieroglyphic texts refer to the gods and goddesses (Shu, Tefnut, Geb, Nut) that came into being as the succeeding generation, brought into existence by the high God Ra. Therefore, we are to understand that there is an outer form of manifestation and perception and there is an inner perspective of higher being.

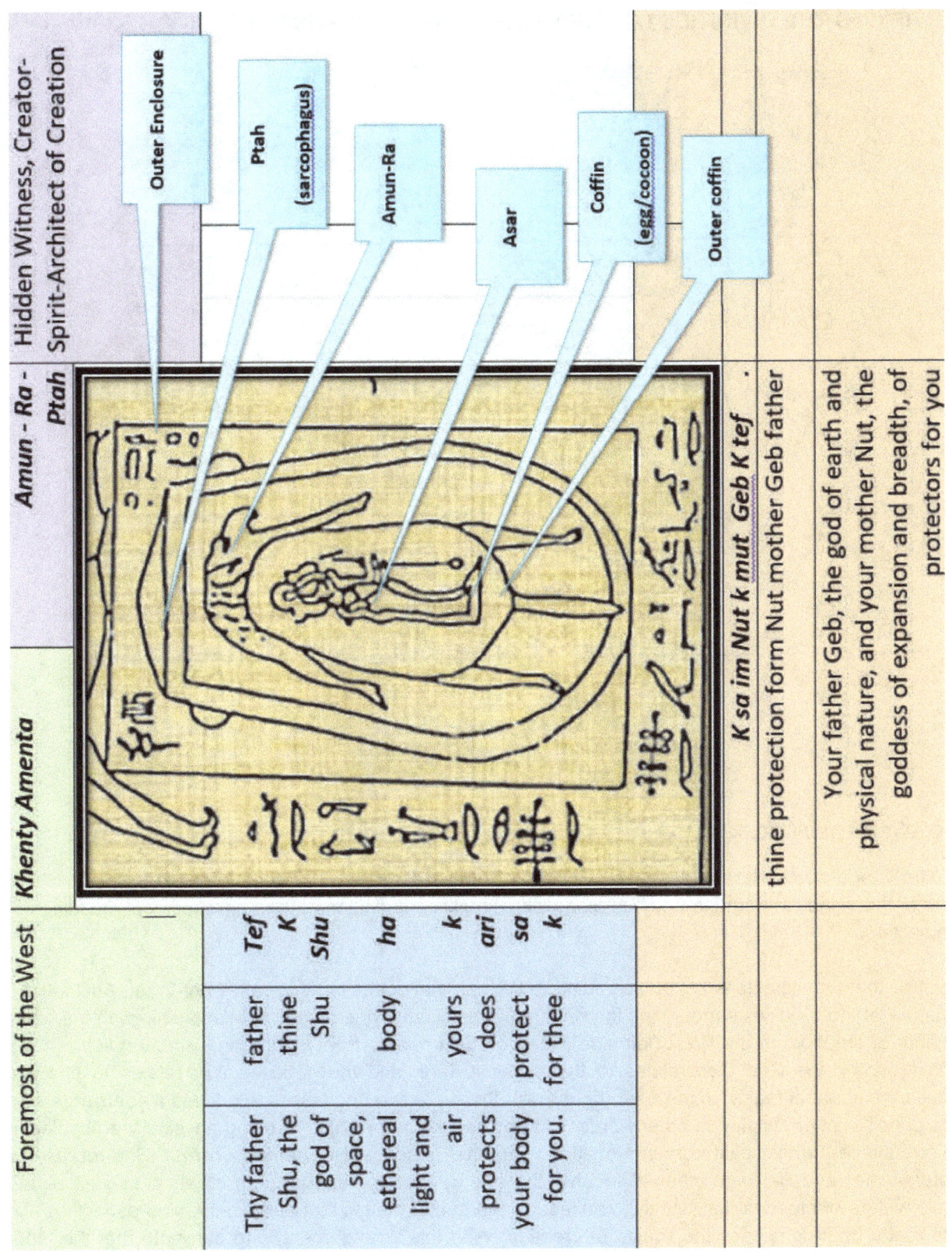

| Amun - Ra - Ptah | Hidden Witness, Creator-Spirit-Architect of Creation |
| Khenty Amenta | Foremost of the West |

Labels on image: Outer Enclosure; Ptah (sarcophagus); Amun-Ra; Asar; Coffin (egg/cocoon); Outer coffin

Tef	K	Shu	ha	k	ari	sa	k
father	thine	Shu	body	yours	does	protect	for thee

Thy father Shu, the god of space, ethereal light and air protects your body for you.

K sa im Nut k mut Geb K tef .
thine protection form Nut mother Geb father

Your father Geb, the god of earth and physical nature, and your mother Nut, the goddess of expansion and breadth, of protectors for you

EGYPTIAN BOOK OF THE DEAD HIEROGLYPH TRANSLATIONS Vol. 5

IDENTIFYING THE DIVINITIES OF THE VIGNETTE OF PAPYRUS SALT

Description & summary

The image above, from the Ancient Egyptian Papyrus Salt 825, has labels for the sections of the center of the vignettes from the papyrus along with simplified definitions of the philosophical meanings of each section.

Notice that the vignette is set up according to the cardinal points North-South-East-West. Additionally, the nature of the divinities surrounding the rectangular enclosure has a special relationship with the basic elements of creation. In the West (left side), the god Shu relates to air/space and ethereal light. In the South (bottom), the God **Geb** relates to the physical earth and the goddess **Nut** relates to physical expansion and astral reality. In the East (right side), there are two goddesses. Goddess **Nebethet** relates to the principle of physicality, in other words, she represents the principle of being physically embodied in time and space. Further east from her location is another goddess. Her name is **Tefnut**. She represents moisture/water and life force inherent in Shu, the energy that courses through creation as well as the cosmic waters of creation that, subtly, manifest as the subtle matter that composes mind as well as the gross matter that composes the liquids of creation. With this arrangement, one can note that the inner divinities Asar, Amun Ra and Ptah are cosmic and subtle while the external divinities, Shu, Tefnut,

EGYPTIAN BOOK OF THE DEAD HIEROGLYPH TRANSLATIONS Vol. 5

Nebehet, Geb, Nut are of a grosser, more "coagulated" substance in comparison to the cosmic ones. Within the vignette, there are three references to the concept of protection. In this manner, the Osiris, the subtle soul, is enveloped by the gross matter of creation, along with the subtle energy contained in the fluids of Creation. These encasements may be likened to the Ancient Egyptian concept of burial whereby the mummy of the deceased is placed within a coffin and that coffin is placed within another coffin or sarcophagus and those encasements are placed within another rectangular succeeding larger encasements.

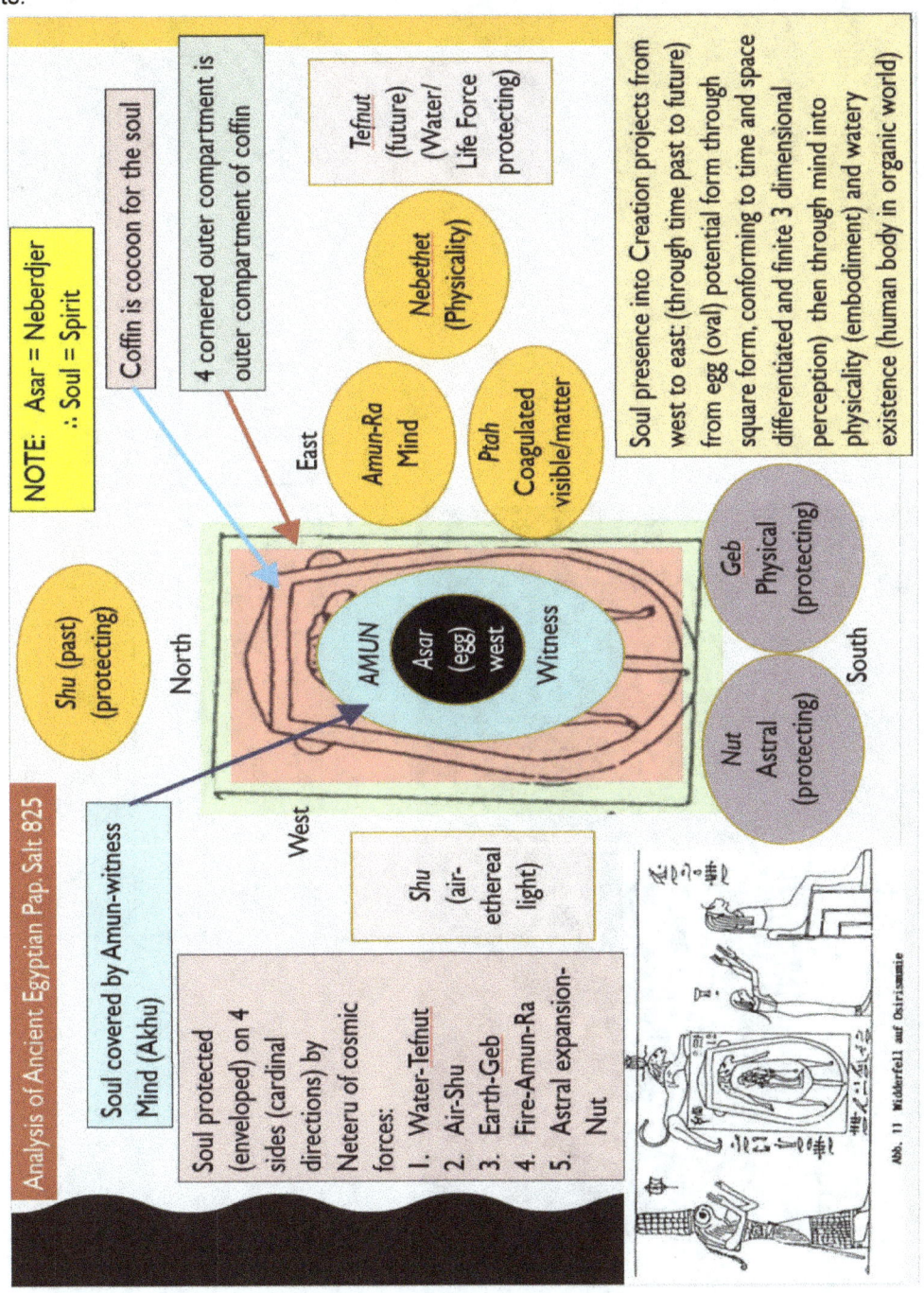

EGYPTIAN BOOK OF THE DEAD HIEROGLYPH TRANSLATIONS Vol. 5

The papyrus Salt is, in literal two-dimensional form, rendering the concept that is found in three-dimensional form in the Ancient Egyptian royal tombs, such as the one belonging to Pharaoh **Tutankhamun** (images of the tomb of Tutankhamun are included on the next pages).

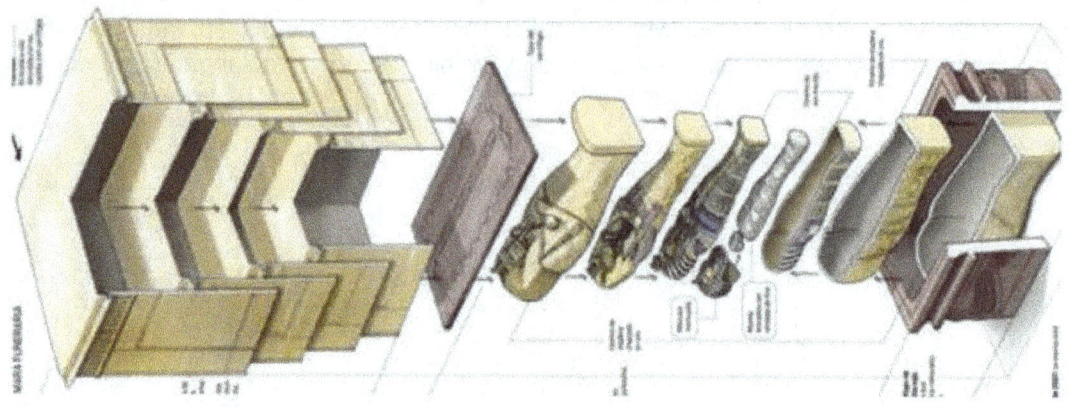

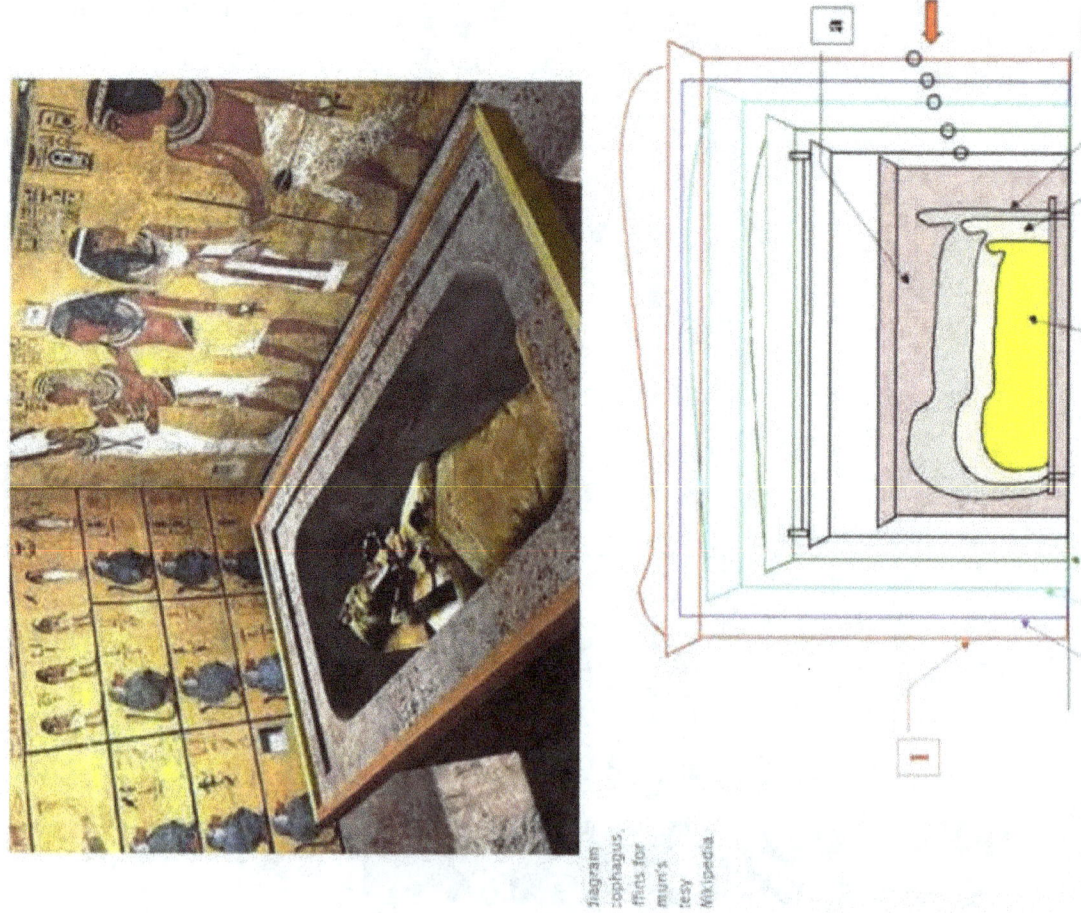

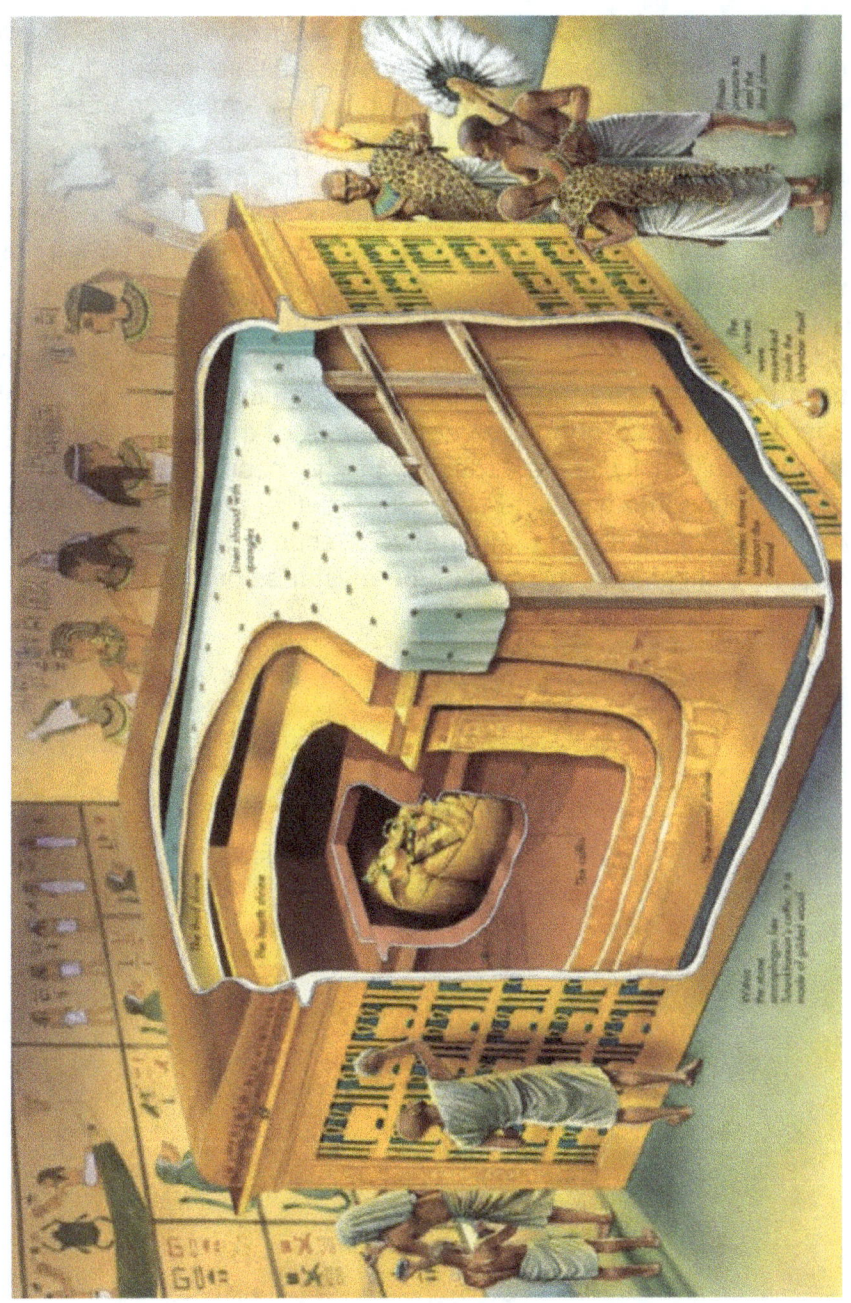

CONCLUSION

The components of the Trinity (Amun-Ra-Ptah) are subtle encasements that surround the Soul, Asar, who is at the same time the soul of the Royal Person and the soul of every object (including human beings) in time and space. These three principles, Amun/witness, Ra/mind and Ptah/ physicality/coagulated energy that has taken form and substance, surround the soul and allow the soul to have perceptions and experiences through them. The implication of this finding means that honoring and worshiping them leads to knowing about them and the realization that they are not realities but encasements through which the soul perceives the reality that passes through them, like seeing something through layers. They define the nature of perception and the format of the physical perceived realities, both in the waking and dream states. Some layers may be clear (like glass) while others are more opaque. The combination of these may also cause a mirroring effect like a mirage, whereby the soul loses grip on its own reality and identity as it views itself through the reality of the prism of the Trinity. In such a case the soul may be considered as being deluded as to its true nature and identity, which is the project of the Temple rituals, wisdom, and architecture to restore when interacting with a qualified, well-balanced, and thoroughly initiated and purified human being. This process leads to the unveiling of the soul's perceptions such that the perceptions that have been conditioned by the encasing elements of the Trinity become understood for what they are and do not further delude the mind as to the nature of reality and about its ultimate essential being. In a sense, they become transparent instead of opaque determiners of the reality of the soul. Rather, they become understood, intuitionally, as extensions of the cosmic mind of the Transcendental Absolute Soul, that extends into time and space in order to perceive and experience time and space but beyond that have no abiding importance. Becoming established in this clarified form of perception awareness constitutes the goal of the mysteries of the temple.

THE CONCEPT OF OM AS A DESCRIPTION OF MANIFEST WITNESSING CONSCIOUSNESS IN ANCIENT EGYPTIAN PHILOSOPHY

The image below is an Ancient Egyptian demotic hieroglyph for Om. The demotic script was a late Ancient Egyptian script that was used in the very late period in Ancient Egyptian history. While Om is most commonly known as a Sanskrit mantra (word of power from India), it also appears in the Ancient Egyptian texts and is closely related to the Kamitan Amun in sound and Amen of Christianity (which derived from Ancient Egyptian religion (see the books, *Mystical Journey From Jesus to Christ* by this author, and also *African Origins of Western Religion*). More importantly, it has the same meaning as Amun,

Below you will find the ancient glyphs of the ancient Egyptian OM symbol. Note the similarity to the Indian symbol that follows. The set of demotic symbols is composed of two parts. The first part looks like number three (3). The second part looks like the mathematical fraction one quarter (1/4). However, the two parts together actually are a word that is translated as "OM" or "AM". Indeed, the term is similar to the Indian Om or AUM term signifying the name and sound of the Transcendental Divine. In the book, African Origins Volume 3, a further discussion about this term was introduced, showing the similarities. From a religious studies comparative standpoint, it was noted that early India was in contact with Ancient Egypt and several Indian religious tenets, symbols, philosophical wisdom insights, and iconographies can be correlated to the earlier Ancient Egyptian ones. Therefore, it is not surprising to find several Ancient Egyptian terms and wisdom teachings that can be matched to what later came to be known as Indian religion and philosophy.

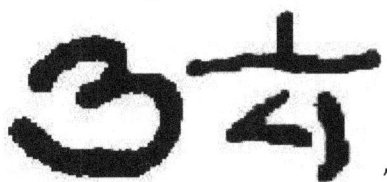

"Om" from the Ancient Egyptian Leyden Papyrus

The ancient African text containing the term OM is found in the Leyden Magical Papyrus in which the Supreme Being is described as follows:

> "Great is thy name, Heir is thy name, Excellent is thy name, Hidden is thy name, Mighty one
> of the gods and goddesses is thy name, "He whose name is hidden from all the gods and goddesses is thy name, OM ( ), Mighty Am is thy name; All the gods and

goddesses is thy name..."

We know that OM is the name of Amun because of the epithet "Hidden" and OM is the nameless Ancient divinity because of the epithet "name is hidden". OM is also the ancient divinity Neberdjer (All-encompassing Divinity) because of the epithet "All the gods and goddesses" so OM is the name given to the most ancient divinities of Kamit (Egypt) dating to the Pre Dynastic era (prior to 5000 BCE).

Om is a powerful sound; it represents the primordial sound of creation. Thus it appears in Ancient Egypt as Om or Am, in modern-day India as Om, and in Christianity as Amen, being derived from Amun. One Indian Tantric scripture (Tattva Prakash) states that Om or AUM can be used to achieve the mental state free of physical identification and can bring union with Brahman (the Absolute transcendental Supreme Being - God) if it is repeated 300,000 times... Om may also be used for engendering mental calm prior to beginning the recitation of a longer set of words of power or it may be used alone as described above. Thus, Om can be used before chanting the names of the Trinity, for example, Om Amun Ra Ptah, to achieve the goal of the Temple, the restoration of one's true identity. This hekau (chant, words of power, mantra) of Om Amun Ra Ptah, when chanted with an understanding of the Temple rituals, wisdom, and architecture by a qualified, well-balanced and thoroughly initiated and purified human being who understands the Trinity as extensions of the cosmic mind of the Transcendental Absolute Soul, that extends into time and space in order to perceive and experience time and space but beyond that have no abiding importance, the goal of the mysteries of the temple have been achieved.

Above: The Indian Sanskrit Symbol "Aum" or "Om"

From Subtle to Gross-The Absolute Manifesting as Three: Principles of experience: Amun-Ra-Ptah

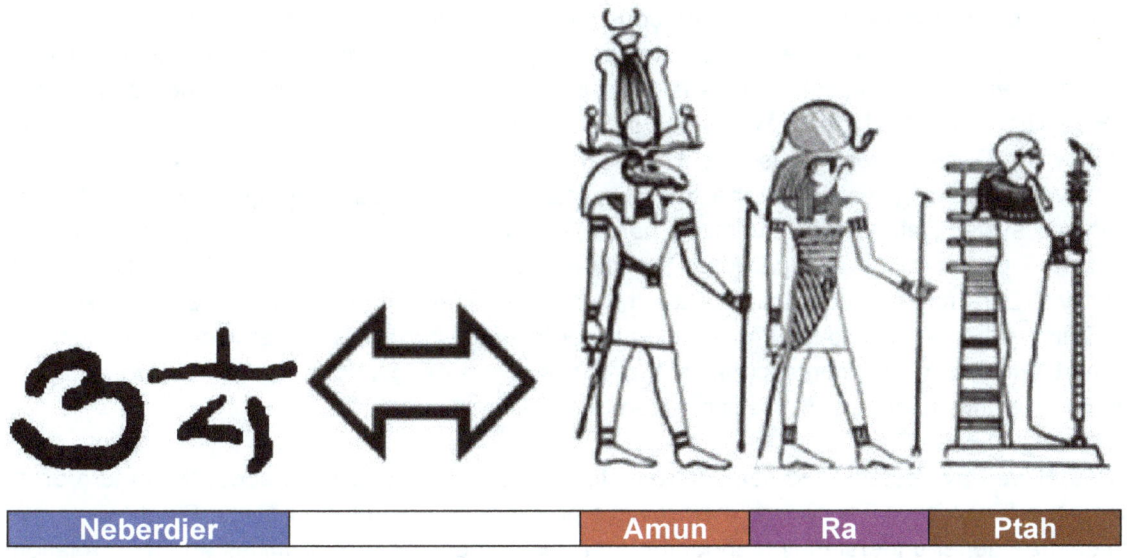

Description in summary

Ancient Egyptian "OM"

In the image above, an Ancient Egyptian demotic glyph for Om has been presented in relation to the Trinity of Amun, Ra, and Ptah.

So, the Ancient Egyptian wisdom provides the understanding that the Transcendental Being, referred to by the Om, expresses Itself in time and space as a Trinity, here, Amun, Ra, Ptah, which constitutes the operation of conscious awareness in terms of relative existence. In other words, the Transcendent exists outside of time and space while encompassing time and space just as a person sleeping on a bed having the dream (dreamer), transcends the dream, and yet encompasses the dream which the dreamer has given rise to. Furthermore, the dream is composed of the mind of the dreamer. In the same way, the Trinity is the matrix composing the three dream components that constitute time and space and the venue for mental perceptions, all of which occur within and is sustained by the Transcendental Absolute Consciousness (Neberdjer). Thus, Creation is a dream of time and space in the mind of the Absolute, Transcendental Consciousness, Neberdjer, through the Trinity of perceptions experienced by the Soul (Asar/Osiris). Another important point to be understood is that the transcendental essence, the "Om," and the Trinity, are not separate and incompatible natures. In other words, the Trinity is composed of the same transcendent consciousness just as the dream of a human being who is asleep, is composed of the mind of the same person who is sleeping.

EGYPTIAN BOOK OF THE DEAD HIEROGLYPH TRANSLATIONS Vol. 5

The Trinity, therefore, is not a separate or alien existence. Rather, it is composed of the transcendent consciousness and it is supported by that same consciousness and cannot exist without it. Thus, the Transcendental Absolute manifests itself through the Trinity of conscious experience in time and space which requires three aspects of mind for conscious perception. Those three aspects are witnessing subject (Amun), next is the object to be perceived (Ptah), and then there is required an interacting medium in order for the witness subject to be able to perceive the objects; that perception medium is mind (Ra). Therefore, the human experience in time and space requires these three aspects, which are afforded by the Transcendental Absolute. However, when these three aspects, the seer, seen, and sight are perceived as abiding realities by the limited human personality, as its opaque physical body, its brain, and nervous system, along with its limited perception of self-identity, then the cosmic Trinity becomes limited to the perception of an individual personality in time and space. That limitation relegates the personality to an erroneous conclusion about the nature of itself and the nature of existence. That limited state of being, when an individual human being regards himself or herself as an individual soul, a physical body, and using the limited mental capacity that is not aware of cosmic existence, but only the existence of its local time and space reality, this is referred to as spiritual ignorance.

Now that we have established some introductory fundamental principles about the nature of the gods that compose the Cosmic Trinity, and their relative position regarding the Absolute Spirit, we can proceed now to gain a deeper understanding about the qualities of these cosmic divinities and their relationship to human beings as components of human consciousness (ability to perceive and cognize with the mind, intellect and sense of existence as a living entity) with the help of the Ancient Egyptian Scripture known as the Egyptian Book of the Dead.

EGYPTIAN BOOK OF THE DEAD HIEROGLYPH TRANSLATIONS Vol. 5

	Amun	**Ra**	**Ptah**
	I	See/interact	That
	Witnessing / Identity Illumining cosmic mind Beyond thought/form/name	Cosmic Mind Thought behind the concept of physicality	Physicality
	Idea	Kheperu{Creations}	Forms
		images of objects in the cosmic mind	Tat {Language Representing forms}
	Seer	Sight	Seen
	Soul Consciousness illumining mind	Mind/thought/feeling/memories/desires/senses	Body

EGYPTIAN BOOK OF THE DEAD HIEROGLYPH TRANSLATIONS Vol. 5

Description and summary

In the *Hymn to Amun-Ra*[1] scripture that follows, we learn important insights about the nature of the divinity (Amun-Ra), as well as its relationship to human existence. In this text, we learn the momentous teaching that Amun is a conscious witness that does not sleep. Further, we learned that this witnessing aspect of divine consciousness is awake and aware within men and women even when they are asleep. Moreover, we additionally learn that this divinity is not only hidden within human beings and thereby constitutes the true source of their capacity for conscious awareness, but we also learn that this divinity is hidden within all objects. This means that the objects of creation, even those that appear to be non-sentient, actually have a divine presence. Furthermore, the scripture informs us that this divinity is within the objects, of Creation, but also it is established within the god **Tem**, the solar aspect of divinity that brings creation into being (Khepera) and also dissolves creation (Tem), at the end of time, along with the creator spirit **Ra-Herakty**, who is the sustainer of creation.

Therefore, this witnessing consciousness is the source from which arises the Creator Spirit, Ra, and the production of the Creator Spirit which is Creation. This momentous realization, that within the human being there is this immortal witnessing consciousness divinity that has brought them into conscious awareness, and which sustains their lives, causes those who hear it to express feelings of jubilation.

The realization of the significance of this mystery brought forth by the hymn, which is that witnessing consciousness is within a human being and that that same witnessing consciousness is the cosmic witness Divinity, is indeed a most important realization of human life, the understanding and the discovery of that divine consciousness that lies within every human being, that realization, causes jubilation because it allays the ordinary human egoistic stresses over worldly human anxieties, tensions, and traumas that inevitably culminate in their death. With this realization, it is possible to understand that the witnessing consciousness divinity that lies within, which transcends human vicissitudes and human mortality, can be relied upon so as to let go of the illusory stresses of limited human mortal life. This realization affords the opportunity to discover the divine presence within oneself and in the outer world and partake of its qualities, which include immortality, the silence, and coolness of inner peace, and the discovery of existence beyond ego culminating in the experience of transcendental all-encompassing existence, Neberdjer This is the goal of Ancient Egyptian religion, the purpose of the Egyptian Book of the Dead and the mission of the Ancient Egyptian Temple.

---

[1] See the book *African Religion Vol. 2 Theban Theology - Egyptian Yoga Volume 2*

HYMN TO AMUN-RA, The Hidden Awake and Aware Among Us[2]

Precept A-Amun-Ra is witnessing Consciousness in the Sleep State

Precept A.

A.1 *sedjer resu her neb remteju sedjeru*
A.2 sleep awakeaware/watchful person all men women sleeping
A.3 in the sleep state of consciousness [Amun-Ra] is awake and aware and watchful of men and women while they are sleeping.

AMUN established in objects. Amun is witnessing consciousness that sustains the Creator Divinity and the Objects of Creation

Precept B.
B.1 *Amun men {mdj}*
B.2 Hidden Creator-Spirit established (founded)
B.3 The hidden divinity, who is the witnessing consciousness of the Divine, is established, founded, latent, hidden...

---

[2] Hieratic and Hieroglyphic text: Hymne à Ammon-Ra des papyrus égyptiens du Musée de Boulaq. Translations by Dr. Muata Ashby ©2019

EGYPTIAN BOOK OF THE DEAD HIEROGLYPH TRANSLATIONS Vol. 5

Precept C.
- C.1 chetu{fig}   nebt   Temu   (Ra)Herakty
- C.2 things/objects all   Creator-Spirit   Sustainer-Creator-Spirit
- C.3 ...in all objects that exist including the beginning and ending Creator Spirit and the sustainer Creator Spirit.

Precept D.
- D.1. aau
- D.2. praises/adorations people
- D.3. Praises and adorations are uttered by people...

Precept E.
- E.1. n-k   im   djed   senu   er   awuu
- E.2. to-thee   form   speech   theirs   as-to   expansiveness
- E.3. ...about you (Amun-Ra) in the form of verbal expansions about your glory.

Examples of the Henu Pose:

EGYPTIAN BOOK OF THE DEAD HIEROGLYPH TRANSLATIONS Vol. 5

Precept F.
- F.1   Henu   {remteju}   n-k
- F.2   The Henu jubilation posture is practiced {by men and women} to-thee
- F.3   There is so much adulation and happiness that the jubilation posture is practiced in honor...

Precept G-Amun is witnessing consciousness that rests within us and sustains the individual human existence and ego conscious awareness.

Precept G.
- G1   en   urd   {ndjs}   k   im   n-u
- G2   of   resting   {small} thee within   of-us
- G3   ...of your resting (latent/hidden/quiescent/supporting/upholding) {small/undetected/atomic/infinitesimal} within us, supporting the existence of created names and forms of Creation as well as the consciousness that supports our existence and conscious awareness of ourselves as conscious living beings in time and space.

EGYPTIAN BOOK OF THE DEAD HIEROGLYPH TRANSLATIONS Vol. 5

Description & summary

The following short Scriptures are presented here as complements to the *Hymn to Amun-Ra* (above). They will provide further insights into some particular statements given in the hymn. The first text is entitled "Stele of Adoration to Ra-Herakty & Tem as One". These divinities were mentioned in the *Hymn to Amun-Ra* above [Verse/Precept C]. This stele has four columns of text. Through the text, we learn that the divinity being identified is the sustainer Creator Spirit. Beginning at column number two, we learned that the two divinities mentioned in Verse/Precept "C" of the *Hymn to Amun-Ra*, Ra-Herakty & Tem, who were represented in the text as if they were two separate entities, are presented in the stele as being one and the same. In other words, they are not separate divinities, but rather aspects of each other and as we learned in the *Hymn to Amun-Ra*, they are as if emanations from the witnessing self (Amun) within. In this context, Amun being the witnessing consciousness within Ra-Herakty-Tem and since Ra is the mind aspect of the Trinity (Amun-Ra-Ptah), then it follows that we are to understand that consciousness is the inner reality that is the source of the capacity of awareness, the witnessing mind. Since the *Hymn to Amun-Ra* also informed us that the witnessing consciousness aspect of the Trinity is established within objects, we are additionally informed that the God Ptah (fashioner of objects as the architect of Creation) is also a product of the Cosmic Witnessing Self.

So, creation, as well as the perception of creation, are both sustained by the witnessing consciousness just as it sustains the conscious awareness of humans even as they sleep. In other words, the witnessing consciousness aspect of the time and space reality that human beings consider to be "creation" or "existence" in "time and space" is actually a production of and is sustained by Consciousness (Neberdjer). This means that Consciousness (Neberdjer) sustains the mind and the objects that the mind is aware of and the fact that perceptions and the objects of perception are not realities in and of themselves. Rather, the truth behind mental perceptions and the objects perceived by the mind is Consciousness (Neberdjer) perceiving and sustaining them. In other words, the Trinity of consciousness (Amun-Ra-Ptah/Seer/Sight/Seen) is sustained by Neberdjer (Absolute) which means that Neberdjer is the higher and ultimate truth, while the Trinity composing time and space and conscious awareness, is only a temporary manifestation of the Absolute, which the limited mind refers to as "time and space reality".

Therefore, creation and the objects, as well as the names and forms of creation (names and forms that have been assigned by ignorant, unenlightened and limited human minds), have no independent existence without the conceptualization that brought them into existence (conscious awareness) in their current apparent state of substance and form. The names given to the objects of creation are therefore productions of the limited understanding of the human mind. Thus, those names that have been given do not and cannot represent the totality of knowledge about those objects being named since the human mind and intellect are incapable of fathoming the depths of their existence and can only perceive their surface/external (Amun-Ra-Ptah) form and appearance. If the human being were to turn towards the Royal Road of the

Ancient Egyptian Temple, that path would lead to proving, as a matter of intuitional experience, the illusory myth of creation and time and space as well as the limitations of human existence. It would also prove the erroneousness of the conclusions, based on the limited human mental intellectual capacity, that human existence begins with physical birth, continues on, and then ends with physical death. Then, with that discovery of one's Neberdjer Consciousness (in the form of Amun), the jubilation mentioned in the above *Hymn to Amun-Ra*, would be experienced.

Stele of Adoration to Ra-Herakty & Tem as One

*Cross-reference- HYMN TO AMUN-RA, The Hidden Awake and Aware Among Us [VERSE C]

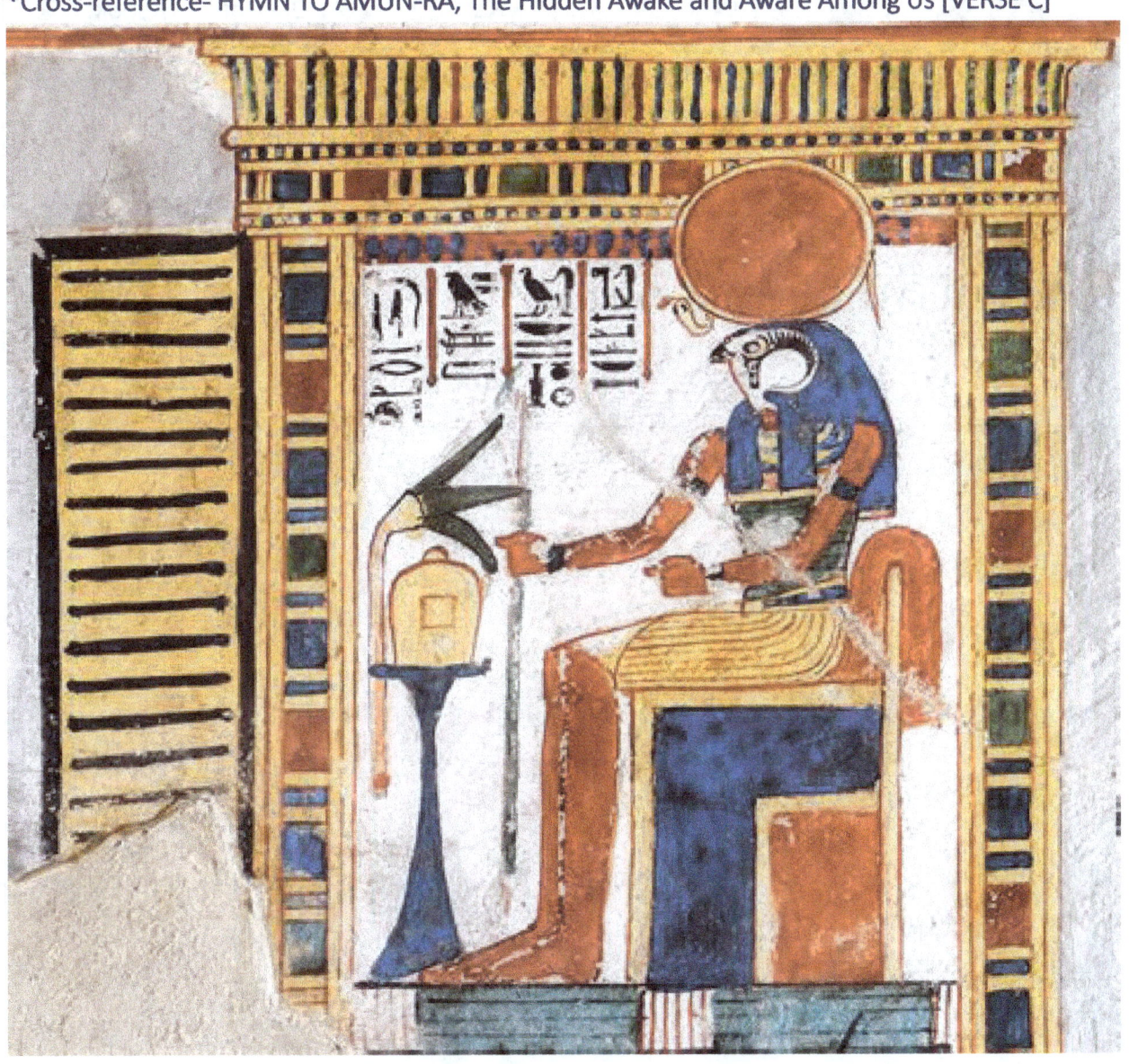

Stele of Ra-Herakty and Temu Col. 1 2 3 4	Transliteration Col. 1	Translation Col. 1	Contextual Translation Col. 1
	Medu dje in Ra	Words Spoken By Creator-Spirit	These words are now being spoken by the Creator Spirit…

Stele of Ra-Herakty and Temu Col. 1 2 3 4	Transliteration Col. 2	Translation Col. 2	Contextual Translation Col. 2
	Herakty *Tem*	of two horizons conclusions	…the divinity who encompasses from east to west, beginning to ending, the sustainer of Creation, time and space as Ra Herakty), and the divinity of conclusion and dissolutions and ending Creation time and space (Temu).

EGYPTIAN BOOK OF THE DEAD HIEROGLYPH TRANSLATIONS Vol. 5

Stele of Ra-Herakty and Temu Col. 1 2 3 4	Transliteration Col. 3	Translation Col. 3	Contextual Translation Col. 3
	u *neb tawy* *Anu*	(Ending of the name of Temu) Lord two lands Heliopolis	Who is lord of the two lands of upper and lower Egypt and thereby the duality of existence, what is above and below. The city of Heliopolis, the first city of Creation…

Stele of Ra-Herakty and Temu Col. 1 2 3 4	Transliteration Col. 4	Translation Col. 4	Contextual Translation Col. 4
	Neter **aah** **{mdj}** **Neb** **Pet**	Divinity Great {figurative} Lord heaven	*Ra-Herakty-Temu* is the Great Divinity of Heliopolis and the lord of Heaven.

Description & summary

The second Ancient Egyptian text that will be used to complement the wisdom presented in the *Hymn to Amun-Ra* comes from the Ancient Egyptian wisdom texts known as the Precepts of **Ani**. The theme here is about praying with loving hearts. This text is presented specifically relating to Verse/Precept "E" of *Hymn to Amun-Ra*. In Verse/Precept E, the hymn speaks of how people's praises grow in expansiveness. This statement can be taken as meaning that it is getting louder and louder. Here, in the precepts of Sage Ani, the text speaks of how speech should be conducted in the Temple. So, while loud praises and exaltations may be appropriate in certain venues, it is important to remember that within the temple context, the speech is to remain silent and reverential, instead of exuberant, boisterous, or otherwise agitated. While loud praises may be appropriate for a festive context of spiritual worship such as public rituals and spiritual festivities, inside the temple or the personal worship room at home, praises grow in expansiveness not by outward loud prayers, but by praying in silence with a loving heart, and by being silent and cool, as we discussed, from the teachings of Sage Amenemopet above.

Precepts of Ani- Pray in silence with a loving heart

*Cross-referencePrecepts of Ani (below)to- HYMN TO AMUN-RA, The Hidden Awake and Aware Among Us [VERSE E-above]

Precept H.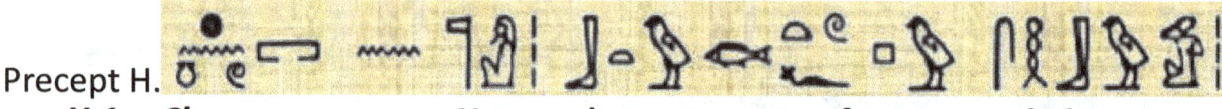

- **H.1.** Chenu   n   Neteru betu   tu - f   pu   sehebu
- **H.2.** Inner-Temple of   Divinities violation to- them those reveling, loud, festive sounds
- **H.3.** It is important for a spiritual aspirant to understand that reveling and shouting and festive behaviors are fine for public rituals outside but are violations of the internal temple behavior rules since these cause mental disturbance, agitations, and distractions from the promotion of silence and stillness in the mind that are necessities for attaining the deeper experience of the temple.

Precept I.

- I.1. **Senemehu**   n – k   im   ab   mert
- I.2. Prayers   of-thee   in   heart devotional/loving
- I.3. When in the temple, a spiritual aspirant should have a heart(mind) that has devotional/loving feeling.

Precept J.

- J.1. **Iu**   medtu   f   nebt   amunu –   {per}
- J.2. Its   words   yours   all   hidden- {chamber}
- J.3. The words contemplated in the personality (mind) should not be audible but rather in silence, with solemnity, and confined to the hidden chamber of the heart(mind) in the form of thought with feeling.

Temple of Amun-Ra at Abu Simbel Sanctuary Text Translation

Description and summary

Having gained important wisdom about the nature of the cosmic Trinity and its source as well as how and where it manifests within time and space objects as well as the essence of human existence, we can now proceed to enter the sanctuary (Holy of Holies), of the temple. On both the North and South walls, there are images of a divine boat and offerings to Amun (on the south{left}) side) and to Ra-Herakty (on the north{right} side) [image below]. For the purpose of this study of the wisdom of spiritual mystic identity that is contained in the temple architecture, iconography, and hieroglyphic texts, we will concentrate on the sculptured sitting images within the sanctuary west wall along with their corresponding hieroglyphic texts.

Before looking at the four characters within the sanctuary and their texts in detail, there is an important iconographical and architectural principle to be highlighted. The principle is non-duality. Notice that the sanctuary room is a single enclosure with only one entrance that faces towards the east. The seated characters face east with their backs towards the west. This west to east movement, according to the Temple Directional Movement Matrix, is of Creation. The special highlight though, is that this creative movement that starts in the west and goes towards the east is presided over by four entities that have come into manifestation in the oneness of this room. In other words, further west of their backs there is the unmanifest, Neberdjer (Om). Where their backs begin to emerge from the wall, is the beginning of the four principles they represent; this is also the beginning of their manifestation in time and space. Therefore, Creation occurs/manifests *concomitantly* with the appearance of these principles of conscious awareness. Amun-Ra-Ptah are cosmic principles, witnessing self-mind-physicality, which allows human mental perception to be possible. In other words, Creation and awareness in mental principles occurs at the same time and is/are co-dependent. Creation cannot exist without "something" being aware of it; that "something" that is aware, is Transcendental Consciousness (Neberdjer), manifesting as Amun. Thus, the infinite Absolute (Neberdjer) is consciousness that is aware of time and space Creation and that perceives itself as Creation and objects in Creation, through the trinity of Amun-Ra-Ptah. The Royal Person is the living manifestation (Soul) of Absolute Divinity (Neberdjer) within that Creation that is sustained by the three principles.

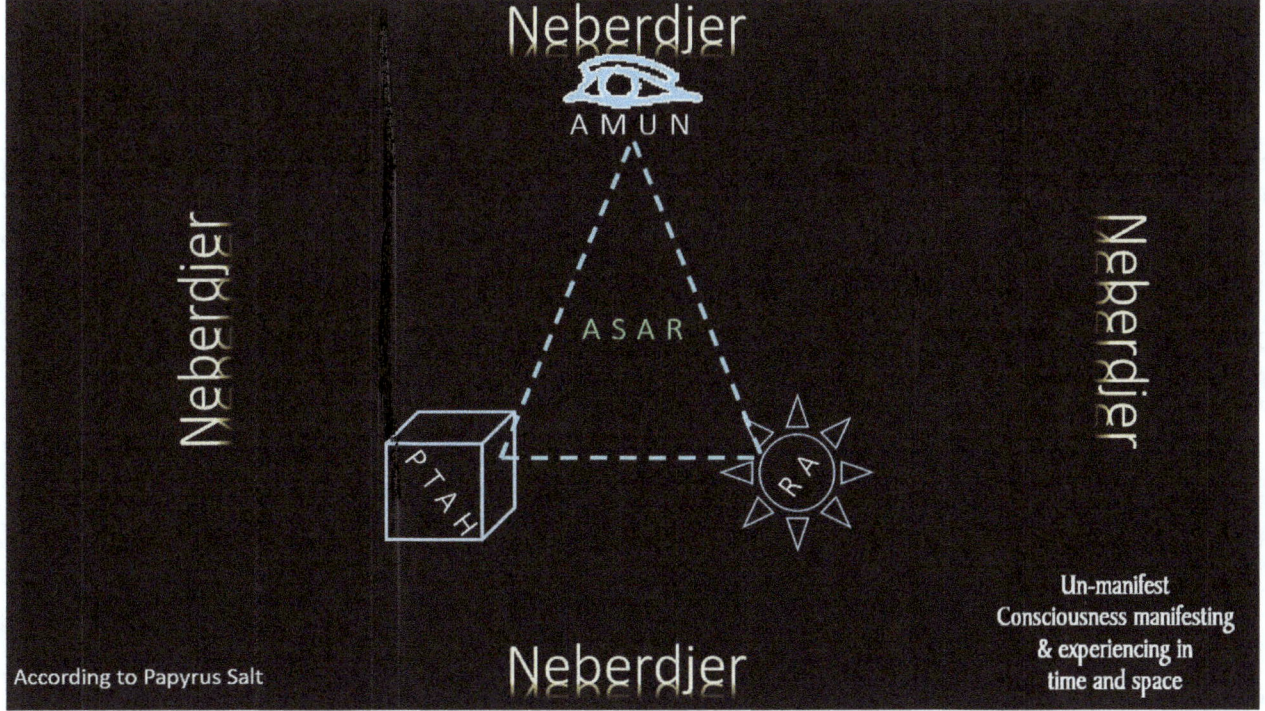

Furthermore, the principles Amun-Ra-Ptah and Asar (the Soul/Royal Person) are manifestations of Neberdjer (the Absolute) consciousness and as such have no independent reality from Neberdjer (Absolute Consciousness). Thus, the Creation is not an absolute reality but only a temporary manifestation sustained by Consciousness that appears at the same time as Consciousness becomes aware of Creation. Creation cannot exist without conscious awareness being aware of it. Therefore, consciousness and awareness of Creation are one and the same which also means that Creation is a perception of and within cosmic consciousness. As a human being is able to perceive Creation, through mind (Amun-Ra-Ptah), the limitation of mind prevents understanding that the nature of their ability to be conscious and aware in itself and conscious and aware of Creation are sustained by the same source, Cosmic Consciousness, which itself is sustained by the Transcendental Absolute. If a human being were to realize their innate Absolute nature, at the same time the illusoriness of the Creation is removed and it is recognized as a manifestation of the same Absolute, as their own conscious awareness, mind, and body are as well. Thus, in the sanctuary room, there is an origin of oneness in the movement from west to east, and also from east to west, an end of duality. So, in the sanctuary, there are no more names and forms but only the beginning and end of things. The movement from here is west towards the Absolute, and east towards Creation and duality. Finally, in this room, where the four characters appear, it is also an indication that the four characters are in reality four manifestations of a single essential being that has come into manifestation. This finding sheds light on the Ancient Egyptian emphasis on number four.

Boat Pedestal Containing the Divine Image of the Temple Tutelary Divinity

The four seated figures in the sanctuary are, from left to right: The God Ptah, The God Amun-Ra, The Royal Person (human and Divine), and The God Ra-Herakty. In the following image, the same figures can be seen in a drawing from an early 19th-century explorer that depicts the colors that the sculpture was found with, at that time. This finding of the predominance of blue on the left, south side of the temple, while having a predominance of the two personalities on the right side being painted in red, indicates some remnants of the wisdom of color that existed in the temple in ancient times. These same colors are characteristic of Ancient Egyptian iconography and confirmed by the fact that other depictions of these personalities have been found rendered similarly in other temples of Ancient Egypt. This finding provides an additional dimension to the experience of the message of the temple. The color blue relates to source conscious awareness (Amun) and its conceptualization (Ptah). The color red symbolizes the expression of the source consciousness through movement, expansion, fire and light energies that illumine the conceptualizations of the conscious awareness which are the Creations manifesting as concepts (objects) in the mind and objects in the physical world, both of which appear in time and space awareness.

Also, it is fitting that the sitting figures should be colored and placed as they are because the God Ptah and the God Amun-Ra, with bodies colored in blue, relate to the south and to sustenance and provisioning for the Royal Person. On the north side of the temple, axis sit the Gods, colored in red, Ramses and Ra-Herakty, who represent dynamic action in the world of time and space, which is witnessed and supported by the south. Blue is the color of coolness and source consciousness while red is the color of movement and dynamic action in time and space. Notice that the Royal Person, Ramses, has a body-colored in red and wears a crown colored in blue. From this color matrix and in consideration of the iconographical context of the room, the seated postures and the overall wisdom of manifestation, we may see this presentation as an indication of the dual capacity of the Royal person; he or she is capable of both manifestation with a body as well as experiencing transcendental source consciousness.

Southern wall boat **Northern wall boat**

The walls of the north and south sides of the sanctuary room contain dual (Holographic) images of a Divine Boat and there is a pedestal in the center of the room where an actual ceremonial boat would have been placed, where the two wall images meet at the center of the room, on the axis of the temple. Therefore, the two boat images would come together symbolically in the center of the room where there would be a "physical" boat. In this context, the holographic convergence concept evokes a boat in the center of the room regardless of if there is a physical one there or not. The virtual boat exists in the conceptualization of the mind and thus the physical boat exists at the "physical" level of mind, which is composed of subtle matter; and that boat is the higher vessel of the soul's spiritual journey. The images on the south side wall depict an offering to Amsu and on the north side to Ra-Herakty. Thus, in a coming into Creation (duality) east to west movement, we may think of the boat that is on the pedestal at the center of the room as becoming two boats; in other words, becoming dual and instituting movement from west to east, i.e. creative movement. It means that Amun-Ra has become Amun "and" Ra-Herakty from this point onwards moving east, the movement of the boat is in duality, the fundamental feature of time and space relative reality. Likewise, as one enters the sanctuary, moving west, as the two images of the boats on the south and north walls converge (holographic convergence) on the center on the pedestal, this represents a movement from duality to oneness, a dissolution of Creation.

EGYPTIAN BOOK OF THE DEAD HIEROGLYPH TRANSLATIONS Vol. 5

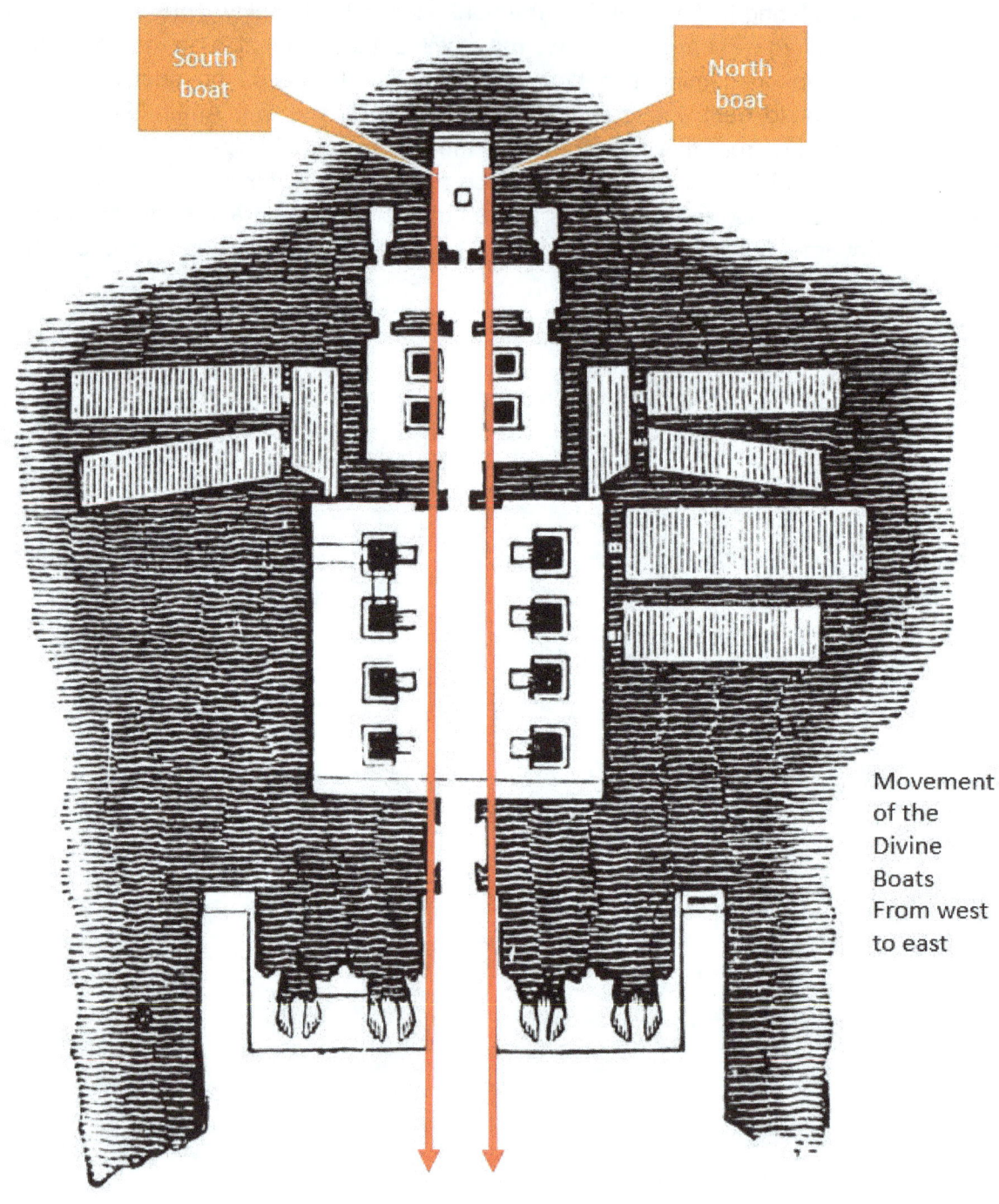

South boat

North boat

Movement of the Divine Boats From west to east

EGYPTIAN BOOK OF THE DEAD HIEROGLYPH TRANSLATIONS Vol. 5

Description and summary

The following images render the four divinities with the colors that they are found rendered and as depicted in other parts of this temple and other temples of Ancient Egypt.

| Ptah | Amun | Royal Person(Rameses) | Ra-Herakty |

Below: Image from the sanctuary of the Temple of Amun-Ra

EGYPTIAN BOOK OF THE DEAD HIEROGLYPH TRANSLATIONS Vol. 5

Description and summary

The following image depicts the three cosmic divinities and Rameses in the form of statues as found in an Ancient Egyptian tomb.

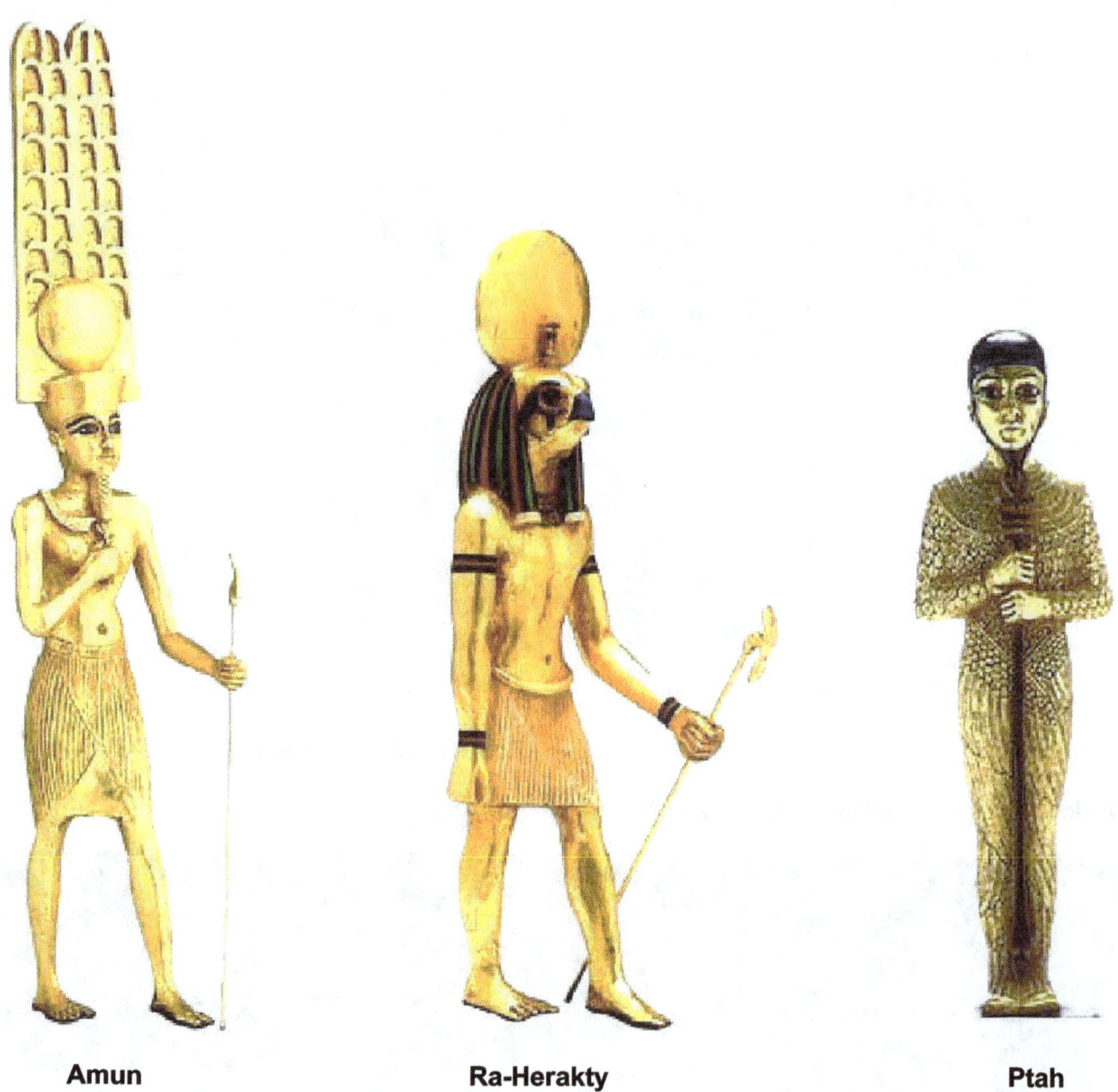

Amun   **Ra-Herakty**   **Ptah**

EGYPTIAN BOOK OF THE DEAD HIEROGLYPH TRANSLATIONS Vol. 5

Temple of Amun-Ra at Abu Simbel Sanctuary Translation

Description and Summary

Next, we will proceed to read the hieroglyphic text in the sanctuary west wall above the four seated figures. There are seven relevant columns of text on the wall. The text of column number one relates to and identifies the God Ptah. The text of column number two relates to and identifies the God Amun-Ra. The text of columns 3-4 relates to and identifies the Royal Person as human. The final three columns relate to and identify the divinity as Ra-Herakty.

In the final three columns, there is a statement about an act that Ra-Herakty does on behalf of the human (bound/manifest) Royal Person. In the context of the architectural setting where this image of the Royal Person is located and considering the relationships of the Royal Person to the other seated Divinities as outlined throughout the temple panels, this circumscribed aspect may be thought of as a manifest or time and space depiction of a human being expressing in a time and space physical reality.

In column number six, the Royal Person is not described as human anymore, but rather as an unbound or uncircumscribed entity. The divinity then makes a momentous statement in column number seven; he states that he grants manifestation, on the physical plane, of the likeness of the un-manifest (uncircumscribed) aspect of the Royal Person. In other words, there is an un-manifest unbound aspect of the Royal Person that exists in the plane transcending the physical plane. That un-manifest aspect of the Royal Person is being granted the capacity of having its likeness manifest on the physical plane, in time and space. The fact that this grant is being given by the God Ra-Herakty signifies that that which appears with a name and form, in an apparently physical reality, owes its manifestation and form to the nature of mind & senses, which can be seen as an extension of mind, since this divinity, Ra-Herakty, is the divinity of the Cosmic Trinity that presides over the principal of mind, he interaction medium between witnessing consciousness and apparent physical reality in time and space (Amun/witness, Ra/mind and Ptah/physicality/coagulated energy).

Amun is the divinity that sustains conscious awareness in the living-sentient and non-sentient objects of Creation. Ra-Herakty is the divinity that conceptualizes their names and forms for their apparent appearance in time and space relative but temporary reality. Everything conceptualized into apparent existence by Ra-Herakty "exists" in those forms only for a limited, fleeting period. That concept from the cosmic mind (Ra-Herakty, through Djehuty) appears with a physical form that can be perceived with physical senses in time and space and under the jurisdiction of the god Ptah. A deeper implication of this process of coming into apparent existence is that the existence is only apparent and not real, but only a conceptualization sustained by conscious awareness which is itself sustained by consciousness devoid of all qualities of name or form and beyond life or death and time and space. That underlying substratum of apparent time and space existence is the Absolute, e.g. Neberdjer. So the terms "apparent" and "appearance", in this context, signify a projection of mind, as when an idea coms to conscious awareness with form and name; but that form is temporary and replaced by other names and forms. Thus the forms and names are temporary and therefore illusory but the entity that is aware of the names and forms, the appearing objects in the mind and in Creation, is the Absolute essential existence that sustains all the temporary appearances in the mind (thoughts, desires, memories, feelings, etc.) as well as the external appearances perceived by the senses (physical objects in time and space (including people, animals, plants, elements, planets, stars, etc.)).

Therefore, we are to understand that conscious awareness of the human experience is based on the presence of witnessing consciousness within, as was explained by the *Hymn to Amun-Ra*, we explored previously. The interacting medium (mind and senses) allows the witnessing consciousness to experience the presence and absence of objects that appear in temporary time and space. Thus, the capacity of a "living" being to be conscious and aware of anything, at any level, from the rudimentary amoeba to the most erudite college professor, is neither originated by nor sustained by the individual mind, but rather, the consciousness that can be awake and aware. Human beings use the mind to interact with apparent objects and have the capacity of mental functions in order to understand their meaning. Those higher mental functions that allow a human being the possibility of experiencing above simple animal conscious awareness and strive for higher conscious awareness, include cognition, memory, language, and intellect, the capacity of introspection, and capacity for self-identity.

This last feature of mind, self-identity, represents an important key to understanding and achieving personal spiritual enlightenment, the discovery of a Transcendental Self, beyond the human being, the key to understanding degradation, pain, and suffering as well as the downfall of the human being, which can descend to levels below those of ordinary animals. So, while the human being is part animal, it has the capacity, through spiritual evolution, to exceed its instinctual and or unethical behaviors (acting without regard for knowing and following truth in favor of personal desires). At the other extreme of human capacity is spiritual enlightenment that can be achieved when the illusoriness of the ego self-identity is discovered and rejected in favor of seeking the divine grace (Sa-Ankh), spoken of earlier, that leads to the discovery of the higher spiritual identity.

Verse 1

1.1 Medu dje in Ptah Maat Neb

<u>1.2 Words spoken by Architect Creation lord of Righteousness</u>

1.3 These words are spoken by the Divine in the form of the God Ptah, who is Architect of Creation and Lord of Truth and Righteousness

Verse 2.

    2.1 Medu dje in Amun-Ra Neb pet

    <u>2.2 Words spoken by Hidden Creator Spirit Lord Heaven</u>

    2.3 These words are spoken by the Divine in the form of the Hidden Creator Spirit who is Lord of Heaven.

Verse 3.

    3.1 Neb tawy (User-Maat-Ra-Setep-en-Ra)

    <u>3.2 Lord two lands (power/dominion- truth- Creator Spirit- chosen - by –Ra)</u>

    3.3 This is the Royal Person, who is known by the name: (one manifesting the truth of the power and dominion of the Creator-Spirit and chosen by same Creator Spirit, Ra.)

Verse 17.

    17.1.   *Neb chau* (R A-M E S S -A M U N -M E R Y)

    17.2.   Lord thrones (Creator Spirit- Child -Hidden Creator Spirit-beloved)

    17.3.   The Royal Person is a sovereign over thrones and dawnings like the sun and known by the name: (Offspring of the Creator-Spirit and beloved by the Hidden Creator-Spirit).

Verse 18.

    18.1. *Medu dje in Ra-Herakty her ab per*

    18.2. Words spoken by Creator Spirit of the two horizons, innermost reality of the temple of...

    18.3.   These words are being spoken by the Creator-Spirit aspect as the divine that is the sustainer of Creation and who spans from the beginning to end, which is the innermost reality of the temple of...

Verse 19.

19.1. 〕 *Rameses-Amun-mery* 〔

19.2. <u>{unbound} Child of the Creator Spirit who is beloved of the Hidden-Creator-Spirit</u>

19.3. ...the Royal Person who is known as 〔Offspring of the Creator-Spirit and beloved by the Hidden Creator-Spirit〕. and now "unbound", now "uncircumscribed."

Verse 20.

20.1. *Pa di mi ta*

20.2. <u>who is given (by Ra-Herakty) to unbound Ramses material existence (pun with **pad**-matter/cake) likeness on earth</u>

5.3, 6.3, 7.3 [**CONTEXTUAL SUMMARY Verses 5-7**] The Royal person Ramses sits on an equal plane of existence (Cosmic Consciousness) with the 3 cosmic divinities of time and space material manifestation and time/space awareness. Ra-Herakty is the "her ab", the innermost reality of the house (the temple/physical dwelling/body) of Ramses. Ra's aspect (Ra-Herakty) as Divinity of 2 horizons, i.e. of unity encompassing duality, says: "he gives to the "unbound/uncircumscribed" and "un-manifest", "non-physical", "non-manifest" aspect of Ramses, - to that aspect of Ramses, Ra gives material substance (likeness of manifestation) to exist on the physical plane (time and space).

PERTEMHERU CHAPTER 176-Going Into the Hidden Chamber of the Un-manifest and Coming Out as an Enlightened Spirit Being

Description & summary

The following text translation from the "PERT EM HERU" or Ancient Egyptian Book of the Dead (or, as the Ancient Egyptians referred to it: Book of Enlightenment), provides further insights into the teaching of spiritual identity and the philosophy expressed in the Temple and its sanctuary, as well as the Ancient Egyptian scriptures that have been described throughout this volume. The text comes from chapter 176 of the book, entitled "Going into the hidden chamber of the un-manifest and coming out as an enlightened spirit-being." This chapter speaks of the idea of becoming Neberdjer, the all-encompassing divinity, which is eternity and infinity. Doing the act, suggested by the chapter, means joining the two lands, that is, uniting duality into non-duality and thus doing/becoming an enlightened personality, a personality that has discovered the Transcendental Being that exists beyond the temporary and therefore illusory mortal, limited human existence.

Following the context of the Ancient Egyptian Temple being played out on an east-west axis, the text speaks of disdain for moving towards the east. In Ancient Egyptian wisdom, the east is seen as the land of incarnation, of being born. Juxtaposed against the idea of going to the east, indicating incarnation or reincarnation into time and space, is the context of moving towards the West, the place where the sanctuary is found and beyond which there is unmanifest Spirit-Being in Its fullness as opposed to the limited experience of human existence. The text further speaks of the distasteful nature of what happens when one goes to the east to incarnate into time and space whereby unpalatable, uncomfortable, degrading things and sufferings are visited upon the personality. The text alludes to a chopping block, in a subtle way relating to the idea of the god Osiris, who was dismembered by his brother Set/Seth, who sought to usurp his throne. The text continues by proclaiming that the avid initiates should not want anything to happen to them that would be disapproved of by the gods and goddesses, meaning, anything not within the realm of sufferings outside the purview of a life based on ethical conscience. This indicates that this Royal Person has reached the level of seeing him or herself as a god or goddess and along with that self-identity comes self-respect.

EGYPTIAN BOOK OF THE DEAD HIEROGLYPH TRANSLATIONS Vol. 5

Chap 176 Pertemheru chapter 176 becoming Neberdjer on the day of uniting 2 lands if known becoming Shining Spirit

Verse 4.
4.1. **Betu   a   pu   ta   en   abtet   an   aq   a   er   chebt**
4.2. Abomination me that earth to east, not go-in I as to slaughterhouse
4.3. It is something abominable, hateful, disgusting, wicked, sinful, awful, bad to me that while being on the earth plane as a human being I should go to the eastern horizon and be reborn into this abomination called ignorant human life of egoistic suffering! I refuse to go into that slaughterhouse (as what happened to Asar) where bodies, feelings, and minds are placed on the chopping block of anguish, frustrations, and unknown sufferings!

Verse 5.
5.1. **an   aritu n-a   chetu   im   nenu   betu   Neteru   her entet nuk a**
5.2. not   done to-me   things   among   those   hateful   gods   upon which I am
                                                           /goddesses
5.3. I don't want anything to be done upon me which the gods and goddesses find abominable. I am…

Verse 6.
6.1. **as   shuai   abu   her-ab   mesqet   erdi   en   n - f   Neberdjer   achu {mdj} f**
6.2. see pass pure innermost-reality resurrection given -he Absolute-Self shining {fig} he
                                    chamber   Spirit-Being
6.3. …behold, I pass through as a purified personality into the innermost recesses of the resurrection chamber that is given by the **Neberdjer,** Lord-of-utmost-limits, the All-Encompassing-Divinity, the Absolute Transcendental Self, the Universal Consciousness. I go into that resurrection chamber of **Neberdjer** purified and emerge as a Shining-Spirit-Being {fig}.

EGYPTIAN BOOK OF THE DEAD HIEROGLYPH TRANSLATIONS Vol. 5

Verse 7.

7.1. *ra   pu   en   sema {mdj} tawy   embah -a   neb   chetu   ar   rech {mdj}*
7.2. day   that of   uniting {fig} two-lands presence-hand lord   objects as to knowledge
7.3. This occurs on the day when the two lands, the duality of conscious awareness, becomes dissolved into non-dual awareness; this is called "Egyptian Yoga." When this unification occurs and there is an experience of non-duality, not in isolation, but additionally in the presence of the hand of the Lord (Neberdjer) of objects (forms of Creation), then the experiential knowledge...

Verse 8.

8.1. *ra   pu   unn   f   im   ach   aqer {mdj} im   Neterkhert*
8.2. day   that being he   as   shining spirit perfected within lower heaven
8.3. ... on that day (at that time), the person having this experience also is henceforth known as one who has achieved the state of conscious awareness called "Shining Spirit Being," which is a term designating one who has achieved the perfection of conscious awareness also referred to as "Enlightenment." This will be experienced in the netherworld, i.e. in the astral plane or mind, with conscious awareness; as such, one who has achieved this has achieved all that the scriptures allude to and has achieved the highest goal of life on earth, finishing with human existence and reincarnations. The one who has achieved this goal has achieved knowledge of the hidden, un-manifest, but all-pervasive Transcendental Being (Neberdjer) and as such is also transcendental, immortal, eternal and infinite.

8.4. COMMENTARY: enlightenment is a mental concept that from the perspective of the thinking mind can be described as an experience of the personality as a realized effect of experiencing Spirit Being, which is beyond mind, time and space. But enlightenment is experienced in and through the mind as a stable perspective of spiritual self-identity. This means that enlightenment is a mental construct that has nothing to do with Spirit Being or Absolute Consciousness, which is free of all concepts or mental and sensory perceptions, qualities, or definitions. The term "enlightenment" philosophically, conceptually describes a mental realization, in the mind of the individual perceiving person, of being the Absolute as opposed to the reflected personality that the mind is aware of as an individual who was born, is living and dying in time and space.

Description & summary

The following image, which was presented earlier in this text, is now being used to further describe the "projection concept" of the temple in terms of the overall effect of the architecture of the complex as a whole. In a similar manner to how the concept, feeling, and energy of panel #2A projects (moves, propels, transfers) to panel #2B, the same concept applies to the entire temple from east to west and west to east.

When lines (AA, BB, CC, DD) [see on next page] are drawn from the four personalities in the inner shrine to the four personalities in the façade, front of the temple, it is found that the two lines that relate to the north side of the temple (AA, BB) and the two lines that relate to the south side of the temple (CC, DD) encompass six columns and the two personalities on the south facade, totaling the number eight for each set of two arrows.

The number eight was discovered to be an important number within the temple, describing the nature of the divinities, cosmic forces, that act to form and manage Creation that are controlled by the Moon-god Djehuty, the Lord of the City of the Eight. So, the two divinities sitting on either side of the temple axis in the Sanctuary, the Holy of Holies of the temple, encompass the number eight as they project (move, propel, transfer) from East to West. In like fashion, the Lord of the City of the Eight controls the eight principles that manage creation. Additionally, this signifies that there are eight principles in the south or source realm of Creation and eight principles in the north or manifestation realm of Creation; i.e. there are mirrored principles reflecting each other from the Astral Plane (Hypostyle Hall 1) to the Physical plane (Hypostyle Hall 2).

Another important indication given by the architectural and iconographical positioning of the four divinities of the inner sanctuary and the four seated figures on the outside façade is that even though the four external seated figures are identified as Ramses, they are each indeed manifestations of the four inner divinities. Therefore, Ramses is not just human but a composite of the other cosmic principles, which are in reality manifestations of a single unmanifest essence.

EGYPTIAN BOOK OF THE DEAD HIEROGLYPH TRANSLATIONS Vol. 5

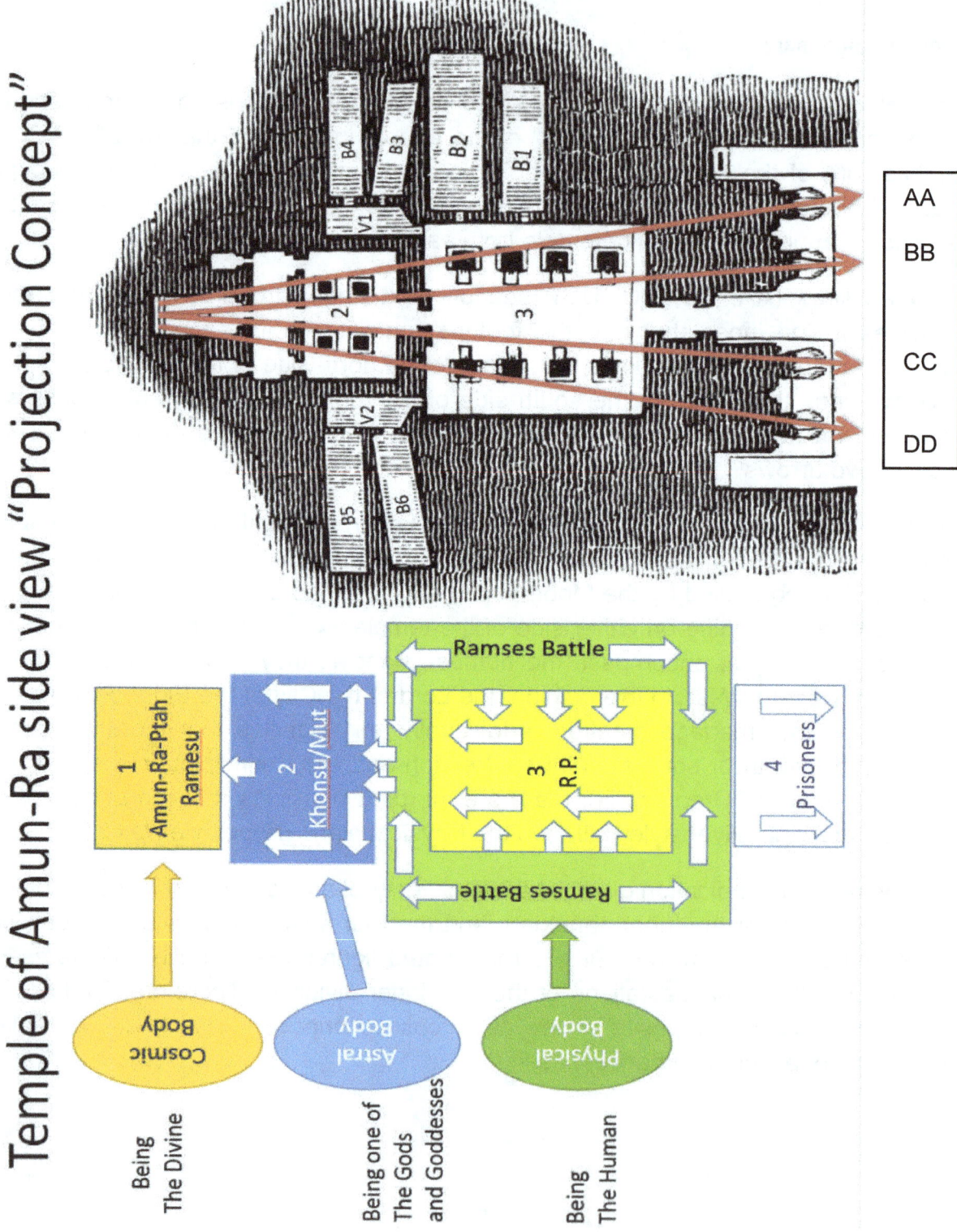

EGYPTIAN BOOK OF THE DEAD HIEROGLYPH TRANSLATIONS Vol. 5

The Projective aspect of the temple of Amun-Ra is founded on the concept of Eight Personalities in One

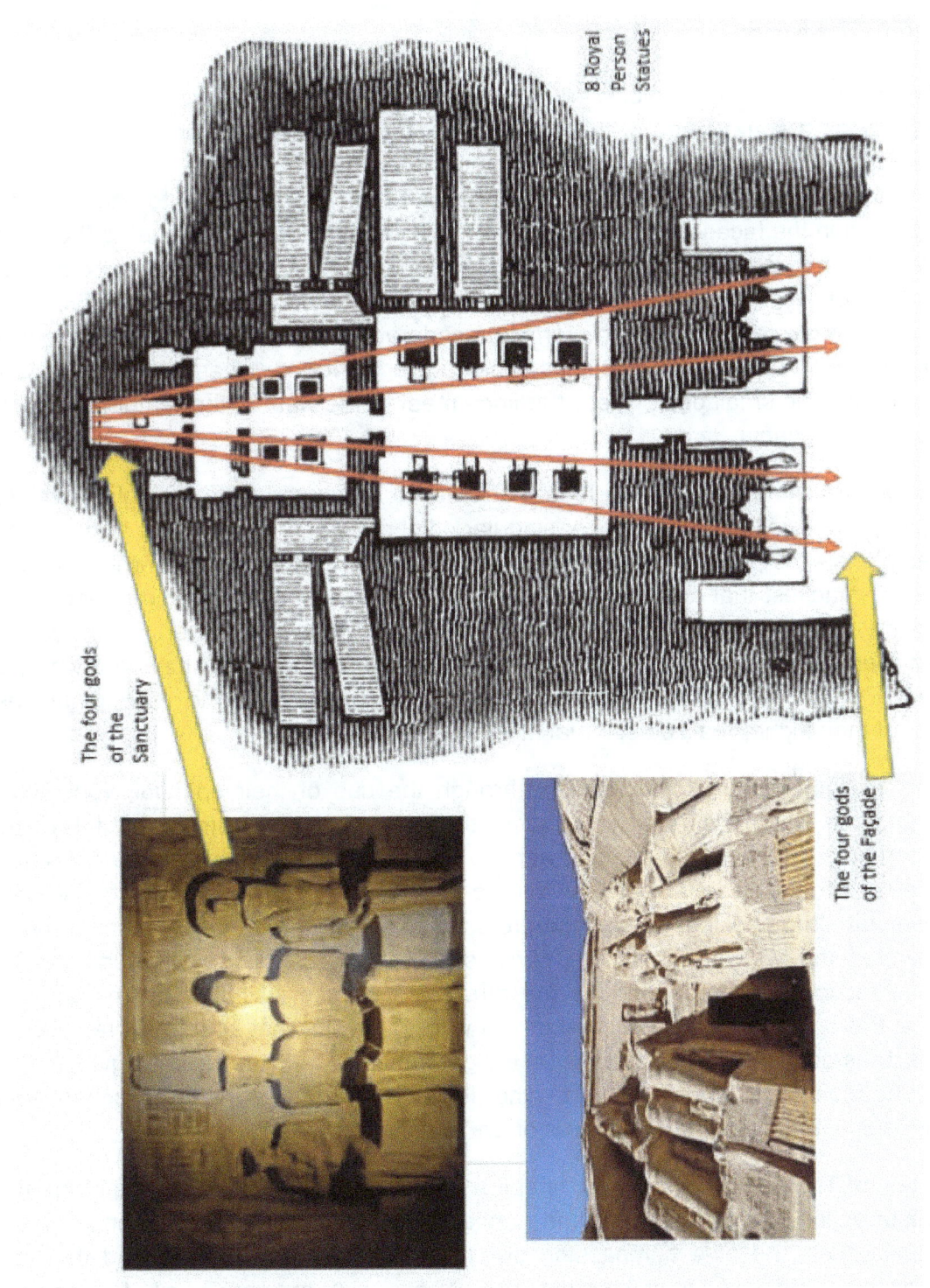

EGYPTIAN BOOK OF THE DEAD HIEROGLYPH TRANSLATIONS Vol. 5

Temple of Amun-Ra "Megaphone" Effect

Description & Summary

Building on the concepts discussed in the previous image, a side view (on next page) of the temple provides a stark image of the architectural concept being applied in a subtle way, and which is experienced even when a human being walks into the temple, unaware of this factor. Just as the four seated personalities in the sanctuary project eastwardly, to each of the massive seated figures in the façade, if lines are drawn from the sanctuary floor level to the floor level of the façade it is noticed, again, that the sanctuary floor height is higher than any other part of the temple. Additionally, if the line is drawn from the roof of the sanctuary (west part of the temple) to the top of the seated figures in the temple façade at the front, (east part of the temple) it can be easily noticed that the geometric lines evoke a **megaphone** type architectural/iconographical context wherein the small point where the lines meet at the west of the temple project out in an ever-expanding manner.

This presentation indicates the idea that creation originated from a single point, which the Ancient Egyptians called a BENBEN or singular point of creation from which all came into being. This idea signals the power of the sanctuary and the source of that power, which is the singular, non-dual un-manifest that appears in a single point in time and space and projects outward to manifest the entire creation. This, therefore, demonstrates and empowers the Royal Person to visualize themselves as majestic personalities, Ramses "The Great", having divine parentage and worthy of being depicted in a megalithic format as metaphoric representations of the grandeur of their higher realized spiritual mystic identity.

This mission of the Royal Person, through the use of their spiritual work and spiritual equipment, their resurrection machine, that is, the temple complex composed of the temple as a kind of computer hardware, the iconographies, and hieroglyphic texts are the software and the Royal Persons themselves, as purified initiated beings, entering the temple, provide themselves as the wetware, the thinking, feeling operators and experiencers of the product of the machine. In this context, the "wetware" is a living, conscious being (possessing competent intellectual and perceptive faculties) that can engage the ritual occurrences inscribed on the walls so as to partake in the ongoing grace and communion with the divine that eventually renders one, who practices it, as one who comes forth as an enlightened being. The Ancient Egyptian term **HEM,** Dignity, and Majesty is accorded to one who achieves this high state of conscious awareness; they are considered as being **Akh sheps** or an "enlightened noble".

The text of The Book of The Dead, chapter 176 (presented above), speaks of the movement into a resurrection chamber wherein the purified personality goes to experience oneness with the Absolute Self, the all-encompassing divinity, **Neberdjer**, and having had this experience emerging from that special communion, no longer with ordinary, limited, ignorant human conscious awareness but rather emerging transformed, having experienced transcendental existence beyond human reality and beyond time and space reality. The term used to describe this process is "Sema Tawy" or "Egyptian Yoga", which is the uniting or harmonization or dissolution of the lower self and the Higher Self. The term used to describe such a person who has achieved this momentous state of consciousness is, as introduced above, "**akh**" or shining spirit. In other words, an illumined being, one who has discovered and achieved a state of awareness with a permanent perception of expanded spiritual existence wherein the self-identity has graduated from limited, ignorant human levels to the level of being one with the Absolute.

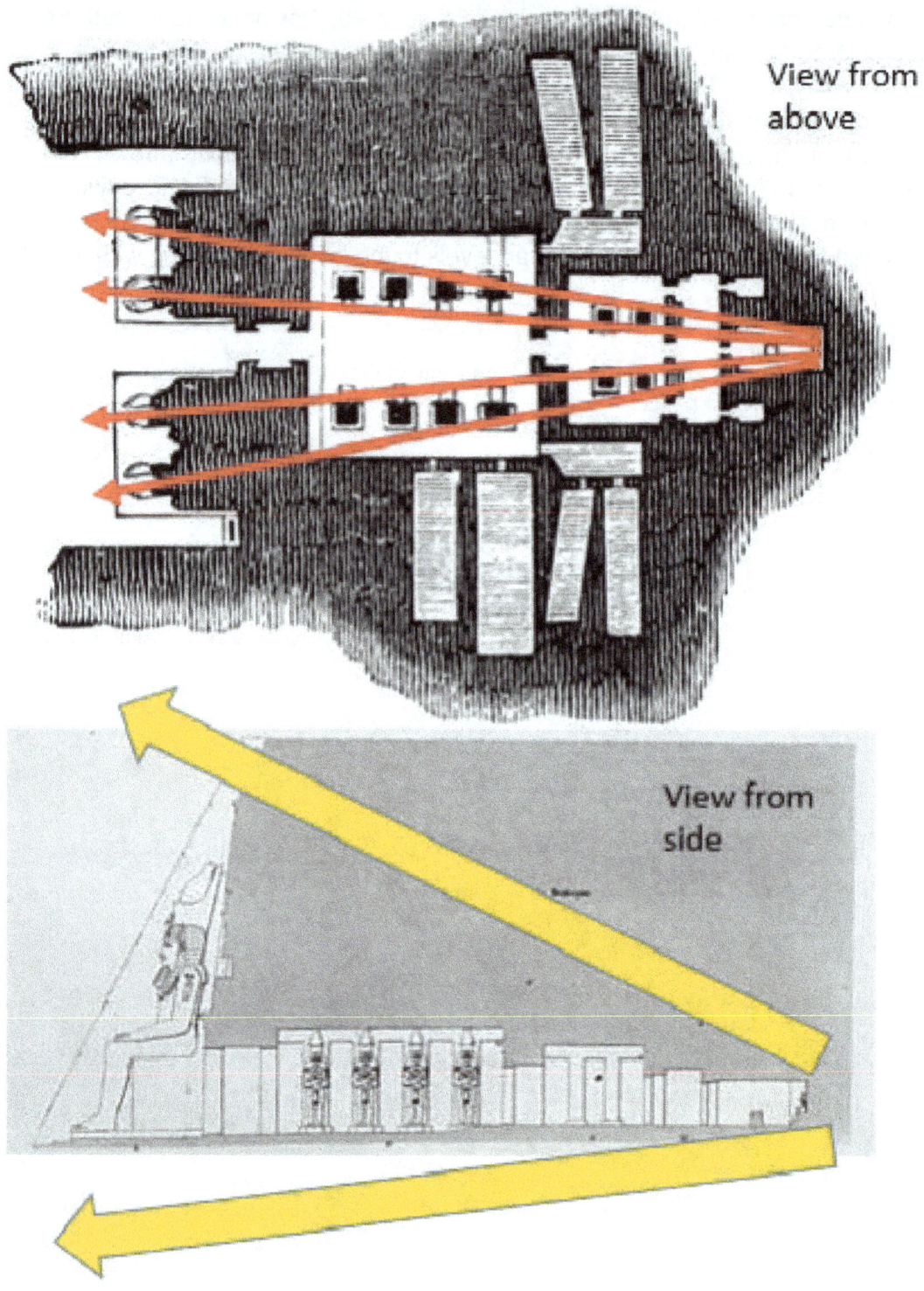

EGYPTIAN BOOK OF THE DEAD HIEROGLYPH TRANSLATIONS Vol. 5

ADDENDUM

Panel #7- My Unbound SELF is THE GREAT DIVINITY, WHO ALSO IS MY FATHER" –[360⁰ Location, Temple Branch #4]

The following panel of the temple is presented as an additional example of the identity themes seen in the previous panels.

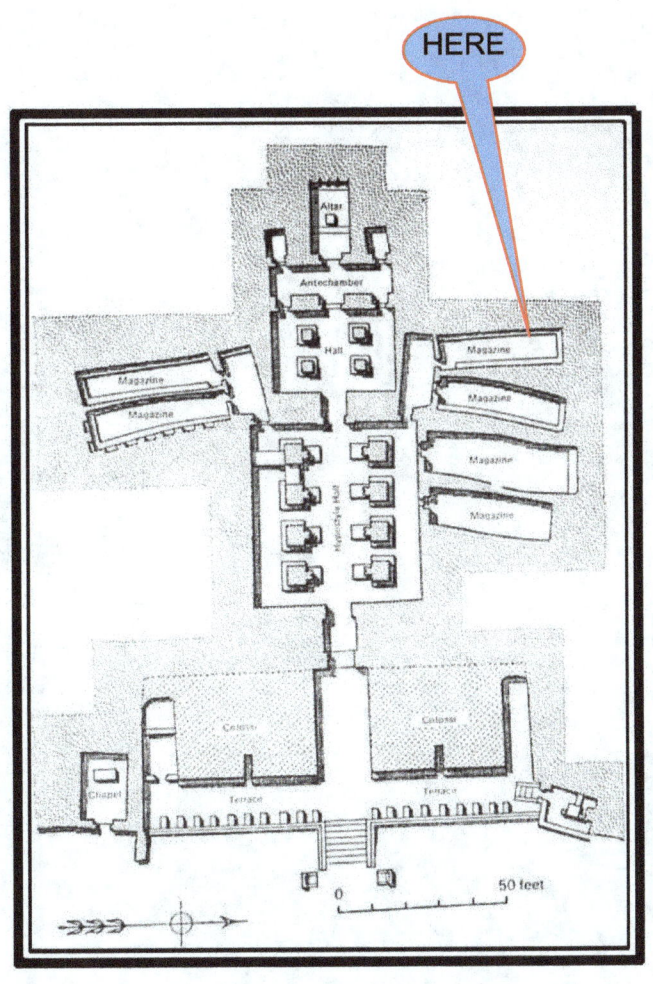

EGYPTIAN BOOK OF THE DEAD HIEROGLYPH TRANSLATIONS Vol. 5

EGYPTIAN BOOK OF THE DEAD HIEROGLYPH TRANSLATIONS Vol. 5

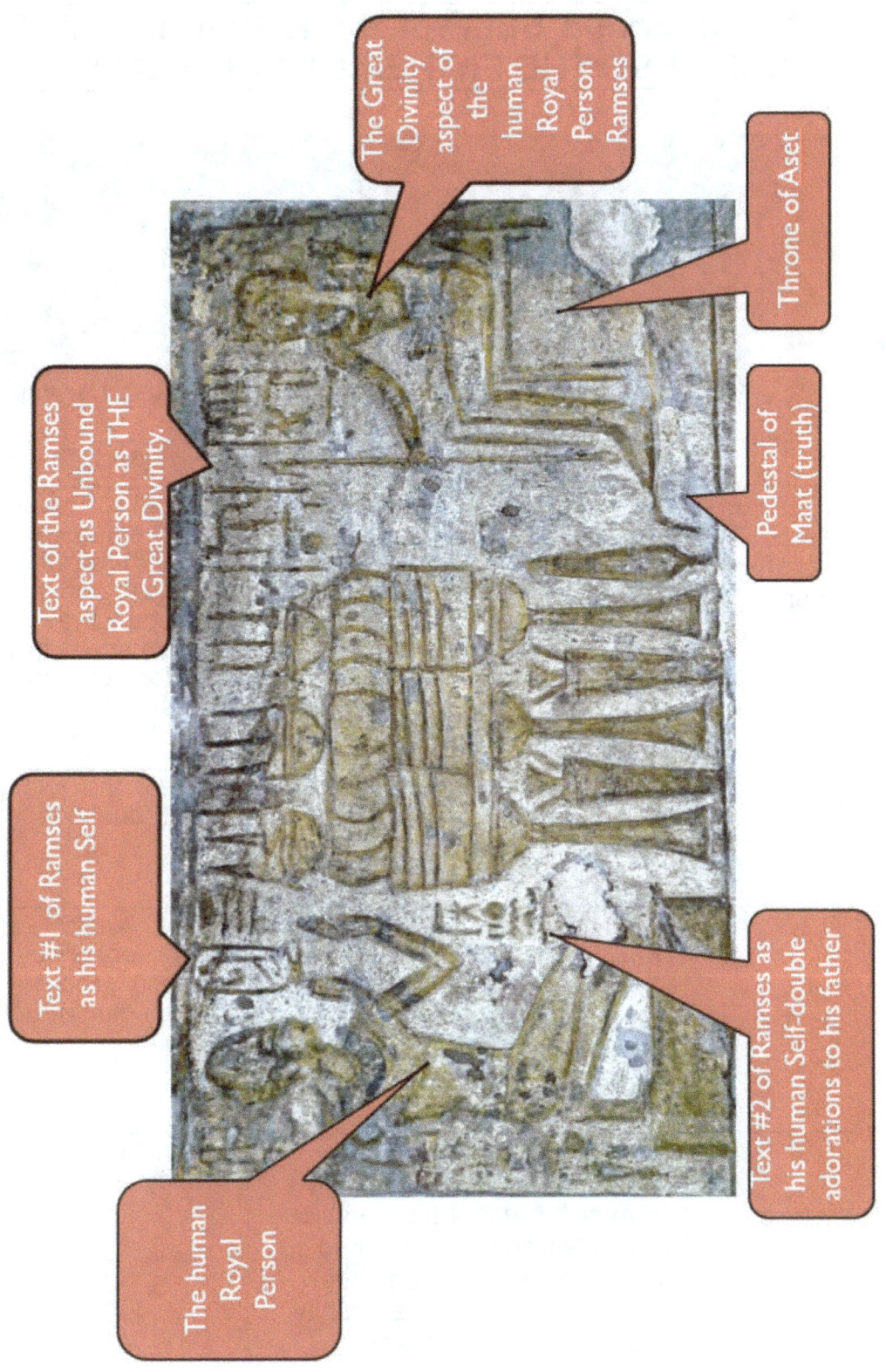

Panel 7- The Unbound SELF of the Human is THE GREAT DIVINITY, AND ALSO THE FATHER OF THE HUMAN

Col.   1   2   3   4

	Transliteration	Translation	Contextual Translation
Col. 1 1st main proforma spiritual name of Ramses	(USER-MAAT-RA-SETEP-EN-RA)	(Power of the truth of the Creator Spirit and chosen by the Creator Spirit)	The Royal Person, Ramses, goes by the name: ("One who exercises dominion backed by the righteousness of the Creator Spirit and who is chosen by that Creator Spirit.")
Col. 2	*neb tawy*	Lord Two-Lands	Lord of the two lands of Egypt (duality)
Col. 3	*Medu dje in Ra... (Note: name is continued into column 4 to be Rameses)*	Words spoken by Ra (continued in next column to be Ramses)...	These words are now being spoken by the Ra (meses) (born of The Creator Spirit)...
Col 4	*...meses (continued from column 3 to be Rameses) pa Neter aah*	...mses (continued from previous column to be Rameses) The Divinity Great	(Ra)mses THE Great Divinity

EGYPTIAN BOOK OF THE DEAD HIEROGLYPH TRANSLATIONS Vol. 5

Col 5 ↓	Transliteration Col. 5	Translation Col. 5	Contextual Translation Col. 5
	Sa Ankh	Protective life-force	This occurrence (the viewing of this panel with the understanding of the mystery (mystic wisdom) and feeling as being the protagonist participant) of this ritual provides a protective life-force *energy/consciousness* originated from Ra/Heru through gods and goddesses and their Divine Manifestations to the Royal Person that sustains life and allows conscious awareness of the Divine. This energy-consciousness is to be applied to the body of the R.P. to make it be like the body of Ra.
	Ha F neb	body his all	
	Ra	Creator Spirit	
	mi	like	
Col. 6 ↑	Col. 6	Col. 6	Col. 6
	Dua Neter sep-sen en tef	Adorations to Divinity twice to father	With upraised arms, I adore the Divinity that is myself and I recognize that my own Higher Self is the father/parent that brought this personality into manifestation (self-begotten). This adoration is performed twice.

EGYPTIAN BOOK OF THE DEAD HIEROGLYPH TRANSLATIONS Vol. 5

INDEX

Ab, 130
Absolute, 56, 148, 192, 203, 204, 205, 206, 211, 218, 234, 242
Absolute Divinity, 218
Abu Simbel, 13, 14, 16, 17, 19, 24, 25, 87, 190, 217, 226
Africa, 16, 246, 252, 254, 255
African Proverbial Wisdom Teachings, 260
African Religion, 242, 248, 251
Akhemu Seku, 83
Akhemu Urdu, 82, 83
Allopathic, 243
Amen, 202, 203
Amenta, 247
Amentet, 126, 249
American Heritage Dictionary, Dictionary, 251
American Theocracy, 254
Amun, 13, 14, 15, 16, 19, 21, 24, 25, 26, 44, 49, 51, 52, 54, 55, 56, 59, 60, 61, 62, 63, 64, 71, 74, 76, 78, 79, 87, 93, 100, 113, 117, 119, 132, 139, 140, 141, 142, 144, 148, 149, 151, 153, 154, 155, 156, 157, 161, 167, 171, 175, 179, 185, 189, 190, 192, 193, 194, 195, 200, 202, 203, 204, 206, 207, 208, 209, 211, 212, 215, 217, 218, 219, 220, 222, 224, 225, 226, 227, 229, 230, 231, 239

Amun-Ra-Ptah, 71, 190, 194, 195, 200, 204, 211, 218
Ancient Egypt, 7, 8, 10, 11, 12, 16, 19, 21, 22, 25, 28, 30, 35, 55, 65, 71, 72, 82, 86, 88, 89, 90, 95, 97, 98, 100, 121, 123, 124, 125, 128, 146, 148, 153, 157, 170, 171, 179, 180, 192, 194, 197, 198, 199, 202, 203, 204, 205, 207, 212, 215, 219, 220, 224, 225, 232, 233, 239, 242, 243, 244, 245, 246, 247, 248, 249, 250, 251, 252, 253, 255, 258, 259, 260, 261, 262, 263, 264, 267
Ancient Egyptian Book of the Dead, 30, 232
Ancient Egyptian Wisdom Texts, 258, 259
anger, 171, 250
Ani, 215
Ankh, 88, 94, 104, 114, 118, 120, 146, 178, 186, 246
Anu, 214, 248
Anu (Greek Heliopolis), 214, 248
Anunian Theology, 248
Ari, 114, 186
Aryan, 244
Asar, 10, 29, 35, 125, 126, 127, 139, 141, 144, 147, 148, 149, 151, 152, 153, 154, 156, 192, 195, 204, 218, 234, 247, 249, 250
Asar and Aset, 247

Asarian Resurrection, 170, 247, 249, 250, 252
Aset, 138, 144, 146, 147, 148, 151, 153, 244, 247, 249, 250
Aset (Isis), 138, 144, 146, 147, 148, 151, 153, 244, 247, 249, 250
Ashanti, 260
Asia XE, 255
Asiatic, 254, 255, 256
Assyrians, 258
Astral, 236, 247
Astral Plane, 236, 247
Atlantis, 252
Aum (Om), 203
Awakening, 247, 263
Awareness, 86, 130
Being, 46, 72, 83, 95, 126, 202, 203, 232, 234, 235, 249
Bhagavad Gita, 258
Bible, 249
Black, 255
Black XE, 255
Boat, Divine, 221
Body, 51, 118, 120, 168, 169, 178, 206, 263
Book of Coming Forth By Day, 247, 248
Book of Enlightenment, 30, 35, 232
Book of the Dead, see also Rau Nu Prt M Hru, 2, 22, 30, 205, 207, 232, 248, 259
Brahman, 203
Buddha, 252, 253, 265
Buddhism, 248, 253
Buddhist, 246, 253

Bull, 142, 144
Catholic, 249
Catholic Church, 249
Child, 51, 62, 74, 93, 113, 119, 139, 141, 144, 161, 167, 175, 185, 186, 230, 231, 249, 250
Christ, 247
Christianity, 202, 203, 242, 248, 249
Church, 249
Civilization, 244, 253, 254, 255, 262, 263
coercion, 254
Collapse, 254, 262, 264
colony, 177
color, 17, 54, 55, 79, 195, 220, 257, 259
Conditioning, 27, 35, 36
Conflict, 260
Conscience, 127
Conscious, 56, 130
Consciousness, 76, 97, 117, 123, 126, 127, 128, 130, 206, 231, 234, 247, 259
Consciousness, human, 65, 82, 205, 242
contentment, 179, 265
Coptic, 247
cosmic force, 95, 123, 127, 160, 236, 249, 253
Cosmic mind, 128
Creation, 15, 75, 83, 89, 90, 123, 126, 132, 148, 160, 192, 193, 198, 204, 207, 210, 211, 213, 214, 218, 228, 230, 235, 236, 247, 248, 259
Crook, 77
Cross, 212, 215
Culture, 246, 252, 256, 263, 264
Death, 254, 262
December, 249
delusion, 37
Demotic, 202, 204

Denderah, 247
Desire, 260
Devotional Love, 245
Diet, 243
Dollar, U.S. Dollar, 264
Duality, 28, 123
Duat, 125, 247
Earth, 83
Edfu, 247
Egoism, 35
Egyptian Book of Coming Forth By Day, 247
Egyptian Mysteries, 1, 10, 65, 243, 250, 251, 260, 261
Egyptian Physics, 248
Egyptian Proverb, 71, 72, 245
Egyptian proverbs, 245
Egyptian religion, 207
Egyptian Yoga see also Kamitan Yoga, 235, 240, 242, 243, 246, 247, 248, 265
Egyptologists, 251, 258
Empire culture, 254
Energy, 97, 130
Enlightenment, 30, 35, 83, 97, 232, 235, 242, 243, 245, 246, 247, 248, 249, 250, 253, 260, 262, 263
Ether, 123
Ethics, 243, 244, 253, 255, 259
Ethiopia, 260
Eucharist, 247
European explorers, 79
evil, 37, 250, 251, 252
Exercise, 247
Existence, 142
Eye, 111, 127
Eye of Heru, 111
Eye of Horus, 127
Faith, 256
Feelings, 36
Female, 123
Finances, 263

Flail, 77
Form, 8
frustration, 38
Galla, 260
Galla culture, 260
Geb, 195, 197, 247
Ghana, 260
global economy, 254
Globalization, 254
God, 26, 35, 41, 48, 54, 55, 56, 67, 70, 71, 72, 75, 77, 79, 83, 86, 89, 90, 95, 103, 110, 112, 113, 124, 125, 128, 130, 131, 132, 138, 140, 142, 143, 145, 146, 148, 153, 155, 157, 159, 164, 170, 190, 194, 195, 197, 203, 211, 219, 220, 226, 228, 245, 245, 248, 252, 257
Goddess, 43, 63, 132, 148, 151, 157, 159, 249, 257
Goddesses, 98, 122, 132, 133, 134, 246, 251
Gods, 90, 98, 122, 132, 133, 134, 220, 246, 251
gods and goddesses, 15, 26, 72, 90, 95, 96, 97, 103, 121, 123, 125, 127, 128, 133, 143, 148, 160, 168, 170, 195, 202, 203, 233, 234, 246, 248, 251, 252
Good, 89, 104, 252
Gospels, 249
Great Pyramid, 83, 84
Greece, 243, 252
Greeks, 121, 258
Hate, 260
Hatha Yoga, 255
Hathor, 111, 247, 249, 250, 265
Hatred, 260
Health, 243, 248
Heart, 130, 250, 256
Heart (also see Ab, mind,

conscience), 130, 250, 256
Heaven, 51, 147, 214, 229, 249
Hekau, 264
Heliopolis, 214
Hermes, 103, 126, 127, 261
Hermes (see also Djehuti, Thoth), 103, 126, 127, 261
Hermetic, 261
Hermeticism, 261
Heru, 30, 96, 97, 111, 127, 139, 141, 144, 145, 147, 148, 151, 153, 154, 156, 168, 170, 176, 246, 247, 248, 249, 250, 252, 259
Heru (see Horus), 30, 96, 97, 111, 127, 139, 141, 144, 145, 147, 148, 151, 153, 154, 156, 168, 170, 176, 246, 247, 248, 249, 250, 252, 259
Hetheru, 111, 250
Hetheru (Hetheru, Hathor), 111, 250
Hieratic, 208
Hieroglyphic, 8, 10, 12, 208, 246, 258, 261
Hieroglyphic Writing, language, 8, 10, 12, 208, 246, 258, 261
Hieroglyphs, 12, 43
High God, 132, 142
Hinduism, 248
Hindus, 251
hope, 257
Horus, 124, 126, 127, 144, 148, 151, 153, 170, 172, 174, 175, 176
Humanity, 250
Iamblichus, 258
Ibis, 103, 110
Identification, 33, 98, 132, 133, 185
illusion, 148

Image, 39, 41, 97, 219
India, 202, 203, 243, 244, 245, 246, 253, 255
Indian Yoga, 244
Indus, 244
Indus Valley, 244
Intellect, 110, 113
Isis, 124, 138, 139, 141, 144, 146, 147, 148, 151, 170, 244, 265
Isis, See also Aset, 124, 138, 139, 141, 144, 146, 147, 148, 151, 170, 244, 265
Islam, 242
Jesus, 247, 249, 265
Jesus Christ, 247
Judaism, 242
Justice, 43
Ka, 142, 154
Kamit (Egypt), 203, 251
Kamitan, 202, 243, 252
Karma, 245
Karnak, 59, 64, 97
Kemetic, 253, 256, 260, 263, 265, 267
Khemn, see also ignorance, 251
Khepesh, 83
Khonsu, 56, 132, 139, 141, 143, 144, 145, 147, 148, 153
King, 249, 252
Kingdom, 15, 97, 177, 249
Kingdom of Heaven, 249
Krishna, 249
Kush, 16
Kybalion, 261
Lake, 177
Life, 28, 118, 120, 147, 168, 178, 246, 252, 256, 257, 259
Life Force, 246
Lotus, 19
Love, 245, 265
Lower Egypt, 52, 94, 114, 146, 147, 161, 186

Maat, 39, 41, 42, 43, 52, 56, 67, 75, 78, 113, 114, 119, 120, 151, 180, 228, 229, 245, 249, 250, 252, 253, 256, 259, 260, 261, 262, 263
Maat Philosophy, 250, 253, 256, 262
Malawi, 260
Male, 41, 123
Matrix, 192, 218
Matter, 248
media, 254
Meditation, 243, 245, 246, 267
Medu Neter, 251, 264
Memphite Theology, 248
Meskhenet, 245
Metaphysics, 248, 259
Middle East, 242
Middle Kingdom, 177
Min, 139, 141, 144, 147, 154, 247
Mind, 123, 130, 191, 206, 263
Moon, 110, 125, 127, 130, 131, 132, 160, 236
Music, 257
Mut, 56, 63, 64, 65, 132, 146, 147, 148, 153, 154
Mysteries, 1, 10, 65, 148, 243, 250, 251, 258, 260, 261
mystical philosophy, 65, 254, 259
Mysticism, 244, 247, 248, 250, 253, 255
Nature, 35
Neberdjer, 56, 123, 148, 192, 203, 204, 206, 211, 218, 232, 234, 235, 239, 242
Nebethet, see also Nebthet, 197
Nefer, 88, 89, 104
Nehast, 251
neo-con, 254

Neter, 75, 78, 85, 88, 89, 94, 104, 114, 117, 147, 161, 175, 186, 214, 245, 246, 245, 247, 251, 252, 254, 258, 260, 263, 264
Neterian, 14, 35, 36, 89, 121, 179, 251, 252, 253, 263, 264, 265
Neterianism, 261, 263
Neteru, 35, 127, 215, 234, 251
New Kingdom, 15
Nigeria, 260
Nile River, 15, 177
Nubia, 16, 176, 177
Nut, 195, 197, 247
Om, 202, 203, 204
Orion Star Constellation, 249
Orthodox, 251
Osiris, 10, 35, 100, 124, 126, 127, 128, 148, 152, 153, 154, 155, 156, 170, 192, 194, 195, 198, 204, 233, 252
Pa Neter, 161, 186
Parent, 167
Part 4- From Identification as a Human to Identification as one of the Gods and Goddesses, 132
Peace, 260, 262, 263
Peace (see also Hetep), 260, 262, 263
Persians, 258
Pert Em Heru, See also Book of the Dead, 247
Pharaoh, 199, 263
Philae, 247
Philosophical, 31
Philosophy, 10, 35, 131, 242, 243, 244, 245, 248, 250, 253, 255, 256, 262, 263
Physical, 83, 236
physical world, 48, 124, 220
Pole Star, 85
Prayers, 216
pressure, 32
priests and priestesses, 10, 29, 65, 90, 98, 148, 153, 243, 246, 252
Proverbial Wisdom, 260
Psychology, 248, 261
Ptah, 70, 71, 72, 75, 77, 78, 83, 124, 132, 155, 156, 189, 190, 192, 193, 194, 195, 200, 204, 206, 211, 218, 219, 220, 224, 225, 226, 228, 248
Pyramid, 83, 84, 97
Pyramid Texts, 97
Queen, 64, 146, 147, 252
Ra, 10, 13, 14, 15, 16, 19, 21, 24, 25, 26, 39, 40, 41, 42, 43, 44, 49, 51, 52, 54, 55, 56, 59, 61, 71, 74, 76, 78, 87, 93, 95, 96, 97, 100, 113, 114, 117, 119, 120, 121, 123, 126, 127, 128, 130, 139, 141, 142, 144, 148, 149, 151, 153, 154, 155, 156, 157, 161, 167, 168, 170, 172, 175, 176, 178, 179, 185, 186, 189, 190, 192, 194, 195, 200, 204, 206, 207, 208, 209, 211, 212, 213, 214, 215, 217, 218, 219, 220, 222, 224, 225, 226, 227, 229, 230, 231, 239, 245, 246, 247
Racism, 260
Reality, 267
Realization, 244
Reflection, 130
Religion, 242, 244, 247, 248, 249, 250, 251, 252, 253, 255, 263, 264, 265
Resurrection, 170, 247, 249, 250, 252
Righteousness, 228
Ritual, 250
Rituals, 249
Roman, 177, 258
Romans, 258
Rome, 252
Sage Amenemope, 86, 124
Sages, 242, 247, 248, 250, 253, 265
Saints, 248, 265
Sanskrit, 202, 203
Sebai, 253, 257, 261, 263
See also Ra-Hrakti, 10, 13, 14, 15, 16, 19, 21, 24, 25, 26, 39, 40, 41, 42, 43, 44, 49, 51, 52, 54, 55, 56, 59, 61, 71, 74, 76, 78, 87, 93, 95, 96, 97, 100, 113, 114, 117, 119, 120, 121, 123, 126, 127, 128, 130, 139, 141, 142, 144, 148, 149, 151, 153, 154, 155, 156, 157, 161, 167, 168, 170, 172, 175, 176, 178, 179, 185, 186, 189, 190, 192, 194, 195, 200, 204, 206, 207, 208, 209, 211, 212, 213, 214, 215, 217, 218, 219, 220, 222, 224, 225, 226, 227, 229, 230, 231, 239, 245, 246, 247
Self (see Ba, soul, Spirit, Universal, Ba, Neter, Heru)., 51, 74, 93, 96, 103, 113, 119, 139, 141, 144, 161, 162, 163, 167, 170, 172, 175, 185, 187, 211, 234, 246, 244, 245, 247, 250, 257
Sema, 252, 260, 262, 264
Sema Tawi, 264
Serpent, 110, 148
Serpent Power, 110, 148
Serpent Power (see also Kundalini and Buto), 110, 148

Serpent Power see also Kundalini Yoga, 110, 148
Set, 29, 170, 252
Seti I, 246
Sex, 247
Sexism, 260
Shedy, 243
Shen, 88
Sheps, 113
Shetaut Neter, 78, 247, 251, 252, 254, 260, 263, 264
Shetaut Neter See also Egyptian Religion, 78, 247, 251, 252, 254, 260, 263, 264
Shu (air and space), 128, 130, 195, 197
Sirius, 249
skin, 55
slavery, 251
society, 243, 251, 253, 256, 259, 260, 261, 262, 264
Soul, 20, 125, 130, 206, 218, 252, 263
Spirit, 15, 35, 43, 51, 52, 56, 59, 61, 62, 72, 74, 77, 78, 93, 95, 97, 113, 114, 119, 120, 121, 123, 126, 127, 129, 130, 131, 139, 141, 142, 144, 148, 151, 161, 167, 168, 170, 175, 176, 178, 185, 205, 206, 208, 209, 213, 229, 230, 231, 232, 234, 235, 245, 246
Spiritual discipline, 243
Spirituality, 243, 256, 263, 264, 265
Sublimation, 247
Sudan, 16, 177
sun, 128, 130, 131
Sun Gods, 128
Superpower, 254
Superpower Syndrome, 254
Superpower Syndrome Mandatory Conflict XE, 254
Supreme Being, 95, 202, 203, 249
Tantra, 247
Tawi, 264
Tefnut (moisture), 195, 197
Tem, 207, 211, 212, 213
Temple, 13, 14, 15, 19, 24, 25, 39, 49, 53, 64, 67, 70, 71, 79, 87, 97, 98, 100, 102, 132, 135, 136, 137, 149, 151, 154, 163, 172, 179, 180, 189, 190, 192, 201, 203, 207, 212, 215, 217, 218, 219, 226, 232, 233, 239, 242, 247, 250, 263, 267
Temple of Aset, 247
Temu, 209, 213, 214
The Absolute, 204, 242
The Black, 255
The God, 72, 75, 79, 110, 140, 145, 219, 246
The Gods, 246
Theban Theology, 242
Thebes, 59, 63, 64, 242, 246
Theocracy, 254
Theology, 148, 242, 248
Thoth, 103
Thoughts, 36
Thoughts (see also: Mind), 36
Time, 61, 190
time and space, 25, 27, 32, 38, 56, 84, 89, 123, 124, 128, 144, 147, 148, 153, 160, 164, 170, 190, 191, 193, 197, 200, 204, 205, 210, 211, 212, 213, 217, 218, 220, 222, 226, 227, 231, 233, 239, 240, 251
Tomb, 131, 246
Tomb of Seti I, 246
transcendental reality, 251
Transcendental Self, 234
Tree, 259
Tree of Life, 259
Triad, 242
Trinity, 54, 55, 56, 71, 132, 133, 135, 140, 148, 190, 191, 194, 195, 200, 204, 205, 211, 217, 226, 247
Truth, 75, 151
Tutankhamun, 199
Tutankhamun, Pharaoh, 199
Understanding, 131, 251, 262
United States of America, 27, 254
Universal Consciousness, 234, 247
Upanishads, 248, 258
Ur, 63
USA, West, 89
Vedic, 244
Violence, 260
Waset, 63, 242
Wealth, Money, 263
Western, West, 38, 52, 100, 127, 197, 233, 236
White, 262
Wisdom, 36, 40, 46, 82, 86, 128, 130, 189, 245, 246, 258, 259, 263
Wisdom (also see Djehuti, Aset), 36, 40, 46, 82, 86, 128, 130, 189, 245, 246, 258, 259, 263
World War II, 254
Yoga, 235, 240, 242, 243, 244, 246, 247, 248, 250, 252, 253, 255, 265
Yoga of Devotion (see Yoga of Divine Love), 265
Yogic, 255, 260
Yoruba, 260

EGYPTIAN BOOK OF THE DEAD HIEROGLYPH TRANSLATIONS Vol. 5

Other Books From C M Books
https://aerbook.com/store/Egyptian_Yoga_Books

P.O.Box 570459
Miami, Florida, 33257
(305) 378-6253 Fax: (305) 378-6253

Prices subject to change.

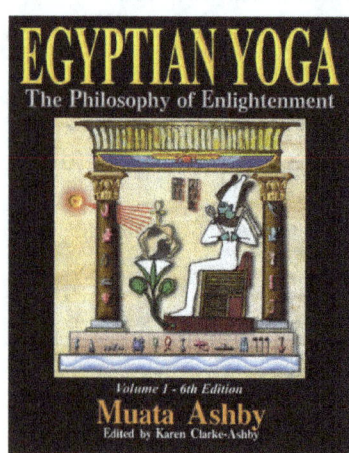

1. *EGYPTIAN YOGA: THE PHILOSOPHY OF ENLIGHTENMENT* An original, fully illustrated work, including hieroglyphs, detailing the meaning of the Egyptian mysteries, tantric yoga, psycho-spiritual and physical exercises. Egyptian Yoga is a guide to the practice of the highest spiritual philosophy which leads to absolute freedom from human misery and to immortality. It is well known by scholars that Egyptian philosophy is the basis of Western and Middle Eastern religious philosophies such as *Christianity*, *Islam*, *Judaism*, the *Kabala*, and Greek philosophy, but what about Indian philosophy, Yoga and Taoism? What were the original teachings? How can they be practiced today? What is the source of pain and suffering in the world and what is the solution? Discover the deepest mysteries of the mind and universe within and outside of yourself. 8.5" X 11" ISBN: 1-884564-01-1 Soft $19.95

2. *EGYPTIAN YOGA: African Religion Volume 2*- Theban Theology U.S. In this long awaited sequel to *Egyptian Yoga: The Philosophy of Enlightenment* you will take a fascinating and enlightening journey back in time and discover the teachings which constituted the epitome of Ancient Egyptian spiritual wisdom. What are the disciplines which lead to the fulfillment of all desires? Delve into the three states of consciousness (waking, dream and deep sleep) and the fourth state which transcends them all, Neberdjer, "The Absolute." These teachings of the city of Waset (Thebes) were the crowning achievement of the Sages of Ancient Egypt. They establish the standard mystical keys for understanding the profound mystical symbolism of the Triad of human consciousness. ISBN 1-884564-39-9 $23.95

3. *THE KEMETIC DIET: GUIDE TO HEALTH, DIET AND FASTING* Health issues have always been important to human beings since the beginning of time. The earliest records of history show that the art of healing was held in high esteem since the time of Ancient Egypt. In the early 20th century, medical doctors had almost attained the status of sainthood by the promotion of the idea that they alone were "scientists" while other healing modalities and traditional healers who did not follow the "scientific method' were nothing but superstitious, ignorant charlatans who at best would take the money of their clients and at worst kill them with the unscientific "snake oils" and "irrational theories". In the late 20th century, the failure of the modern medical establishment's ability to lead the general public to good health, promoted the move by many in society towards "alternative medicine". Alternative medicine disciplines are those healing modalities which do not adhere to the philosophy of allopathic medicine. Allopathic medicine is what medical doctors practice by an large. It is the theory that disease is caused by agencies outside the body such as bacteria, viruses or physical means which affect the body. These can therefore be treated by medicines and therapies The natural healing method began in the absence of extensive technologies with the idea that all the answers for health may be found in nature or rather, the deviation from nature. Therefore, the health of the body can be restored by correcting the aberration and thereby restoring balance. This is the area that will be covered in this volume. Allopathic techniques have their place in the art of healing. However, we should not forget that the body is a grand achievement of the spirit and built into it is the capacity to maintain itself and heal itself. Ashby, Muata ISBN: 1-884564-49-6 $28.95

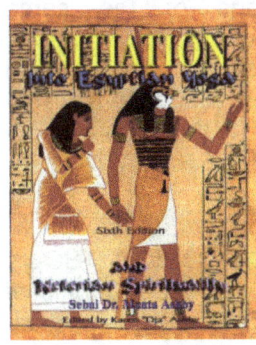

4. INITIATION INTO EGYPTIAN YOGA Shedy: Spiritual discipline or program, to go deeply into the mysteries, to study the mystery teachings and literature profoundly, to penetrate the mysteries. You will learn about the mysteries of initiation into the teachings and practice of Yoga and how to become an Initiate of the mystical sciences. This insightful manual is the first in a series which introduces you to the goals of daily spiritual and yoga practices: Meditation, Diet, Words of Power and the ancient wisdom teachings. 8.5" X 11" ISBN 1-884564-02-X Soft Cover $24.95 U.S.

5. *THE AFRICAN ORIGINS OF CIVILIZATION, RELIGION AND YOGA SPIRITUALITY AND ETHICS PHILOSOPHY* HARD COVER EDITION Part 1, Part 2, Part 3 in one volume 683 Pages Hard Cover First Edition Three volumes in one. Over the past several years I have been asked to put together in one volume the most important evidences showing the correlations and common teachings between Kamitan (Ancient Egyptian) culture and religion and that of India. The questions of the history of Ancient Egypt, and the latest archeological evidences showing civilization and culture in Ancient Egypt and its spread to other countries, has intrigued many scholars as well as mystics over the years. Also, the possibility that Ancient Egyptian Priests and Priestesses migrated to Greece, India and other countries to carry on the traditions of the Ancient Egyptian Mysteries, has been speculated over the years as well. In chapter 1 of the book *Egyptian Yoga The Philosophy of Enlightenment*, 1995, I first introduced the

deepest comparison between Ancient Egypt and India that had been brought forth up to that time. Now, in the year 2001 this new book, THE AFRICAN ORIGINS OF CIVILIZATION, MYSTICAL RELIGION AND YOGA PHILOSOPHY, more fully explores the motifs, symbols and philosophical correlations between Ancient Egyptian and Indian mysticism and clearly shows not only that Ancient Egypt and India were connected culturally but also spiritually. How does this knowledge help the spiritual aspirant? This discovery has great importance for the Yogis and mystics who follow the philosophy of Ancient Egypt and the mysticism of India. It means that India has a longer history and heritage than was previously understood. It shows that the mysteries of Ancient Egypt were essentially a yoga tradition which did not die but rather developed into the modern day systems of Yoga technology of India. It further shows that African culture developed Yoga Mysticism earlier than any other civilization in history. All of this expands our understanding of the unity of culture and the deep legacy of Yoga, which stretches into the distant past, beyond the Indus Valley civilization, the earliest known high culture in India as well as the Vedic tradition of Aryan culture. Therefore, Yoga culture and mysticism is the oldest known tradition of spiritual development and Indian mysticism is an extension of the Ancient Egyptian mysticism. By understanding the legacy which Ancient Egypt gave to India the mysticism of India is better understood and by comprehending the heritage of Indian Yoga, which is rooted in Ancient Egypt the Mysticism of Ancient Egypt is also better understood. This expanded understanding allows us to prove the underlying kinship of humanity, through the common symbols, motifs and philosophies which are not disparate and confusing teachings but in reality expressions of the same study of truth through metaphysics and mystical realization of Self. (HARD COVER) ISBN: 1-884564-50-X $45.00 U.S. 81/2" X 11"

6. *AFRICAN ORIGINS BOOK 1 PART 1* African Origins of African Civilization, Religion, Yoga Mysticism and Ethics Philosophy-<u>Soft Cover</u> $24.95 ISBN: 1-884564-55-0

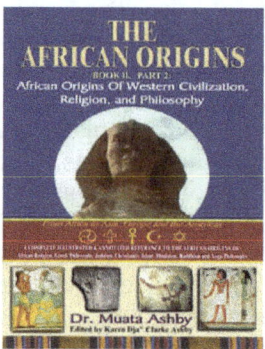

7. *AFRICAN ORIGINS BOOK 2 PART 2* African Origins of Western Civilization, Religion and Philosophy (Soft) -<u>Soft Cover</u> $24.95 ISBN: 1-884564-56-9

8. *EGYPT AND INDIA AFRICAN ORIGINS OF Eastern Civilization, Religion, Yoga Mysticism and Philosophy-*<u>Soft Cover</u> $29.95 (Soft) ISBN: 1-884564-57-7

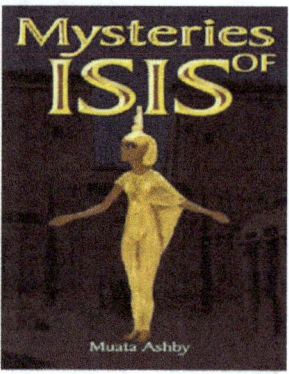

9. *THE MYSTERIES OF ISIS:* **The Ancient Egyptian Philosophy of Self-Realization** - There are several paths to discover the Divine and the mysteries of the higher Self. This volume details the mystery teachings of the goddess Aset (Isis) from Ancient Egypt- the path of wisdom. It includes the teachings of her temple and the disciplines that are enjoined for the initiates of the temple of Aset as they were given in ancient times. Also, this book includes the teachings of the main myths of Aset that lead a human being to spiritual enlightenment and immortality. Through the

EGYPTIAN BOOK OF THE DEAD HIEROGLYPH TRANSLATIONS Vol. 5

study of ancient myth and the illumination of initiatic understanding the idea of God is expanded from the mythological comprehension to the metaphysical. Then this metaphysical understanding is related to you, the student, so as to begin understanding your true divine nature. ISBN 1-884564-24-0 $22.99

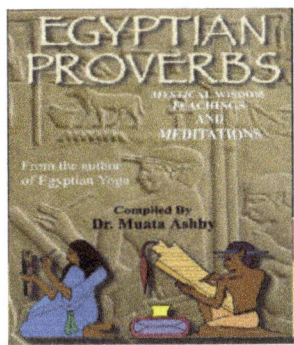

10. *EGYPTIAN PROVERBS:* collection of —Ancient Egyptian Proverbs and Wisdom Teachings -How to live according to MAAT Philosophy. Beginning Meditation. All proverbs are indexed for easy searches. For the first time in one volume, ——Ancient Egyptian Proverbs, wisdom teachings and meditations, fully illustrated with hieroglyphic text and symbols. EGYPTIAN PROVERBS is a unique collection of knowledge and wisdom which you can put into practice today and transform your life. $14.95 U'S ISBN: 1-884564-00-3

11. *GOD OF LOVE: THE PATH OF DIVINE LOVE The Process of Mystical Transformation and The Path of Divine Love* This Volume focuses on the ancient wisdom teachings of "Neter Merri" –the Ancient Egyptian philosophy of Divine Love and how to use them in a scientific process for self-transformation. Love is one of the most powerful human emotions. It is also the source of Divine feeling that unifies God and the individual human being. When love is fragmented and diminished by egoism the Divine connection is lost. The Ancient tradition of Neter Merri leads human beings back to their Divine connection, allowing them to discover their innate glorious self that is actually Divine and immortal. This volume will detail the process of transformation from ordinary consciousness to cosmic consciousness through the integrated practice of the teachings and the path of Devotional Love toward the Divine. 5.5"x 8.5" ISBN 1-884564-11-9 $22.95

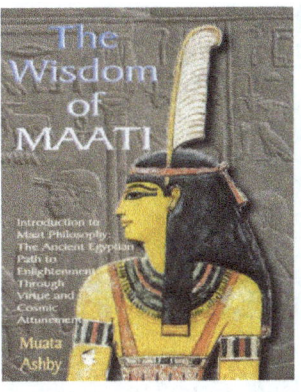

12. *INTRODUCTION TO MAAT PHILOSOPHY: Spiritual Enlightenment Through the Path of Virtue* Known commonly as Karma in India, the teachings of MAAT contain an extensive philosophy based on ariu (deeds) and their fructification in the form of shai and renenet (fortune and destiny, leading to Meskhenet (fate in a future birth) for living virtuously and with orderly wisdom are explained and the student is to begin practicing the precepts of Maat in daily life so as to promote the process of purification of the heart in preparation for the judgment of the soul. This judgment will be understood not as an event that will occur at the time of death but as an event that occurs continuously, at every moment in the life of the individual. The student will learn how to become allied with the forces of the Higher Self and to thereby begin cleansing the mind (heart) of impurities so as to attain a higher vision of reality. ISBN 1-884564-20-8 $22.99

13. **MEDITATION The Ancient Egyptian Path to Enlightenment** Many people do not know about the rich history of meditation practice in Ancient Egypt. This volume outlines the theory of meditation and presents the Ancient Egyptian Hieroglyphic text which give instruction as to the nature of the mind and its three modes of expression. It also presents the texts which give instruction on the practice of meditation for spiritual Enlightenment and unity with the Divine. This volume allows the reader to begin practicing meditation by explaining, in easy to understand terms, the simplest form of meditation and working up to the most advanced form which was practiced in ancient times and which is still practiced by yogis around the world in modern times. ISBN 1-884564-27-7 $22.99

14. *THE GLORIOUS LIGHT MEDITATION* TECHNIQUE OF ANCIENT EGYPT New for the year 2000. This volume is based on the earliest known instruction in history given for the practice of formal meditation. Discovered by Dr. Muata Ashby, it is inscribed on the walls of the Tomb of Seti I in Thebes Egypt. This volume details the philosophy and practice of this unique system of meditation originated in Ancient Egypt and the earliest practice of meditation known in the world which occurred in the most advanced African Culture. ISBN: 1-884564-15-1 $16.95 (PB)

15. *THE SERPENT POWER: The Ancient Egyptian Mystical Wisdom of the Inner Life Force.* This Volume specifically deals with the latent life Force energy of the universe and in the human body, its control and sublimation. How to develop the Life Force energy of the subtle body. This Volume will introduce the esoteric wisdom of the science of how virtuous living acts in a subtle and mysterious way to cleanse the latent psychic energy conduits and vortices of the spiritual body. ISBN 1-884564-19-4 $22.95

16. **EGYPTIAN YOGA** *The Postures of The Gods and Goddesses* Discover the physical postures and exercises practiced thousands of years ago in Ancient Egypt which are today known as Yoga exercises. Discover the history of the postures and how they were transferred from Ancient Egypt in Africa to India through Buddhist Tantrism. Then practice the postures as you discover the mythic teaching that originally gave birth to the postures and was practiced by the Ancient Egyptian priests and priestesses. This work is based on the pictures and

EGYPTIAN BOOK OF THE DEAD HIEROGLYPH TRANSLATIONS Vol. 5

teachings from the Creation story of Ra, The Asarian Resurrection Myth and the carvings and reliefs from various Temples in Ancient Egypt 8.5" X 11" ISBN 1-884564-10-0 Soft Cover $21.95 Exercise video $20

17. *SACRED SEXUALITY: ANCIENT EGYPTIAN TANTRA YOGA: The Art of Sex* Sublimation and Universal Consciousness This Volume will expand on the male and female principles within the human body and in the universe and further detail the sublimation of sexual energy into spiritual energy. The student will study the deities Min and Hathor, Asar and Aset, Geb and Nut and discover the mystical implications for a practical spiritual discipline. This Volume will also focus on the Tantric aspects of Ancient Egyptian and Indian mysticism, the purpose of sex and the mystical teachings of sexual sublimation which lead to self-knowledge and Enlightenment. ISBN 1-884564-03-8 $24.95

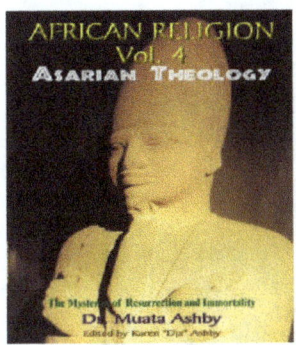

18. *AFRICAN RELIGION Volume 4: ASARIAN THEOLOGY: RESURRECTING OSIRIS* The path of Mystical Awakening and the Keys to Immortality NEW REVISED AND EXPANDED EDITION! The Ancient Sages created stories based on human and superhuman beings whose struggles, aspirations, needs and desires ultimately lead them to discover their true Self. The myth of Aset, Asar and Heru is no exception in this area. While there is no one source where the entire story may be found, pieces of it are inscribed in various ancient Temples walls, tombs, steles and papyri. For the first time available, the complete myth of Asar, Aset and Heru has been compiled from original Ancient Egyptian, Greek and Coptic Texts. This epic myth has been richly illustrated with reliefs from the Temple of Heru at Edfu, the Temple of Aset at Philae, the Temple of Asar at Abydos, the Temple of Hathor at Denderah and various papyri, inscriptions and reliefs. Discover the myth which inspired the teachings of the *Shetaut Neter* (Egyptian Mystery System - Egyptian Yoga) and the Egyptian Book of Coming Forth By Day. Also, discover the three levels of Ancient Egyptian Religion, how to understand the mysteries of the Duat or Astral World and how to discover the abode of the Supreme in the Amenta, *The Other World* The ancient religion of Asar, Aset and Heru, if properly understood, contains all of the elements necessary to lead the sincere aspirant to attain immortality through inner self-discovery. This volume presents the entire myth and explores the main mystical themes and rituals associated with the myth for understating human existence, creation and the way to achieve spiritual emancipation - *Resurrection*. The Asarian myth is so powerful that it influenced and is still having an effect on the major world religions. Discover the origins and mystical meaning of the Christian Trinity, the Eucharist ritual and the ancient origin of the birthday of Jesus Christ. Soft Cover ISBN: 1-884564-27-5 $24.95

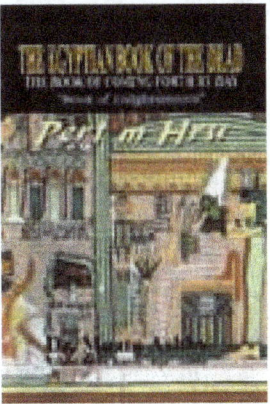

19. *THE EGYPTIAN BOOK OF THE DEAD MYSTICISM OF THE PERT EM HERU* " I

EGYPTIAN BOOK OF THE DEAD HIEROGLYPH TRANSLATIONS Vol. 5

Know myself, I know myself, I am One With God!–From the Pert Em Heru "The Ru Pert em Heru" or "Ancient Egyptian Book of The Dead," or "Book of Coming Forth By Day" as it is more popularly known, has fascinated the world since the successful translation of Ancient Egyptian hieroglyphic scripture over 150 years ago. The astonishing writings in it reveal that the Ancient Egyptians believed in life after death and in an ultimate destiny to discover the Divine. The elegance and aesthetic beauty of the hieroglyphic text itself has inspired many see it as an art form in and of itself. But is there more to it than that? Did the Ancient Egyptian wisdom contain more than just aphorisms and hopes of eternal life beyond death? In this volume Dr. Muata Ashby, the author of over 25 books on Ancient Egyptian Yoga Philosophy has produced a new translation of the original texts which uncovers a mystical teaching underlying the sayings and rituals instituted by the Ancient Egyptian Sages and Saints. "Once the philosophy of Ancient Egypt is understood as a mystical tradition instead of as a religion or primitive mythology, it reveals its secrets which if practiced today will lead anyone to discover the glory of spiritual self-discovery. The Pert em Heru is in every way comparable to the Indian Upanishads or the Tibetan Book of the Dead." – $28.95 ISBN# 1-884564-28-3 Size: 8½" X 11

20. *African Religion VOL. 1- ANUNIAN THEOLOGY THE MYSTERIES OF RA* The Philosophy of Anu and The Mystical Teachings of The Ancient Egyptian Creation Myth Discover the mystical teachings contained in the Creation Myth and the gods and goddesses who brought creation and human beings into existence. The Creation myth of Anu is the source of Anunian Theology but also of the other main theological systems of Ancient Egypt that also influenced other world religions including Christianity, Hinduism and Buddhism. The Creation Myth holds the key to understanding the universe and for attaining spiritual Enlightenment. ISBN: 1-884564-38-0 $19.95

21. *African Religion VOL 3: Memphite Theology: MYSTERIES OF MIND* Mystical Psychology & Mental Health for Enlightenment and Immortality based on the Ancient Egyptian Philosophy of Menefer -Mysticism of Ptah, Egyptian Physics and Yoga Metaphysics and the Hidden properties of Matter. This volume uncovers the mystical psychology of the Ancient Egyptian wisdom teachings centering on the philosophy of the Ancient Egyptian city of Menefer (Memphite Theology). How to understand the mind and how to control the senses and lead the mind to health, clarity and mystical self-discovery. This Volume will also go deeper into the philosophy of God as creation and will explore the concepts of modern science and how they correlate with ancient teachings. This Volume will lay the ground work for the understanding of the philosophy of universal consciousness and the initiatic/yogic insight into who or what is God? ISBN 1-884564-07-0 $22.95

22. *AFRICAN RELIGION VOLUME 5: THE GODDESS AND THE EGYPTIAN MYSTERIES THE PATH OF THE GODDESS THE GODDESS PATH* The Secret Forms of the Goddess and the Rituals of Resurrection The Supreme Being may be worshipped as father or as mother. *Ushet Rekhat* or *Mother Worship*, is the spiritual process of worshipping the Divine in the form of the Divine Goddess. It celebrates the most important forms of the Goddess including *Nathor, Maat, Aset, Arat, Amentet and Hathor* and explores their mystical meaning as well as the rising of *Sirius,* the star of Aset (Aset) and the new birth of Hor (Heru). The end of the year is a time of reckoning, reflection and engendering a new or renewed positive movement toward attaining spiritual Enlightenment. The Mother Worship devotional meditation ritual, performed on five days during the month of December and on New Year's Eve, is based on the Ushet Rekhit. During the ceremony, the cosmic forces, symbolized by Sirius - and the constellation of Orion ---, are harnessed through the understanding and devotional attitude of the participant. This propitiation draws the light of wisdom and health to all those who share in the ritual, leading to prosperity and wisdom. $14.95 ISBN 1-884564-18-6

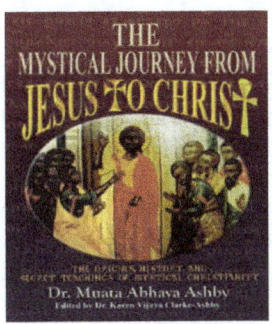

23. *THE MYSTICAL JOURNEY FROM JESUS TO CHRIST* Discover the ancient Egyptian origins of Christianity before the Catholic Church and learn the mystical teachings given by Jesus to assist all humanity in becoming Christlike. Discover the secret meaning of the Gospels that were discovered in Egypt. Also discover how and why so many Christian churches came into being. Discover that the Bible still holds the keys to mystical realization even though its original writings were changed by the church. Discover how to practice the original teachings of Christianity which leads to the Kingdom of Heaven. $24.95 ISBN# 1-884564-05-4 size: 8½" X 11"

24. *THE STORY OF ASAR, ASET AND HERU:* An Ancient Egyptian Legend (For Children) Now for the first time, the most ancient myth of Ancient Egypt comes alive for children. Inspired by the books *The Asarian Resurrection: The Ancient Egyptian Bible* and *The Mystical Teachings of The Asarian Resurrection, The Story of Asar, Aset and Heru* is an easy to understand and thrilling tale which inspired the children of Ancient Egypt to aspire to greatness and righteousness. If you and your child have enjoyed stories like *The Lion King* and *Star Wars you will love The Story of Asar, Aset and Heru.* Also, if you know the story of Jesus and Krishna you will discover than Ancient Egypt had a similar myth and that this myth carries important spiritual teachings for living a fruitful and fulfilling life. This book may be used along with *The Parents Guide To The Asarian Resurrection Myth: How to Teach Yourself and Your Child the Principles of Universal Mystical Religion.* The guide provides some background to the Asarian Resurrection myth and it also gives insight into the mystical teachings contained in it which you may introduce to your child. It is designed for parents who wish to grow spiritually with their children and it serves as an introduction for those who would like to study the Asarian Resurrection Myth in depth and to practice its teachings. 8.5" X 11" ISBN: 1-884564-31-3 $12.95

25. THE PARENTS GUIDE TO THE AUSARIAN RESURRECTION MYTH: How to Teach Yourself and Your Child the Principles of Universal Mystical Religion. This insightful manual brings for the timeless wisdom of the ancient through the Ancient Egyptian myth of Asar, Aset and Heru and the mystical teachings contained in it for parents who want to guide their children to understand and practice the teachings of mystical spirituality. This manual may be used with the children's storybook *The Story of Asar, Aset and Heru* by Dr. Muata Abhaya Ashby. ISBN: 1-884564-30-5 $16.95

26. HEALING THE CRIMINAL HEART. Introduction to Maat Philosophy, Yoga and Spiritual Redemption Through the Path of Virtue Who is a criminal? Is there such a thing as a criminal heart? What is the source of evil and sinfulness and is there any way to rise above it? Is there redemption for those who have committed sins, even the worst crimes? Ancient Egyptian mystical psychology holds important answers to these questions. Over ten thousand years ago mystical psychologists, the Sages of Ancient Egypt, studied and charted the human mind and spirit and laid out a path which will lead to spiritual redemption, prosperity and Enlightenment. This introductory volume brings forth the teachings of the Asarian Resurrection, the most important myth of Ancient Egypt, with relation to the faults of human existence: anger, hatred, greed, lust, animosity, discontent, ignorance, egoism jealousy, bitterness, and a myriad of psycho-spiritual ailments which keep a human being in a state of negativity and adversity ISBN: 1-884564-17-8 $15.95

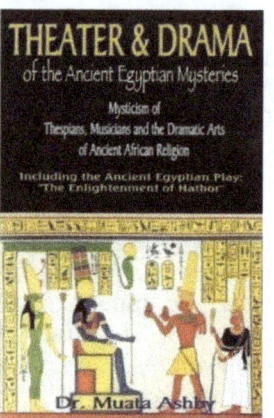

27. TEMPLE RITUAL OF THE ANCIENT EGYPTIAN MYSTERIES--THEATER & DRAMA OF THE ANCIENT EGYPTIAN MYSTERIES: Details the practice of the mysteries and ritual program of the temple and the philosophy an practice of the ritual of the mysteries, its purpose and execution. Featuring the Ancient Egyptian stage play-"The Enlightenment of Hathor' Based on an Ancient Egyptian Drama, The original Theater -Mysticism of the Temple of Hetheru 1-884564-14-3 $19.95 By Dr. Muata Ashby

28. GUIDE TO PRINT ON DEMAND: SELF-PUBLISH FOR PROFIT, Spiritual Fulfillment and Service to Humanity Everyone asks us how we

produced so many books in such a short time. Here are the secrets to writing and producing books that uplift humanity and how to get them printed for a fraction of the regular cost. Anyone can become an author even if they have limited funds. All that is necessary is the willingness to learn how the printing and book business work and the desire to follow the special instructions given here for preparing your manuscript format. Then you take your work directly to the non-traditional companies who can produce your books for less than the traditional book printer can. ISBN: 1-884564-40-2 $16.95 U. S.

29. *Egyptian Mysteries: Vol. 1,* Shetaut Neter What are the Mysteries? For thousands of years the spiritual tradition of Ancient Egypt, S*hetaut Neter,* "The Egyptian Mysteries," "The Secret Teachings," have fascinated, tantalized and amazed the world. At one time exalted and recognized as the highest culture of the world, by Africans, Europeans, Asiatics, Hindus, Buddhists and other cultures of the ancient world, in time it was shunned by the emerging orthodox world religions. Its temples desecrated, its philosophy maligned, its tradition spurned, its philosophy dormant in the mystical *Medu Neter,* the mysterious hieroglyphic texts which hold the secret symbolic meaning that has scarcely been discerned up to now. What are the secrets of *Nehast* {spiritual awakening and emancipation, resurrection}. More than just a literal translation, this volume is for awakening to the secret code *Shetitu* of the teaching which was not deciphered by Egyptologists, nor could be understood by ordinary spiritualists. This book is a reinstatement of the original science made available for our times, to the reincarnated followers of Ancient Egyptian culture and the prospect of spiritual freedom to break the bonds of *Khemn,* "ignorance," and slavery to evil forces: *Såaa* . ISBN: 1-884564-41-0 $19.99

30. *EGYPTIAN MYSTERIES VOL 2:* Dictionary of Gods and Goddesses This book is about the mystery of neteru, the gods and goddesses of Ancient Egypt (Kamit, Kemet). Neteru means "Gods and Goddesses." But the Neterian teaching of Neteru represents more than the usual limited modern day concept of "divinities" or "spirits." The Neteru of Kamit are also metaphors, cosmic principles and vehicles for the enlightening teachings of Shetaut Neter (Ancient Egyptian-African Religion). Actually they are the elements for one of the most advanced systems of spirituality ever conceived in human history. Understanding the concept of neteru provides a firm basis for spiritual evolution and the pathway for viable culture, peace on earth and a healthy human society. Why is it important to have gods and goddesses in our lives? In order for spiritual evolution to be possible, once a human being has accepted that there is existence after death and there is a transcendental being who exists beyond time and space knowledge, human beings need a connection to that which transcends the ordinary experience of human life in time and space and a means to understand the transcendental reality beyond the mundane reality. ISBN: 1-884564-23-2 $21.95

EGYPTIAN BOOK OF THE DEAD HIEROGLYPH TRANSLATIONS Vol. 5

31. *EGYPTIAN MYSTERIES VOL. 3* The Priests and Priestesses of Ancient Egypt This volume details the path of Neterian priesthood, the joys, challenges and rewards of advanced Neterian life, the teachings that allowed the priests and priestesses to manage the most long lived civilization in human history and how that path can be adopted today; for those who want to tread the path of the Clergy of Shetaut Neter. ISBN: 1-884564-53-4 $24.95

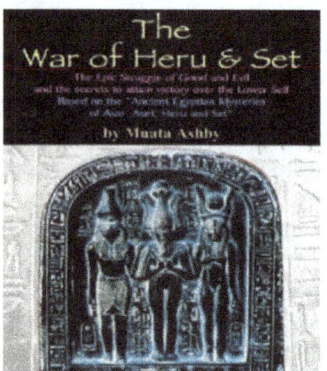

32. *The War of Heru and Set:* The Struggle of Good and Evil for Control of the World and The Human Soul This volume contains a novelized version of the Asarian Resurrection myth that is based on the actual scriptures presented in the Book Asarian Religion (old name –Resurrecting Osiris). This volume is prepared in the form of a screenplay and can be easily adapted to be used as a stage play. Spiritual seeking is a mythic journey that has many emotional highs and lows, ecstasies and depressions, victories and frustrations. This is the War of Life that is played out in the myth as the struggle of Heru and Set and those are mythic characters that represent the human Higher and Lower self. How to understand the war and emerge victorious in the journey o life? The ultimate victory and fulfillment can be experienced, which is not changeable or lost in time. The purpose of myth is to convey the wisdom of life through the story of divinities who show the way to overcome the challenges and foibles of life. In this volume the feelings and emotions of the characters of the myth have been highlighted to show the deeply rich texture of the Ancient Egyptian myth. This myth contains deep spiritual teachings and insights into the nature of self, of God and the mysteries of life and the means to discover the true meaning of life and thereby achieve the true purpose of life. To become victorious in the battle of life means to become the King (or Queen) of Egypt.Have you seen movies like The Lion King, Hamlet, The Odyssey, or The Little Buddha? These have been some of the most popular movies in modern times. The Sema Institute of Yoga is dedicated to researching and presenting the wisdom and culture of ancient Africa. The Script is designed to be produced as a motion picture but may be addapted for the theater as well. $21.95 copyright 1998 By Dr. Muata Ashby ISBN 1-8840564-44-5

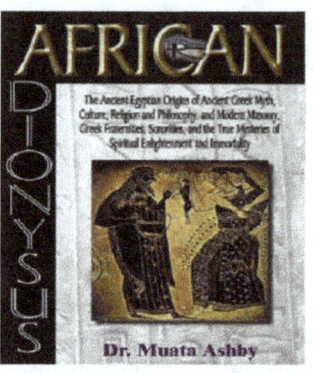

33. *AFRICAN DIONYSUS: From Egypt to Greece:* The Kamitan Origins of Greek Culture and Religion ISBN: 1-884564-47-X FROM EGYPT TO GREECE This insightful manual is a reference to Ancient Egyptian mythology and philosophy and its correlation to what later became known as Greek and Rome mythology and philosophy. It outlines the basic tenets of the mythologies and shoes the ancient origins of Greek culture in Ancient Egypt. This volume also documents the origins of the Greek alphabet in Egypt as well as Greek religion, myth and philosophy of the gods and goddesses from Egypt from the myth of Atlantis and archaic period with the Minoans to the Classical period. This volume also acts as a resource for Colleges students who would like to set up fraternities and sororities based on the original Ancient Egyptian principles of Sheti and Maat philosophy. ISBN: 1-884564-47-X $22.95 U.S.

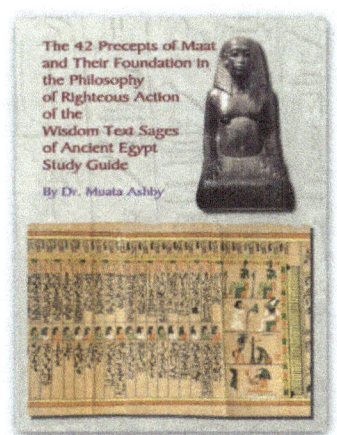

34. THE FORTY TWO PRECEPTS OF MAAT, THE PHILOSOPHY OF RIGHTEOUS ACTION AND THE ANCIENT EGYPTIAN WISDOM TEXTS Advanced Studies This manual is designed for use with the 1998 Maat Philosophy Class conducted by Dr. Muata Ashby. This is a detailed study of Maat Philosophy. It contains a compilation of the 42 laws or precepts of Maat and the corresponding principles which they represent along with the teachings of the ancient Egyptian Sages relating to each. Maat philosophy was the basis of Ancient Egyptian society and government as well as the heart of Ancient Egyptian myth and spirituality. Maat is at once a goddess, a cosmic force and a living social doctrine, which promotes social harmony and thereby paves the way for spiritual evolution in all levels of society. ISBN: 1-884564-48-8 $16.95 U.S.

35. THE SECRET LOTUS: Poetry of Enlightenment
Discover the mystical sentiment of the Kemetic teaching as expressed through the poetry of Sebai Muata Ashby. The teaching of spiritual awakening is uniquely experienced when the poetic sensibility is present. This first volume contains the poems written between 1996 and 2003. **1-884564--16 -X $16.99**

36. The Ancient Egyptian Buddha: The Ancient Egyptian Origins of Buddhism
This book is a compilation of several sections of a larger work, a book by the name of African Origins of Civilization, Religion, Yoga Mysticism and Ethics Philosophy. It also contains some additional evidences not contained in the larger work that demonstrate the correlation between Ancient Egyptian Religion and Buddhism. This book is one of several compiled short volumes that has been compiled so as to facilitate access to specific subjects contained in the larger work which is over 680 pages long. These short and small volumes have been specifically designed to cover one subject in a brief and low cost format. This present volume, The Ancient Egyptian Buddha: The Ancient Egyptian Origins of Buddhism, formed one subject in the larger work; actually it was one chapter of the larger work. However, this volume has some new additional evidences and comparisons of Buddhist and Neterian (Ancient Egyptian) philosophies not previously discussed. It was felt that this subject needed to be discussed because even in the early 21st century, the idea persists that Buddhism originated only in India independently. Yet there is ample evidence from ancient writings and perhaps more importantly, iconographical evidences from the Ancient Egyptians and early Buddhists themselves that prove otherwise. This handy volume has been designed to be accessible to young adults and all others who would like to have an easy reference with documentation on this important subject. This is an

EGYPTIAN BOOK OF THE DEAD HIEROGLYPH TRANSLATIONS Vol. 5

important subject because the frame of reference with which we look at a culture depends strongly on our conceptions about its origins. in this case, if we look at the Buddhism as an Asiatic religion we would treat it and it's culture in one way. If we id as African [Ancient Egyptian] we not only would see it in a different light but we also must ascribe Africa with a glorious legacy that matches any other culture in human history and gave rise to one of the present day most important religious philosophies. We would also look at the culture and philosophies of the Ancient Egyptians as having African insights that offer us greater depth into the Buddhist philosophies. Those insights inform our knowledge about other African traditions and we can also begin to understand in a deeper way the effect of Ancient Egyptian culture on African culture and also on the Asiatic as well. We would also be able to discover the glorious and wondrous teaching of mystical philosophy that Ancient Egyptian Shetaut Neter religion offers, that is as powerful as any other mystic system of spiritual philosophy in the world today. ISBN: 1-884564-61-5 $28.95

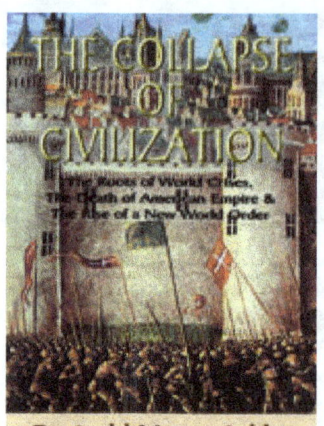

37. The Death of American Empire: Neo-conservatism, Theocracy, Economic Imperialism, Environmental Disaster and the Collapse of Civilization

This work is a collection of essays relating to social and economic, leadership, and ethics, ecological and religious issues that are facing the world today in order to understand the course of history that has led humanity to its present condition and then arrive at positive solutions that will lead to better outcomes for all humanity. It surveys the development and decline of major empires throughout history and focuses on the creation of American Empire along with the social, political and economic policies that led to the prominence of the United States of America as a Superpower including the rise of the political control of the neo-con political philosophy including militarism and the military industrial complex in American politics and the rise of the religious right into and American Theocracy movement. This volume details, through historical and current events, the psychology behind the dominance of western culture in world politics through the "Superpower Syndrome Mandatory Conflict Complex" that drives the Superpower culture to establish itself above all others and then act hubristically to dominate world culture through legitimate influences as well as coercion, media censorship and misinformation leading to international hegemony and world conflict. This volume also details the financial policies that gave rise to American prominence in the global economy, especially after World War II, and promoted American preeminence over the world economy through Globalization as well as the environmental policies, including the oil economy, that are promoting degradation of the world ecology and contribute to the decline of America as an Empire culture. This volume finally explores the factors pointing to the decline of the American Empire economy and imperial power and what to expect in the aftermath of American prominence and how to survive the decline while at the same time promoting policies and social-economic-religious-political changes that are needed in order to promote the emergence of a beneficial and sustainable culture. **$25.95soft** 1-884564-25-9, Hard Cover **$29.95** 1-884564-45-3

38. The African Origins of Hatha Yoga: And its Ancient Mystical Teaching

The subject of this present volume, The Ancient Egyptian Origins of Yoga Postures, formed one subject in the larger works, African Origins of Civilization Religion, Yoga Mysticism and Ethics Philosophy and the Book Egypt and India is the section of the book African Origins of Civilization. Those works contain the collection of all correlations between Ancient Egypt and India. This volume also contains some additional information not contained in the previous work. It was felt that this subject needed to be discussed more directly, being treated in one volume, as opposed to being contained in the larger work along with other subjects, because even in the early 21st century, the idea persists that the Yoga and specifically, Yoga Postures, were invented and developed only in India. The Ancient Egyptians were peoples originally from Africa who were, in ancient times, colonists in India. Therefore it is no surprise that many Indian traditions including religious and Yogic, would be found earlier in Ancient Egypt. Yet there is ample evidence from ancient writings and perhaps more importantly, iconographical evidences from the Ancient Egyptians themselves and the Indians themselves that prove the connection between Ancient Egypt and India as well as the existence of a discipline of Yoga Postures in Ancient Egypt long before its practice in India. This handy volume has been designed to be accessible to young adults and all others who would like to have an easy reference with documentation on this important subject. This is an important subject because the frame of reference with which we look at a culture depends strongly on our conceptions about its origins. In this case, if we look at the Ancient Egyptians as Asiatic peoples we would treat them and their culture in one way. If we see them as Africans we not only see them in a different light but we also must ascribe Africa with a glorious legacy that matches any other culture in human history. We would also look at the culture and philosophies of the Ancient Egyptians as having African insights instead of Asiatic ones. Those insights inform our knowledge bout other African traditions and we can also begin to understand in a deeper way the effect of Ancient Egyptian culture on African culture and also on the Asiatic as well. When we discover the deeper and more ancient practice of the postures system in Ancient Egypt that was called "Hatha Yoga" in India, we are able to find a new and expanded understanding of the practice that constitutes a discipline of spiritual practice that informs and revitalizes the Indian practices as well as all spiritual disciplines. $19.99 ISBN 1-884564-60-7

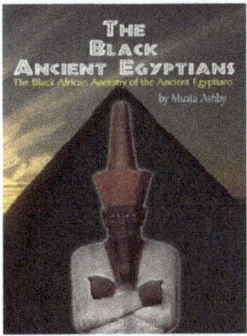

39. The Black Ancient Egyptians

This present volume, The Black Ancient Egyptians: The Black African Ancestry of the Ancient Egyptians, formed one subject in the larger work: The African Origins of Civilization, Religion, Yoga Mysticism and Ethics Philosophy. It was felt that this subject needed to be discussed because even in the early 21st century, the idea persists that the Ancient Egyptians were peoples originally from Asia Minor who came into North-East Africa. Yet there is ample evidence from ancient writings and perhaps more importantly, iconographical evidences from the Ancient Egyptians themselves that proves otherwise. This handy volume has been designed to be accessible to young adults and all others who would like to have an easy reference with documentation on this important subject. This is an important subject because the frame of reference with which we look at a culture depends strongly on our conceptions about its origins. in this case, if we look at the Ancient Egyptians as Asiatic peoples we would treat them and their culture in one way. If we see them as Africans we not only see them in a different light but we also must ascribe Africa with a glorious legacy that matches any other culture in human history. We would also look at the culture and philosophies of the Ancient Egyptians as having African insights instead of Asiatic ones. Those insights inform our knowledge bout other African traditions and we can also begin to understand in a deeper way the effect of Ancient Egyptian culture on African culture and also on the Asiatic as well. ISBN 1-884564-21-6 $19.99

40. The Limits of Faith: The Failure of Faith-based Religions and the Solution to the Meaning of Life

Is faith belief in something without proof? And if so is there never to be any proof or discovery? If so what is the need of intellect? If faith is trust in something that is real is that reality historical, literal or metaphorical or philosophical? If knowledge is an essential element in faith why should there by so much emphasis on believing and not on understanding in the modern practice of religion? This volume is a compilation of essays related to the nature of religious faith in the context of its inception in human history as well as its meaning for religious practice and relations between religions in modern times. Faith has come to be regarded as a virtuous goal in life. However, many people have asked how can it be that an endeavor that is supposed to be dedicated to spiritual upliftment has led to more conflict in human history than any other social factor? ISBN 1884564631 SOFT COVER - $19.99, ISBN 1884564623 HARD COVER -$28.95

41. Redemption of The Criminal Heart Through Kemetic Spirituality and Maat Philosophy

Special book dedicated to inmates, their families and members of the Law Enforcement community. ISBN: 1-884564-70-4 $5.00

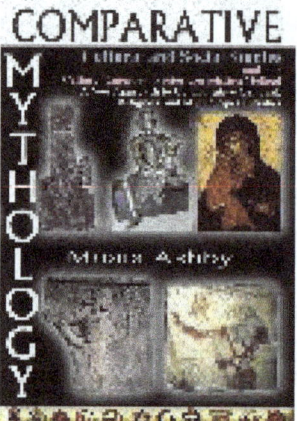

42. COMPARATIVE MYTHOLOGY

What are Myth and Culture and what is their importance for understanding the development of societies, human evolution and the search for meaning? What is the purpose of culture and how do cultures evolve? What are the elements of a culture and how can those elements be broken down and the constituent parts of a culture understood and compared? How do cultures interact? How does enculturation occur and how do people interact with other cultures? How do the processes of acculturation and cooptation occur and what does this mean for the development of a society?

How can the study of myths and the elements of culture help in understanding the meaning of life and the means to promote understanding and peace in the world of human activity? This volume is the exposition of a method for studying and comparing cultures, myths and other social aspects of a society. It is an expansion on the Cultural Category Factor Correlation method for studying and comparing myths, cultures, religions and other aspects of human culture. It was originally introduced in the year 2002. This volume contains an expanded treatment as well as several refinements along with examples of the application of the method. the apparent. I hope you enjoy these art renditions as serene reflections of the mysteries of life. ISBN: 1-884564-72-0

Book price $21.95

43. CONVERSATION WITH GOD: Revelations of the Important Questions of Life
$24.99 U.S.

This volume contains a grouping of some of the questions that have been submitted to Sebai Dr. Muata Ashby. They are efforts by many aspirants to better understand and practice the teachings of mystical spirituality. It is said that when sages are asked spiritual questions they are relaying the wisdom of God, the Goddess, the Higher Self, etc. There is a very special quality about the Q & A process that does not occur during a regular lecture session. Certain points come out that would not come out otherwise due to the nature of the process which ideally occurs after a lecture. Having been to a certain degree enlightened by a lecture certain new questions arise and the answers to these have the effect of elevating the teaching of the lecture to even higher levels. Therefore, enjoy these exchanges and may they lead you to enlightenment, peace and prosperity. Available Late Summer 2007 ISBN: 1-884564-68-2

44. MYSTIC ART PAINTINGS
(with Full Color images) This book contains a collection of the small number of paintings that I have created over the years. Some were used as early book covers and others were done simply to express certain spiritual feelings; some were created for no purpose except to express the joy of color and the feeling of relaxed freedom. All are to elicit mystical awakening in the viewer. Writing a book on philosophy is like sculpture, the more the work is rewritten the reflections and ideas become honed and take form and become clearer and imbued with intellectual beauty. Mystic music is like meditation, a world of its own that exists about 1 inch above ground wherein the musician does not touch the ground. Mystic Graphic Art is meditation in form, color, image and reflected image which opens the door to the reality behind the apparent. I hope you enjoy these art renditions and my reflections on them as serene reflections of the mysteries of life, as visual renditions of the philosophy I have written about over the years. ISBN 1-884564-69-0 $19.95

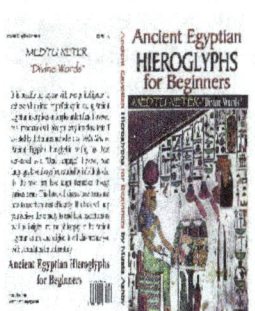

45. ANCIENT EGYPTIAN HIEROGLYPHS FOR BEGINNERS

This brief guide was prepared for those inquiring about how to enter into Hieroglyphic studies on their own at home or in study groups. First of all you should know that there are a few institutions around the world which teach how to read the Hieroglyphic text but due to the nature of the study there are perhaps only a handful of people who can read fluently. It is possible for anyone with average intelligence to achieve a high level of proficiency in reading inscriptions on temples and artifacts; however, reading extensive texts is another issue entirely. However, this introduction will give you entry into those texts if assisted by dictionaries and other aids. Most Egyptologists have a basic knowledge and keep dictionaries and notes handy when it comes to dealing with more difficult texts. Medtu Neter or the Ancient Egyptian hieroglyphic language has been considered as a "Dead Language." However, dead languages have always been studied by individuals who for the most part have taught themselves through various means. This book will discuss those means and how to use them most efficiently. ISBN 1884564429 **$28.95**

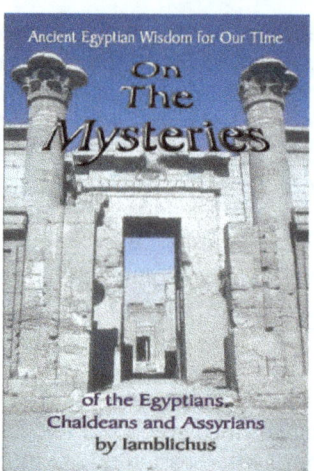

46. ON THE MYSTERIES: Wisdom of An Ancient Egyptian Sage -with Foreword by Muata Ashby

This volume, On the Mysteries, by Iamblichus (Abamun) is a unique form or scripture out of the Ancient Egyptian religious tradition. It is written in a form that is not usual or which is not usually found in the remnants of Ancient Egyptian scriptures. It is in the form of teacher and disciple, much like the Eastern scriptures such as Bhagavad Gita or the Upanishads. This form of writing may not have been necessary in Ancient times, because the format of teaching in Egypt was different prior to the conquest period by the Persians, Assyrians, Greeks and later the Romans. The question and answer format can be found but such extensive discourses and corrections of misunderstandings within the context of a teacher - disciple relationship is not usual. It therefore provides extensive insights into the times when it was written and the state of practice of Ancient Egyptian and other mystery religions. This has important implications for our times because we are today, as in the Greco-Roman period, also besieged with varied religions and new age philosophies as well as social strife and war. How can we understand our times and also make sense of the forest of spiritual traditions? How can we cut through the cacophony of religious fanaticism, and ignorance as well as misconceptions about the mysteries on the other in order to discover the true purpose of religion and the secret teachings that open up the mysteries of life and the way to enlightenment and immortality? This book, which comes to us from so long ago, offers us transcendental wisdom that applied to the world two thousand years ago as well as our world today. ISBN 1-884564-64-X $25.95

47. The Ancient Egyptian Wisdom Texts -Compiled by Muata Ashby

The Ancient Egyptian Wisdom Texts are a genre of writings from the ancient culture that have survived to the present and provide a vibrant record of the practice of spiritual evolution otherwise known as religion or yoga philosophy in Ancient Egypt. The principle focus of the Wisdom Texts is the cultivation of understanding, peace, harmony, selfless service, self-control, Inner fulfillment and spiritual realization. When these factors are cultivated in human life, the virtuous qualities in a human being begin to manifest and sinfulness, ignorance and negativity diminish until a person is able to enter into higher consciousness, the coveted goal of all civilizations. It is this virtuous mode of life which opens the door to self-discovery and spiritual enlightenment. Therefore, the Wisdom Texts are important scriptures on the subject of human nature, spiritual psychology and mystical philosophy. The teachings presented in the Wisdom Texts form the foundation of religion as well as the guidelines for conducting the affairs of every area of social interaction including commerce, education, the army, marriage, and especially the legal system. These texts were sources for the famous 42 Precepts of Maat of the Pert-m-Heru (Book of the Dead), essential regulations of good conduct to develop virtue and purity in order to attain higher consciousness and immortality after death. ISBN1-884564-65-8 $18.95

48. THE KEMETIC TREE OF LIFE
THE KEMETIC TREE OF LIFE: Newly Revealed Ancient Egyptian Cosmology and Metaphysics for Higher Consciousness The Tree of Life is a roadmap of a journey which explains how Creation came into being and how it will end. It also explains what Creation is composed of and also what human beings are and what they are composed of. It also explains the process of Creation, how Creation develops, as well as who created Creation and where that entity may be found. It also explains how a human being may discover that entity and in so doing also discover the secrets of Creation, the meaning of life and the means to break free from the pathetic condition of human limitation and mortality in order to discover the higher realms of being by discovering the principles, the levels of existence that are beyond the simple physical and material aspects of life. This book contains color plates **ISBN: 1-884564-74-7**

$27.95 U.S.

49-MATRIX OF AFRICAN PROVERBS: The Ethical and Spiritual Blueprint
This volume sets forth the fundamental principles of African ethics and their practical applications for use by individuals and organizations seeking to model their ethical policies using the Traditional African values and concepts of ethical human behavior for the proper sustenance and management of society. Furthermore, this book will provide guidance as to how the Traditional African Ethics may be viewed and applied, taking into consideration the technological and social advancements in the present. This volume also presents the principles of ethical culture, and references for each to specific injunctions from Traditional African

Proverbial Wisdom Teachings. These teachings are compiled from varied Pre-colonial African societies including Yoruba, Ashanti, Kemet, Malawi, Nigeria, Ethiopia, Galla, Ghana and many more. ISBN 1-884564-77-1

50- Growing Beyond Hate: Keys to Freedom from Discord, Racism, Sexism, Political Conflict, Class Warfare, Violence, and How to Achieve Peace and Enlightenment--
-INTRODUCTION: WHY DO WE HATE? Hatred is one of the fundamental motivating aspects of human life; the other is desire. Desire can be of a worldly nature or of a spiritual, elevating nature. Worldly desire and hatred are like two sides of the same coin in that human life is usually swaying from one to the other; but the question is why? And is there a way to satisfy the desiring or hating mind in such a way as to find peace in life? Why do human beings go to war? Why do human beings perpetrate violence against one another? And is there a way not just to understand the phenomena but to resolve the issues that plague humanity and could lead to a more harmonious society? Hatred is perhaps the greatest scourge of humanity in that it leads to misunderstanding, conflict and untold miseries of life and clashes between individuals, societies and nations. Therefore, the riddle of Hatred, that is, understanding the sources of it and how to confront, reduce and even eradicate it so as to bring forth the fulfillment in life and peace for society, should be a top priority for social scientists, spiritualists and philosophers. This book is written from the perspective of spiritual philosophy based on the mystical wisdom and sema or yoga philosophy of the Ancient Egyptians. This philosophy, originated and based in the wisdom of Shetaut Neter, the Egyptian Mysteries, and Maat, ethical way of life in society and in spirit, contains Sema-Yogic wisdom and understanding of life's predicaments that can allow a human being of any ethnic group to understand and overcome the causes of hatred, racism, sexism, violence and disharmony in life, that plague human society. ISBN: 1-884564-81-X

52. Guide to Creating a Kemetic Marriage Contract

This marital contract guide reflects actual Ancient Egyptian Principles for Kemetic Marriage as they are to be applied for our times. The marital contract allows people to have a framework with which to face the challenges of marital relations instead of relying on hopes or romantic dreams that everything will workout somehow; in other words, love is not all you need. The latter is not an evolved, mature way of handling one of the most important aspects of human life. Therefore, it behooves anyone who wishes to enter into a marriage to explore the issues, express their needs and seek to avoid costly mistakes, and resolve conflicts in the normal course of life or make sure that their rights and dignity will be protected if any eventuality should occur. Marital relations in Ancient Egypt were not like those in other countries of the time and not like those of present day countries. The extreme longevity of Ancient Egyptian society, founded in Maat philosophy, allowed the social development of marriage to evolve and progress to a high level of order and balance. Maat represents truth, righteous, justice and harmony in life. This meant that the marital partner's rights were to be protected with equal standing before the law. So there was no disparity between rights of men or rights of women. Therefore, anyone who wants to enter into a marriage based on Kemetic principles must first and foremost adhere to this standard…equality in the rights of men and women. This guide demonstrates procedures for following the Ancient Egyptian practice of formalizing marriage with a contract that spells out the important concerns of each partner in the marital relationship, based on Maatian principles [of righteous, truth, harmony and justice] so that the rights and needs of each partner may be protected within the marriage. It also allows the partners to think about issues that arise out of the marital relations so that they may have a foundation to fall back on in the event that those or other unforeseen issues arise and cause conflict in the relationship. By having a document of expressed concerns, needs and steps to be taken to address them, it is less likely that issues which affect the relationship in a negative way will arise, and when they do, they will be better handled, in a more balanced, just and amicable way.

EBOOK ISBN 978-1-937016-59-3,

HARDCOPY BOOK ISBN: 1-884564-82-8

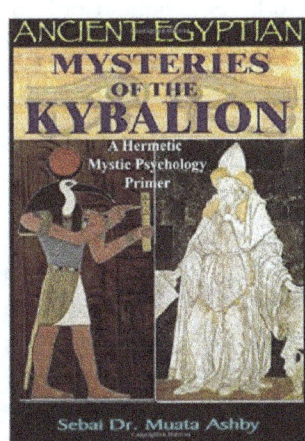

53-Ancient Egyptian Mysteries of The Kybalion: A Hermetic Mystic Psychology Primer Paperback – November 28, 2014

This Volume is a landmark study by a renounced mystic philosopher, Sebai Dr. Muata Ashby. It is study not just to philosophize but to be practiced for the purpose of attaining enlightenment. The book is divided into three sections. Part 1 INTRODUCTION presents a brief history of Hermeticism, its origins in the Ancient Egyptian Mysteries (Neterianism) the Kybalion and the origins of the personality known as Hermes Trismegistus. Part 2 presents the essential teachings of the Kybalion text, a set of MAXIMS, without interpretation. Part 3 presents glosses (commentary and explanation) on the essential teachings of the Kybalion based on the philosophy of the Ancient Egyptian Mysteries as determined by Sebai Dr. Muata Ashby based on studies and translations of original Ancient Egyptian Hieroglyphic texts; the source from which the Kybalion teaching is derived. The Glosses are an edited and expanded version of Lessons given by Sebai Dr. Muata Ashby in the form of lectures on the teachings of the Kybalion.

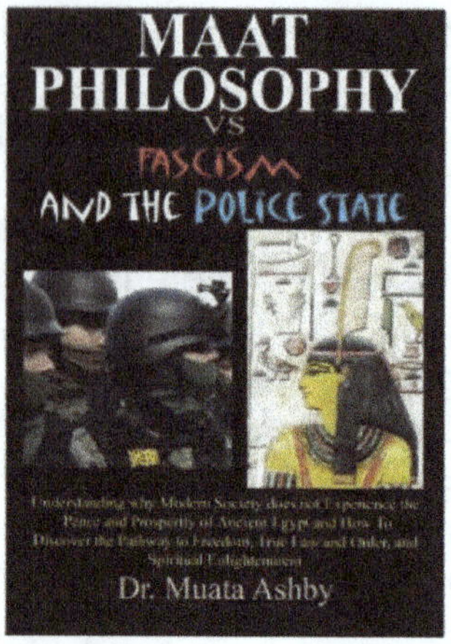

54-Maat Philosophy Versus Fascism and the Police State: Understanding why Modern Society does not Experience the Peace and Prosperity of Ancient Egypt ... Law and Order, and Spiritual Enlightenment Paperback – January 1, 2014

Understanding why Modern Society does not Experience the Peace and Prosperity of Ancient Egypt and How To Discover the Pathway to Freedom, True Law and Order, and Spiritual Enlightenment. Understanding the Corporate State and How Maatian Philosophy can Leads to Freedom, Prosperity and Enlightenment

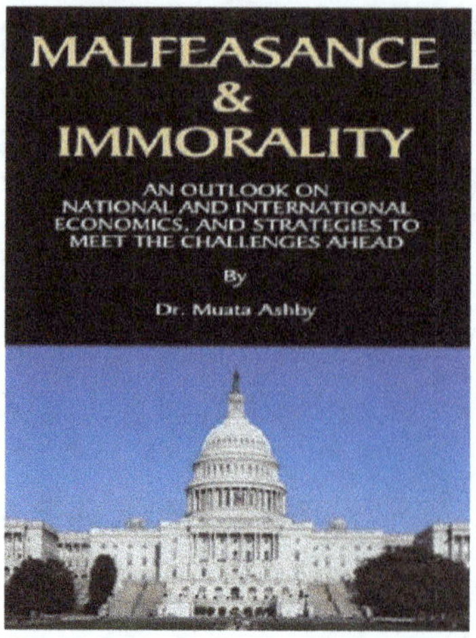

55- MALFEASANCE & IMMORALITY: An Analysis of the World Economic Crash of 2008, the Corrupt Political and Financial Institutions that Caused it and Strategies to Survive the Future Collapse of the Economy

The following is a first ever publication, by the Sema Institute, of a �White Paper�. The term is defined as: A white paper is an authoritative report or guide that often addresses issues and how to solve them. White papers are used to educate readers and help people make decisions. They are often used in politics and business. This paper serves as an update to the book Dollar Crisis: The Collapse of Society and Redemption Through Ancient Egyptian Fiscal & Monetary Policy (2008). That book was a continuation and expansion of issues presented in the book The Collapse of Civilization and the Death of American Empire (2006). Those books contained a detailed analysis of economic and political as well as social issues and how Maat Philosophy could offer insights into the nature of the problem, its sources and possible solutions as well as a means to develop an economic system (Fiscal and Monetary policies) that can work for all members of society. This paper contains an analysis of economic events and possible future outcomes based on those events as well as ideas individuals or groups may use in order to develop plans of action to deal with the possible detrimental events that may occur in the near and intermediate future. It serves as an update to the previous publications. This paper is divided into two parts. The first section is a summary which contains the conclusions of each section of Part 2. This was done so that the reader may have a quick and easy understanding of what is happening with the economy and finally, the actions that should be considered to meet the challenges ahead

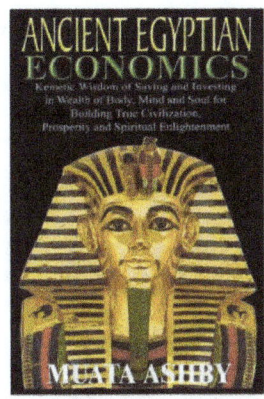

56- ANCIENT EGYPTIAN ECONOMICS

Ancient Egyptian Economics: Kemetic Wisdom of Saving and Investing in Wealth of Body, Mind and Soul for Building True Civilization, Prosperity and Spiritual Enlightenment-----

-Question: Why has the subject of finances and economics become important, I thought the spiritual teachings and Ancient Egyptian Philosophy and money were separate? Answer: Finances and money are an integral part of Ancient Egyptian culture as an instrument for promoting Maat ethics in the form of the well-being of the 'hekat'. The hekat are the people and the "Heka" is the Pharaoh. The Pharaoh was like a shepherd leading a flock and moneys were controlled righteously to promote the welfare of the people. In that tradition we have applied the philosophy of maatian economics to promote the well-being of those who are following this path as well as those who may read the books so they may avoid financial trouble as much as possible and have better capacity to practice the teachings. In order to have a successful life, human beings need a certain amount of money and wealth, but money and wealth are not the goal. They are a foundation that enables the true goal of life, enlightenment, to be realized. Therefore, we are only fulfilling the duty of transmitting wisdom about wealth to promote Maat, righteousness, truth and well-being, for all. This volume explores the mysteries of wealth based on the teachings of the sages of Ancient Egypt and the means to promote prosperity that allows a person to create the conditions for discovering inner peace and spiritual enlightenment. HTP-Peace

57- NETERIAN AWAKENING Journal of Neterian Culture Vol 1-12 In one Volume

This is a single file containing 12 volumes of The Neterian Awakening Journal. The Neterian Awakening Journal was a publication where the culture and community of Shetaut Neter spirituality was explored. In it Sebai Dr. Muata Ashby and Dr. Dja Ashby along with members of the Temple of Shetaut Neter presented articles, festival reviews, Questions and Answer columns and many other important aspects of Neterian culture and spirituality beyond those presented in other volumes of the book series that are useful in understanding the practice of Neterian Spirituality and the path to achieving a ◆Neterian Spiritual Awakening.◆ Part of its mission was: To promote the study of Shetaut Neter (Neterianism, Neterian Religion) as a spiritual path. Instruct the serious followers of Shetaut Neter spirituality who would like to receive literature in between the publication of major books that will fill the needs of their daily spiritual practice. Neterian Awakening Journal explores the varied aspects of Shetaut Neter spirituality not covered in the books. NAJ provides a forum for the development of a Neterian Community of those who wish to follow the Neterian Spiritual Path of African Religious Culture

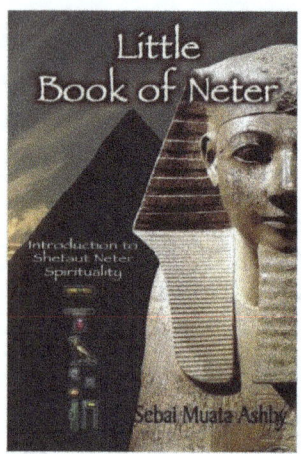

58- Little Book of Neter: Introduction to Shetaut Neter Spirituality and Religion Paperback – June 7, 2007

The Little Book of Neter is a summary of the most important teachings of Shetaut Neter for all aspirants to have for easy reference and distribution. It is designed to be portable and low cost so that all can have the main teachings of Shetaut Neter at easy access for personal use and also for sharing with others the basic tenets of Neterian spirituality.

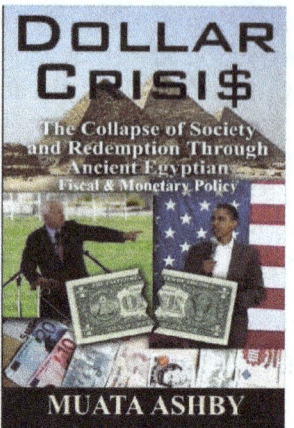

59- Dollar Crisis: The Collapse of Society and Redemption Through Ancient Egyptian Monetary Policy by Muata Ashby (2008-07-24)

This book is about the problems of the US economy and the imminent collapse of the U.S. Dollar and its dire consequences for the US economy and the world. It is also about the corruption in government, economics and social order that led to this point. Also it is about survival, how to make it through this perhaps most trying period in the history of the United States. Also it is about the ancient wisdom of life that allowed an ancient civilization to grow beyond the destructive corruptions of ignorance and power so that the people of today may gain insight into the nature of their condition, how they got there and what needs to be done in order to salvage what is left and rebuild a society that is sustainable, beneficial and an example for all humanity.

60- Devotional Worship Book of Shetaut Neter: Medu Neter song, chant and hymn book for daily practice [Paperback] [2007] (Author) Muata Ashby Paperback – 2007

Ushet Hekau Shedi Sema Tawi Uashu or Ushet means "to worship the Divine," "to propitiate the Divine." Ushet is of two types, external and internal. When you go to pilgrimage centers, temples, spiritual gatherings, etc., you are practicing external worship or spiritual practice. When you go into your private meditation room on your own and your utter words of power, prayers and meditation you are practicing internal worship or spiritual practice. Ushet needs to be understood as a process of not only an outer show of spiritual practice, but it is also a process of developing love for the Divine. Therefore, Ushet really signifies a development in Devotion towards the Divine. This practice is also known as sma uash or Yoga of Devotion. Ushet is the process of discovering the Divine and allowing your heart to flow towards the Divine. This program of life allows a spiritual aspirant to develop inner peace, contentment and universal love, and these qualities lead to spiritual enlightenment or union with the Divine. It is recommended that you see the book "The Path of Divine Love" by Dr. Muata Ashby. This volume will give details into this form of Sema or Yoga.

61- Initiation Into Egyptian Yoga and Neterian Religion Workbook for Beginning and Advancing Aspirants

What is Initiation? The great personalities of the past known to the world as Isis, Hathor, Jesus, Buddha and many other great Sages and Saints were initiated into their spiritual path but how did initiation help them and what were they specifically initiated into? This volume is a template for such lofty studies, a guidebook and blueprint for aspirants who want to understand what the path is all about, its requirements and goals, as they work with a qualified spiritual guide as they tread the path of Kemetic Spirituality and Yoga disciplines. This workbook helps by presenting the fundamental teachings of Egyptian Yoga and Neterian Spirituality with questions and exercises to help the aspirant gain a foundation for more advanced studies and practices

EGYPTIAN BOOK OF THE DEAD HIEROGLYPH TRANSLATIONS Vol. 5

EGIPTIAN BOOK OF THE DEAD HIEROGLYPH TRANSLATIONS SERIES

https://aerbook.com/store/Egyptian_Yoga_Books

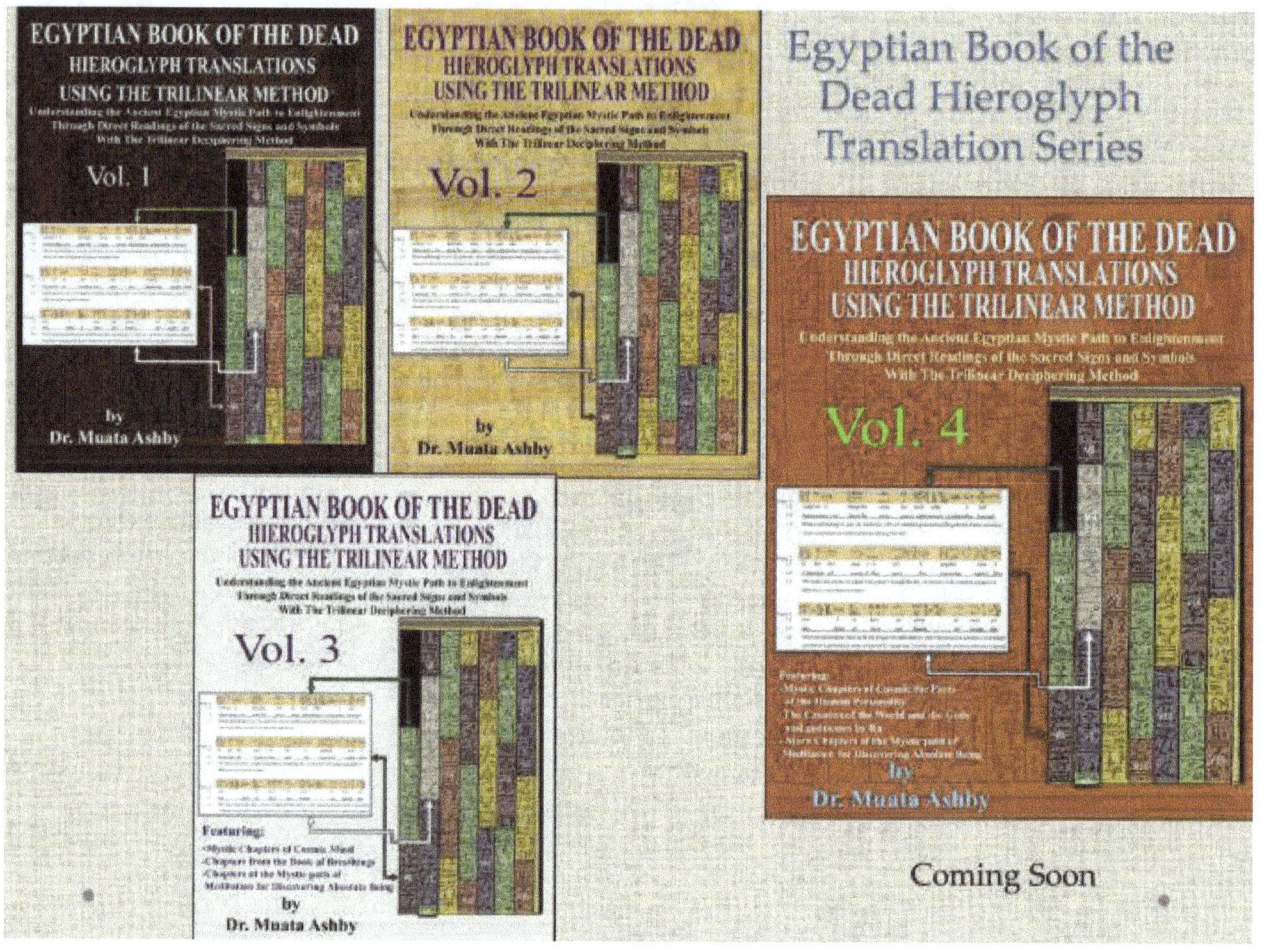

Educational and Mystic Tours to Egypt

Dr. Muata Ashby and Dr. Dja Karen Clarke-Ashby conduct periodic mystic teaching tours to Egypt to explore the wonders of the Ancient Egyptian monuments and wisdom contained in their books, classes and presentations, and meditation. For more information on these trips/spiritual pilgrimages and how to join them, email them at: YogaEgyptTours@gmail.com or KemetMysticTours@gmail.com. You can also visit the website: www.EgyptianYoga.com or www.EgyptianMysteries.org, to find out about their ongoing programs of Online Studies, 360 & Virtual Reality Temple Studies, Ancient Egyptian/Kemetic Devotional Worship and Meditation, Books, Music, Lectures, Retreats, and on the mystery philosophy of Ancient Egypt. To inquire about self-paced distance learning online course and live webinars, email: KemetUniversity@aol.com. To join our email list, email: EgyptianYoga@aol.com and join the email list to be informed of new publications and announcements.

www.Egyptianyoga.com

EGYPTIAN BOOK OF THE DEAD HIEROGLYPH TRANSLATIONS Vol. 5

www.ingramcontent.com/pod-product-compliance
Lightning Source LLC
Chambersburg PA
CBHW081105080526
44587CB00021B/3456